IMAGES
of America

CAMP FORREST AND ITS LEGACY

On the Cover: With bombs exploding around them, the Rangers secure the mock German Village at Camp Forrest. (Courtesy of John Allan.)

IMAGES
of America

CAMP FORREST AND ITS LEGACY

Dr. Elizabeth Taylor

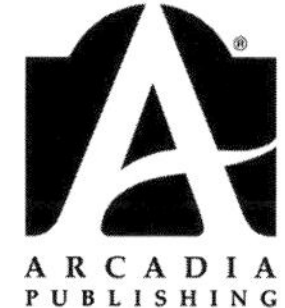

ISBN 9781-4671-6253-1

Published by Arcadia Publishing
Charleston, South Carolina

Printed in the United States of America

Library of Congress Control Number: 2025937160

For all general information, please contact Arcadia Publishing:
Telephone 843-853-2070
Fax 843-853-0044
E-mail sales@arcadiapublishing.com

Visit us on the Internet at www.arcadiapublishing.com

It is with sincere thanks and gratitude to the men and women who devoted their lives in the service and protection of our nation that I dedicate this book. Heroes long gone but not forgotten.

Contents

ACKNOWLEDGMENTS

The images and information in this book came from letters, postcards, diaries, biographies, interviews, newspapers, and other written accounts of life at Camp Forrest and throughout Middle Tennessee during the World War II era. The author is indebted to many individuals and organizations who work to preserve the legacies of Camp Forrest for future generations. I am especially thankful to the following individuals and organizations for their invaluable assistance with this book: John Allan, Sfc. Will Broersma, Tressa Bush, Dr. Peter Cash, Ken Fieth, Jeff Haley, Bessie and Philip Henderson, Sam H. Werner Military Museum, Dr. Joshua Tankersley, Dennis W. Teal, Tennessee State Library and Archives, Tullahoma Fine Arts Center, Louis Varnell, Jimmy Walker, Walter Wallace, Tom Walker, Dot Couch Watson, Capt. Tom Watson, USN (Ret.), Ruth Welborn, and Lt. Col. Russell S. Wolfe Jr.

Many of the images for this book were compiled from the archives of the Albert Gore Research Center, Middle Tennessee State University (MTSU); Camp Forrest Foundation (CFF); Metro Nashville Archives (MNA); National Archives and Records Administration, College Park, Maryland (NARA); and Tennessee State Library and Archives (TSLA); as well as private collections that are cited individually throughout the text.

In preparing this book for publication, the author and Arcadia Publishing made every effort to ensure the information throughout it is correct. However, we acknowledge at the onset the potential for errors, omissions, and misspellings. We apologize in advance should any errors occur and request you notify the publisher with the correct information so we can update the book for future editions.

Introduction

Camp Forrest and Its Legacy is a pictorial history that focuses on the connections and impact this major military installation had on individuals and organizations during World War II. Camp Forrest's influence on daily life throughout this period is sweeping and varied. However, many of its significant operational details have faded with the passage of time. Vintage photographs, personal stories, and historical accounts document the role Camp Forrest played in defense efforts and mobilization for war. The pre–World War II activities in the introduction are not an exhaustive narrative of events and activities during that era. It provides the reader with a broad overview of the local, state, and national events that have a connection to or were affected by Camp Forrest. The captions in each chapter have information on World War II, Camp Forrest, and the units that trained throughout the Middle Tennessee area. In this book, Chapter 1 focuses on military and civilian leaders who had an impact on base operations; Chapter 2 examines the combat units and their training at Camp Forrest; Chapter 3 describes the roles of the combat service and combat service support units; and Chapter 4 details the Middle Tennessee war efforts of civilians and industries.

Pre–World War II National, State, and Local Activities

In 1939, the US Army was ill-prepared for war since there were fewer than 200,000 soldiers at its disposal. With the knowledge that the United States ranked as the 17th largest fighting force in the world, Pres. Franklin Delano Roosevelt's advisors strongly urged him to start preparing for war. With presidential support, Chief of Staff Gen. George C. Marshall began orchestrating a major reorganization of the US Army to promote the faster expansion and mobilization of troops. Marshall became a mediator between the federal government and his military commanders. He routinely defended his military plans and appropriation requests to FDR and Congress. The initial estimate to build up the military was $150 billion ($3.3 trillion in 2025), and the actual costs for the buildup were an estimated $342 billion ($7.5 trillion in 2025).

It had been 20 years since World War I ended, but it was still at the forefront of many American minds. While many Americans held firm against foreign entanglements, leaders at all governmental levels began preparing for the inevitable. Relying on his world war experiences, Marshall knew the importance of appointing experienced senior officers to command positions and the value of well-trained divisions. He also knew that relying on the World War I strategies and doctrines would prove disastrous against Hitler's new army. In Marshall's streamlined military structure, he created three field commands: Army Ground Forces, Army Air Forces, and Army Service Forces.

Marshall appointed Gen. Leslie McNair as commander of US Ground Forces. McNair earned the moniker "the Brains of the Army" by setting in motion specific programs to rapidly mobilize and expand the Army. His responsibilities included the oversight of all Army boards, formal military schools, training centers, mobilization centers, and the special activities of combat arms and the new quasi-arms. Combat arms were the traditional military field branches: infantry, field artillery, cavalry, and coast artillery. Quasi-arms were the new military branches that fell outside of the traditional ones previously outlined. These new branches were airborne, armor, tank destroyer, and antiaircraft artillery. McNair's war preparations and battlefield success initiatives, in part, focused on education. He updated the curriculum at the Command and General Staff College. McNair expected soldiers to understand tactics and work as a team. US soldiers gained tactical advantages over the Axis Powers with scientific and technological equipment and weapons.

On January 14, 1941, FDR issued Executive Order 8633, which ordered about 50 National Guard divisions into active military service. Congress later enacted the Service Extension Act of 1941, which extended military service from 12 months to 30 months. The act also authorized the commander in chief to extend service beyond 30 months if he thought it necessary to ensure national security. Marshall's updated strategies and operations were successful in building a fighting force of over 8 million soldiers by 1942.

Meanwhile, down south, the State of Tennessee also focused on defense efforts and mobilization. Gov. Prentice Cooper's war preparedness initiatives and committees, such as the Civilian Defense Organization and Advisory Committee on Preparedness, educated citizens on the impending war. Unlike most state leaders, Cooper realized war was imminent. As a Tennessee senator, Cooper took part in a 1937 International Rotary–sponsored tour of Europe. During this trip, he had the opportunity to talk with Adolf Hitler. The military preparations he saw throughout Germany, as well as his discussions with Hitler, concerned the World War I veteran. Other Tennessee leaders, such as Sen. Kenneth McKellar, Rep. Tom Stewart, state treasurer John Harton, and Tullahoma mayor Don Campbell, continually promoted the state's resources throughout Washington, DC, to obtain military installations, attract war industries, and secure other defense projects. By the end of World War II, over 300,000 Tennesseans had answered the call to war, and over 280,000 worked in defense-related jobs.

Camp Forrest Becomes a Reality

In late September 1940, the federal government, under Marshall's military expansion program, authorized a permanent Army post in Tullahoma to accommodate over 20,000 soldiers. The quick expansion of the former Tennessee National Guard training site, Camp Peay (future Camp Forrest), was paramount so soldiers could begin training on a grand scale before deploying overseas. State and local Tennessee leaders sprang into action, obtaining more land in the greater Tullahoma area for the proposed expansion of the current garrison. Military personnel began inspecting, surveying, and preparing for the massive construction project, which began on October 10, 1940. Many of the Camp Peay buildings served as housing for the MP (military police) units guarding construction areas. The remaining buildings became administrative offices for military and civilian workers.

Tullahoma's population soared as approximately 35,000 individuals from throughout the southeast besieged the town seeking construction jobs. The area became a boomtown overnight, and the small town of 4,500 residents was initially ill-prepared for the military buildup. Numerous federal and state agencies worked with Tullahoma leaders to provide funding to upgrade the city's infrastructure, construct new homes and apartments, and create byways to reduce military-related traffic congestion.

The final construction costs were approximately $36 million ($791 million in 2025). In approximately 120 days, construction crews built 1,300 buildings, 55 miles of roads, and 5 miles of railroad tracks throughout the cantonment. The buildings included 408 barracks, 158 mess halls, 14 officer's mess buildings, 19 guard houses, 35 warehouses, 20 administration buildings, 30 officer's quarters buildings, a bakery, an ice plant, an incinerator, a cold-storage building, a laundry, a water and sewage treatment facility, four dental clinics, and a 2,000-patient bed hospital complex. Within the Army Ranger training areas, the full-scale model of a German village provided a realistic environment for soldiers to hone immersive and close-quarters combat expertise.

More than 30,000 officers and men from the National Guards in Tennessee, Ohio, Illinois, and Colorado began arriving in March 1941. As one of the newest US Army military installations, Camp Forrest was situated on over 85,000 acres, but the installation and unit-specific buildings (such as barracks, chapels, headquarters, mess halls, and supply rooms), and the combat service support operations were on 13,000 acres (20.3 square miles). Most of its remaining acreage contained combat and maneuver training areas, and four firing ranges. Small arms and field artillery ranges trained soldiers on pistols, rifles, machine guns, grenades, and light artillery.

The 33rd Division (Illinois National Guard) arrived after major construction projects for the base were finished. However, soldiers spent about a month finishing minor construction and cleanup projects. African American Civilian Conservation Corps (CCC) members transferred to Camp Forrest to finish the cleanup and beautification projects, allowing the 33rd Division to focus on training. Camp Forrest life was uneventful throughout the next nine months, until the division took part in the Louisiana Maneuvers in August and September 1941.

Permanently stationed elements from the quartermaster and station hospital did not mobilize to Louisiana. The personnel remained behind to set up these divisions' large-scale infrastructures. Shortages in equipment and supplies throughout the station hospital remedied in the early summer of 1941. Throughout its operation, Camp Forrest employed over 12,000 civilians in the hospital complex; unit-level administrative offices; post exchanges (PX); the laundry; vehicle, tank, and artillery maintenance shops; ordnance depots; and the induction center.

As time progressed, activities on and off base became available to occupy soldiers' free time. Some of the more popular off-duty activities offered included watching movies, playing games, attending religious services, attending Service Club and United Service Organization (USO) events, reading, writing letters home, and shopping. Priests held Catholic Mass on the post every Sunday morning and held dedicated times to hear confessions. Jewish services were every Friday evening. Chaplains held two Protestant services each week. Chaplains for each faith had office hours to offer extra spiritual guidance for those in need. Other recreational activities on post included golfing on the nine-hole course, attending sporting events, practicing at the archery and gun ranges, swimming, playing tennis, and bowling. In town, there were five USO clubs, three movie theaters, a 24-hour bus station, a railroad station, restaurants, bars, and churches of various denominations. With a day pass, soldiers could take a bus or a train trip to visit nearby cities, such as Nashville or Chattanooga.

By July 1941, construction began on a $3 million ($65 million in 2025) Army Air Corps facility five miles north of Camp Forrest. The air-training base William Northern Army Airfield was the state's third largest airfield and an advanced training site for B-24, B-29, and P-39 Airacobra crews; observation plane pilots; and paratroopers.

McNair and the Tennessee Maneuvers

Marshall and McNair sought to educate officers and soldiers on modern warfare by using large-scale training exercises held throughout the United States. During the interwar years of 1935 and 1938, large-scale maneuvers were employed so officers and men could train in realistic combat environments and learn to work as a team. These combat dress rehearsals allowed officers and soldiers to learn from their mistakes. Marshall estimated that the maneuvers in preparation for World War II would cost $40.6 million ($892 million in 2025). He justified this expense during one of his congressional testimonies, explaining it was preferable to make mistakes during a training exercise rather than in a theater of operation. As observers of the 1941 Tennessee Maneuvers, Marshall and McNair saw ways to improve basic and unit combat training. The 1941 Tennessee Maneuvers introduced over 75,000 soldiers from four divisions to the "realities" of war. The Middle Tennessee terrain closely resembled Europe and had ample land to conduct the training simulations. The six maneuvers conducted from 1942 to 1944 required participants to "solve" different scripted combat problems using 22 Middle Tennessee counties as battlefronts. Governmental reports estimate over 850,000 soldiers participated in the 1941 to 1944 Tennessee Maneuvers.

Residents became accustomed to the inconveniences of the battling Red and Blue Armies: soldiers camping out on lawns and porches, continual construction (sometimes destruction) of bridges, and traffic jams. Property owners often sought reparations from the federal government for damage caused by the invading troops. Livestock were often also "victims" of war games; the loud noises caused hens to stop laying eggs and cows to stop giving milk. Everyone believed that tolerance of these inconveniences was a person's patriotic duty.

In the span of 24 hours in the final weeks of 1941, life throughout the nation changed forever with the acts of aggression by Japanese forces at Pearl Harbor on Sunday, December 7. By noon on December 8, with congressional approval, FDR signed the formal declaration of war against Japan. On Thursday, December 11, Nazi Germany and Fascist Italy both formally declared war on America. After the signing of the declarations of war, military orders were issued to units stationed at Camp Forrest to guard vital Tennessee defense industries. In June 1942, Congress approved declarations of war against Axis-aligned Bulgaria, Hungary, and Romania.

From Training Soldiers to Detaining Enemies

In 1942, Camp Forrest transitioned from the induction and training of soldiers to the detention of Enemy Aliens. Enemy Aliens or Civilian Internees were citizens or immigrants in the United States considered suspicious or a threat to national security. Many observers assumed the arrested individuals were engaged in wrongdoing or were traitors. However, there were many individuals falsely accused by the federal government of wrongdoing detained in encampments throughout the United States. The War Department considered establishing an encampment in Crossville, Tennessee, but decided Camp Forrest had resources readily available. For 10 months, authorities detained over 800 individuals of various nationalities in specifically built areas at the cantonment. By mid-1943, the federal government transferred all the enemy aliens to Fort Lincoln in North Dakota and transitioned the post to a prisoner of war (POW) camp.

In June 1943, over 1,500 prisoners of war (POW) captured during the North African campaign began arriving at Camp Forrest. The largest POW population was German; however, the compound held nationalities from other countries, including Italy, Poland, and Austria. By mid-1944, POWs captured in countries such as Italy and France began arriving. By 1946, Camp Forrest detained an average of 20,480 POWs. However, the compound staff evaluated and assigned over 60,000 POWs to other encampments throughout the Southeast.

POWs had access to medical and dental facilities as well as resources for work, recreation, and education. POWs could work on-post (non-war production or non-security clearance areas) and off-post as laborers helping farmers plant and harvest local crops. POWs earned 80¢ a day and could spend money at the PX or save it. After the war, the POW received a voucher for their remaining earnings, which were redeemable at certain US military installations in their home country. In their free time, many POWs created art using materials readily available to them. For example, wood obtained from fallen trees, construction lumber, or food material packages. The Red Cross and the YMCA (Young Men's Christian Association) typically sent recreational supplies such as paints or drawing pencils for the men to use. POWs could also buy art supplies via mail order, the PX, or other art suppliers. Some POWs created artwork as a means of currency to exchange for other material goods or as gifts to repay a person's kindness.

Many German POWs believed Germany was destined to win the war. While some of the detainees did not adhere to Nazi rhetoric, they did consider war reports of the decimation of German forces as propaganda. Recreational activities at the camp drastically reduced after D-Day, and POWs soon learned of Germany's surrender and Hitler's death. The war ended in 1945: Germany surrendered in May and Japan in September. In August 1945, approximately 3,000 sick or wounded but ambulatory German POWs boarded ships for home. In the latter part of 1945, the federal government halted repatriation so that returning American GIs could make it home by Christmas.

Post–World War II Activities

Tennessee state treasurer John Harton and Tullahoma mayor Don Campbell made many trips to Washington, DC, in attempts to convince federal officials not to decommission Camp Forrest and Northern Field. Both men also met with other federal agencies to promote the use of all or at least part of each installation's facilities. In their correspondence with the Veterans Administration, the politicians suggested using the 2,000-bed hospital complex at Camp Forrest for the medical treatment of returning veterans rather than building a new facility. Despite their continual efforts, the War Department cited high operational costs necessitated the installation's closure.

Throughout its operation, Camp Forrest contributed to the US defense mobilization efforts as an induction center, combat training site, Tennessee maneuvers logistic hub, and a civilian internee and prisoner of war facility. The installation exposed military personnel and citizens to diverse cultures; boosted the local, state, and national economies; and afforded many people with opportunities they may have otherwise never had. On June 30, 1946, the federal government decommissioned Camp Forrest.

By August 1946, the Mobile District engineers began the process of dismantling the reservation and selling its assets as surplus. Buyers purchased lumber and entire buildings, such as chapels and barracks, and rebuilt them in new locations throughout the Southeast. In 1951, the federal government approved an Air Force Test Center and Air Force Materiel Command named Arnold Engineering Development Complex (AEDC). The location of the 40,000-acre AEDC complex is on a portion of the original Camp Forrest footprint and is one of the most globally advanced test-flight simulation facilities.

When World War II ended, lives and landscapes at home and abroad changed irrevocably. Many Americans chose to look toward the future and leave the war in the past. Today, eroding tank tracks, decaying chimneys, and concrete slabs are the only physical reminders of the area's military occupation. Over time, most of Northern Airfield's buildings and land were sold, and the installation became the Tullahoma Regional Airport. The recollections of each installation's storied past are still vivid today and commemorate this period in history.

Further Reading

More information on Camp Forrest is available in Dr. Elizabeth Taylor's other books and on the Camp Forrest Foundation website (www.campforrest.com). Her other books include Images of America: *Camp Forrest,* which is a pictorial history of training and daily life at Camp Forrest, and *Voices of Camp Forrest in World War II,* which uses oral histories to document the lives of civilians and soldiers who lived, trained, and worked at Camp Forrest and in Middle Tennessee.

One

Driving Force to Victory

Military Leaders at Camp Forrest

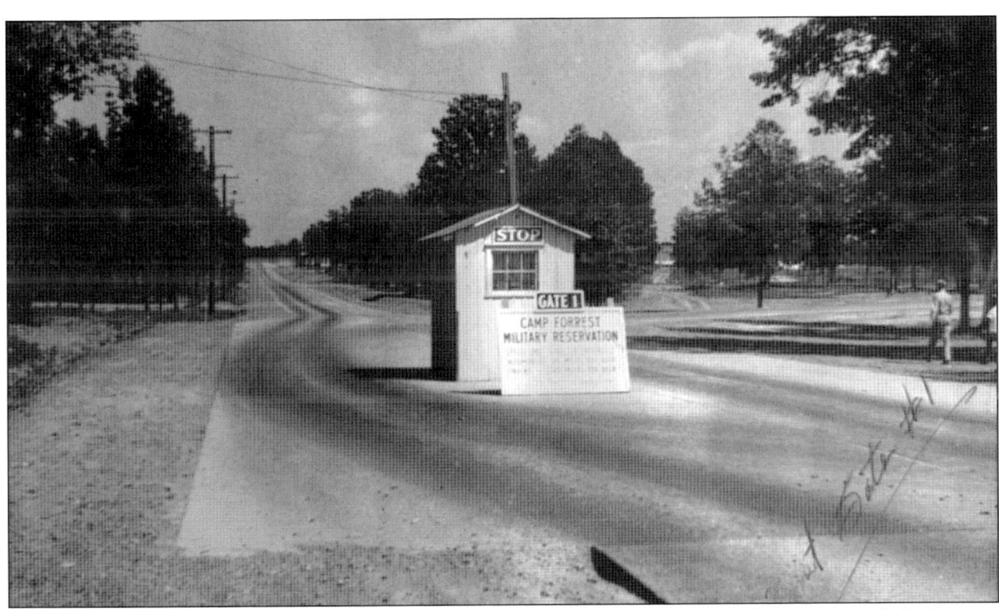

Camp Forrest left an indelible mark on the patriots who passed through Gate 1. While history typically focuses on unit leaders, there are few resources devoted to the symbiotic relationship of individuals and military installations, such as Camp Forrest. Without the dedication of all personnel, delays in mobilization, low morale, and low-quality training were conceivable. This chapter examines many of the civilian and military leaders who came to Camp Forrest, but it is not an exhaustive list. (Courtesy of Dr. Paul Wylie family.)

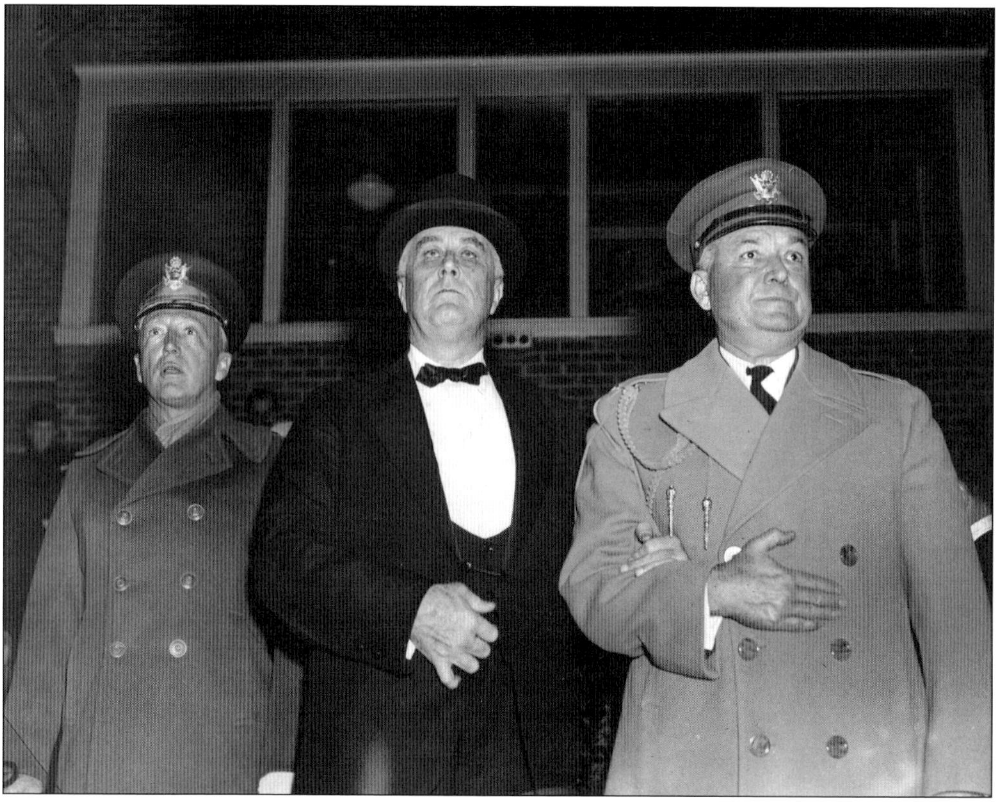

The 80th Division soldiers, equipment, and guns lined both sides of the road to form a three-mile avenue for President Roosevelt's April 1943 inspection tour of military installations. The president complimented Governor Cooper on the beauty of the camp and was especially impressed with the overall excellent health of the soldiers. In the image, Gen. George S. Patton (left), FDR (center), and Gen. Edwin M. Watson, presidential secretary and military aide, attended a horse show that benefitted the Infantile Paralysis Fund. (Courtesy of CFF.)

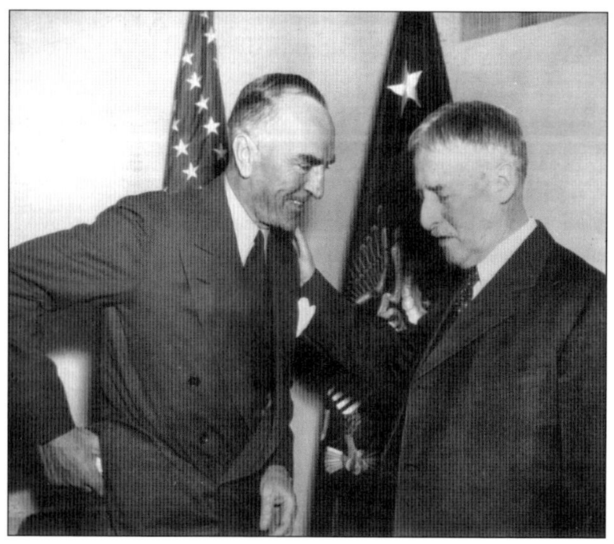

Henry L. Stimson was secretary of war under Presidents Taft and FDR. He visited Camp Forrest several times throughout its operations. On his June 25, 1941, visit, Stimson conferred with various military leaders and reviewed troops during a maneuver exercise. Stimson invoked the May Act (anti-prostitution legislation) in 27 Middle Tennessee counties to prevent the spread of sexually transmitted diseases. Henry L. Stimson (right) congratulates Capt. Eddie Rickenbacker (left) on his return from a secret War Department mission. (Courtesy of CFF.)

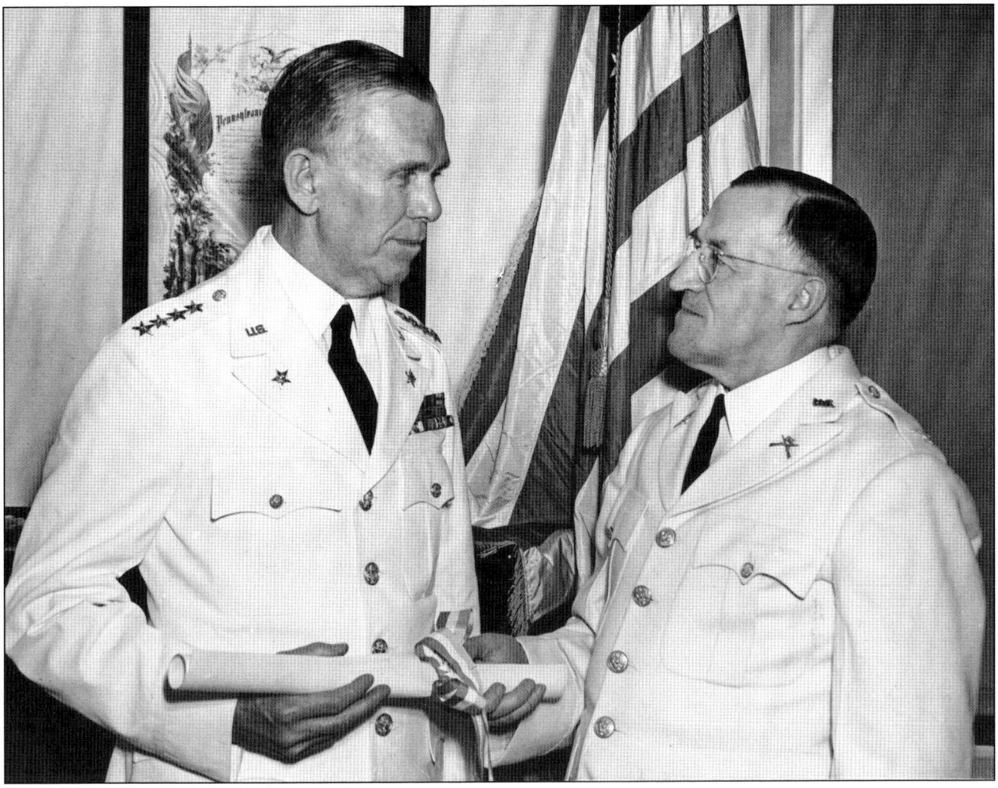

Chief of Staff George C. Marshall requested that Tennessee representatives send recommendations for a new name for Camp Peay. The Army did not name federal installations after local politicians without distinguished military careers. General Orders No. 1 officially changed the post's name to Camp Forrest. Pictured: Col. Frank Hyatt presents General Marshall with an honorary doctorate of military science from the Pennsylvania Military College. (Courtesy of CFF.)

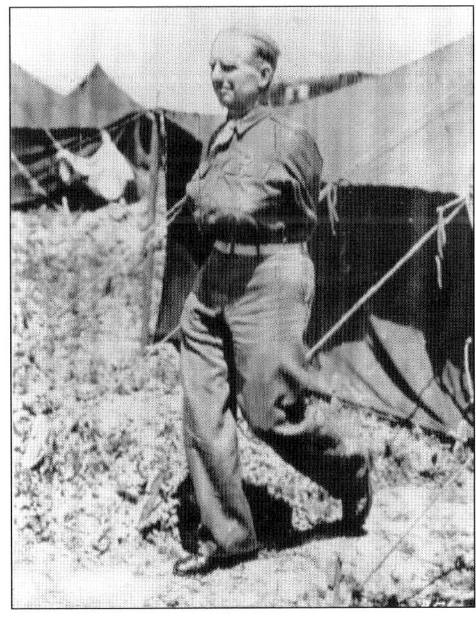

During World War II, Gen. Lesley McNair was commanding general of all US ground forces. He was key in executing Marshall's large-scale war games conducted throughout the United States. The realistic simulations prepared soldiers for combat overseas. He saw the plan in action during the Louisiana Maneuvers and the 1941 Tennessee Maneuvers. McNair died in France on July 25, 1944, from friendly fire during a troop inspection tour. He was the highest-ranking US soldier killed in combat during World War II. (Courtesy of CFF.)

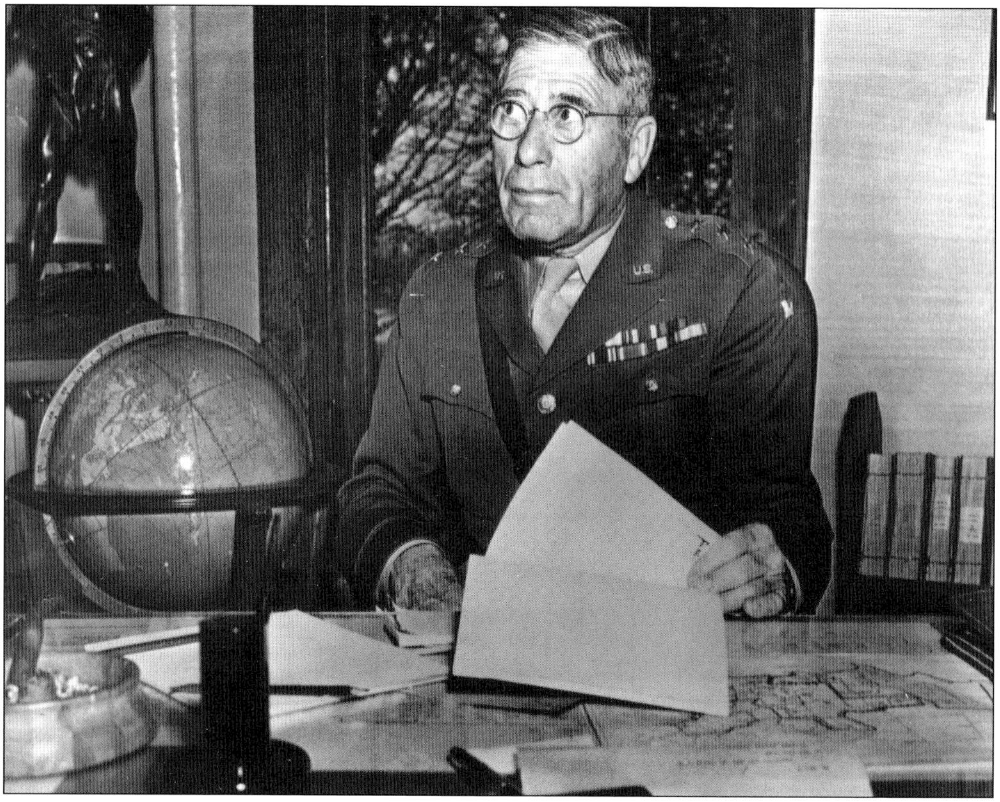

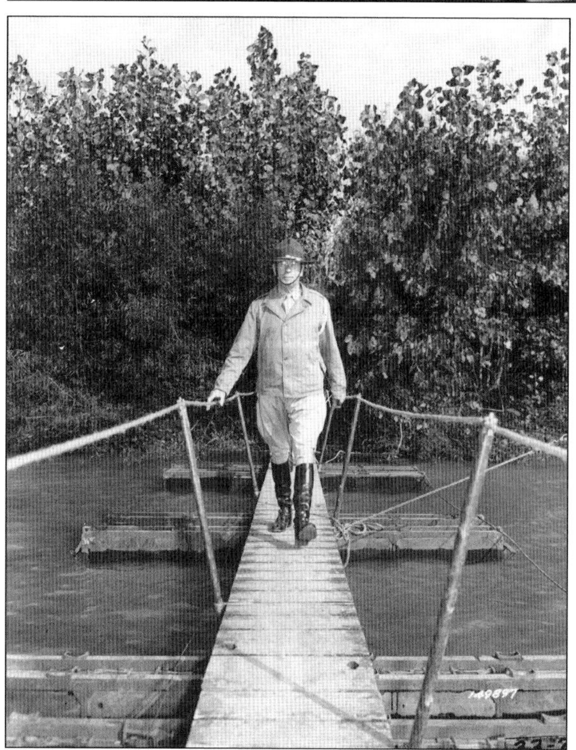

Ben Lear was a stickler for discipline; he expected those under his command to always adhere to the soldier's standards of conduct outlined in the Army regulations. The former equestrian Olympian rose from private to four-star general in a military career spanning 47 years. Throughout the war, he reviewed reports of soldiers returning from the front to discern where to implement improvements to military training and processes. Rather than making Lear's advanced training program a requirement for all soldiers, senior military officials used it to train a small cadre of soldiers. As commander of the Second Army, he took part in the 1941 Tennessee and Louisiana maneuvers. (Both, courtesy of NARA.)

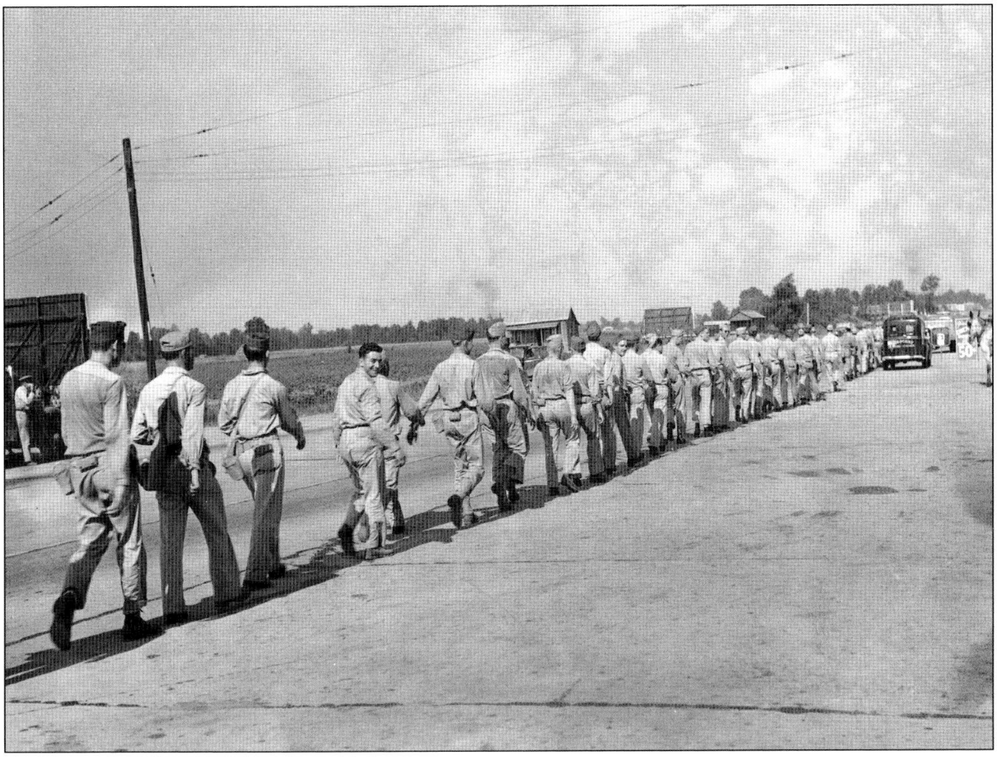

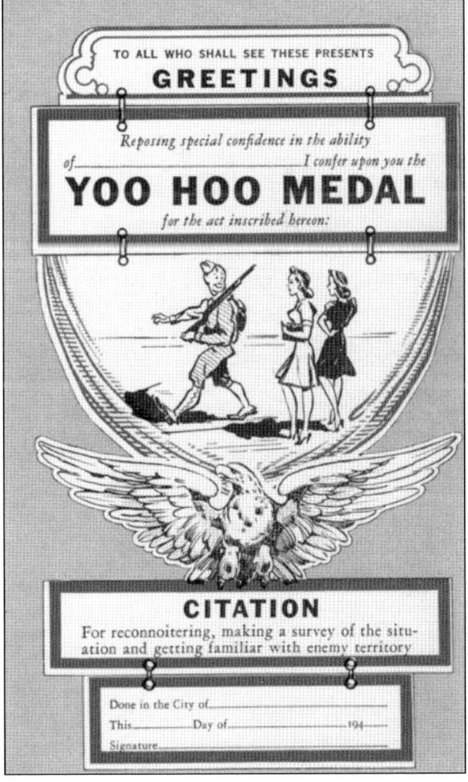

July 9, 1941, marked a turning point in Lear's military career. While golfing with friends at the Memphis Country Club in Memphis, Tennessee, he heard sounds of rowdy catcalls, whistles, and "Yoo Hoos" directed at the shorts-clad women in his party. The offending gang of hooligans were soldiers of the 35th Division from Camp Robinson, Arkansas. Early the next morning, in a letter to the 35th Division commanding officer, Lear described the men's conduct as "a disgrace to the Army, the 35th Division, and their regiment." The 35th Division's punishment for unbecoming behavior was a 15-mile hike under the boiling Tennessee summer sun. He faced criticism throughout the nation for his reaction to the situation; the public decried that the punishment did not fit the crime. For the next five months, the nation laughed at Lear's expense and forever associated him with the nickname "Yoo Hoo." (Both, courtesy of CFF.)

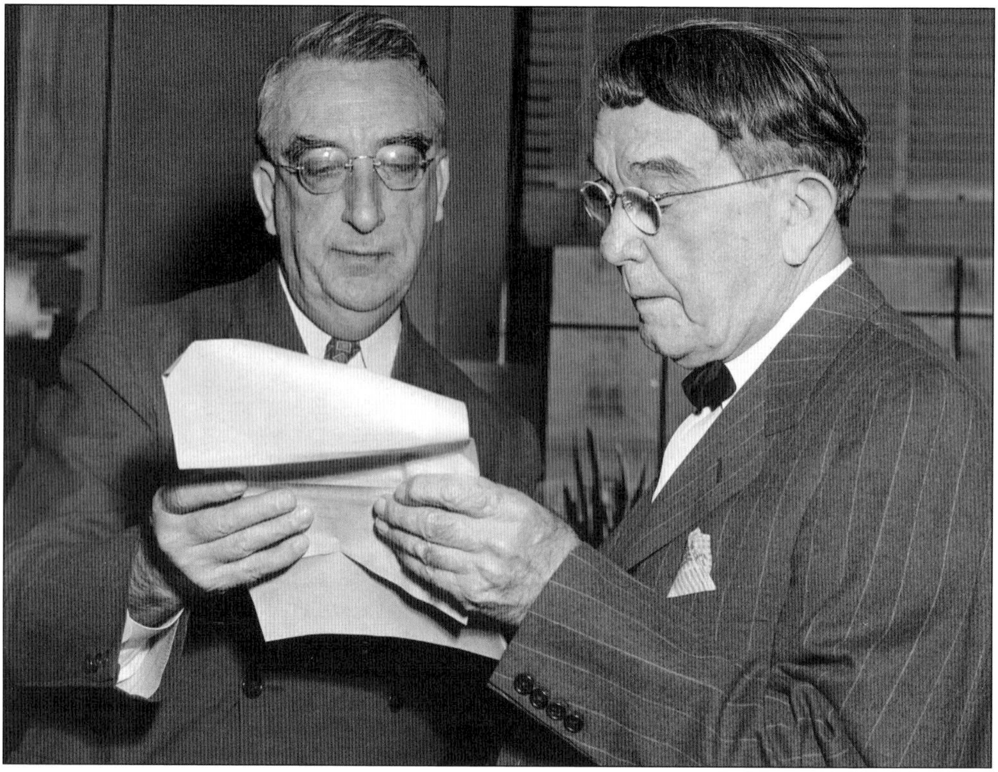

Kenneth McKellar served the State of Tennessee in Congress for over four decades and was a Senate Appropriations Committee member from 1923 to 1953. He was pivotal in securing numerous civilian and military defense industries for his home state. Pictured here, economic stabilization director Fred Vinson (left) and Tennessee senator Kenneth McKellar discuss phases of milk shortages that would occur unless price ceilings increased. (Courtesy of CFF.)

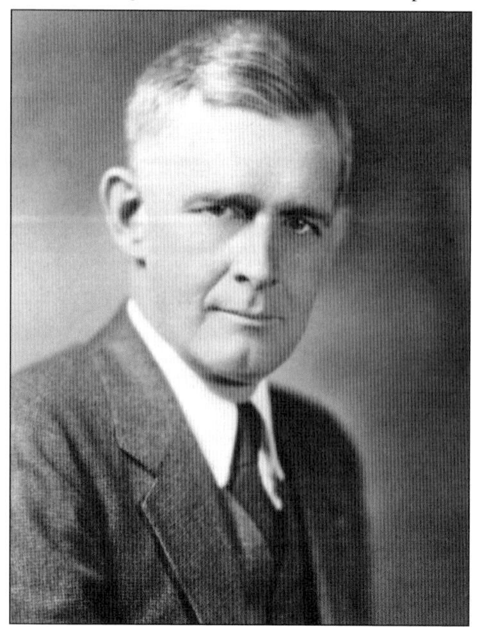

Arthur Thomas Stewart was a senator for the State of Tennessee from 1939 to 1949. He was a proponent of national preparedness and served on the Senate Armed Services Committee. He worked closely with other Tennessee senators to secure military installations, such as Camp Forrest, in his home state. The senator helped secure federal funding for repairs and upgrades to Tullahoma's infrastructure when it became strained from the rapid influx of people seeking employment opportunities. (Courtesy of CFF.)

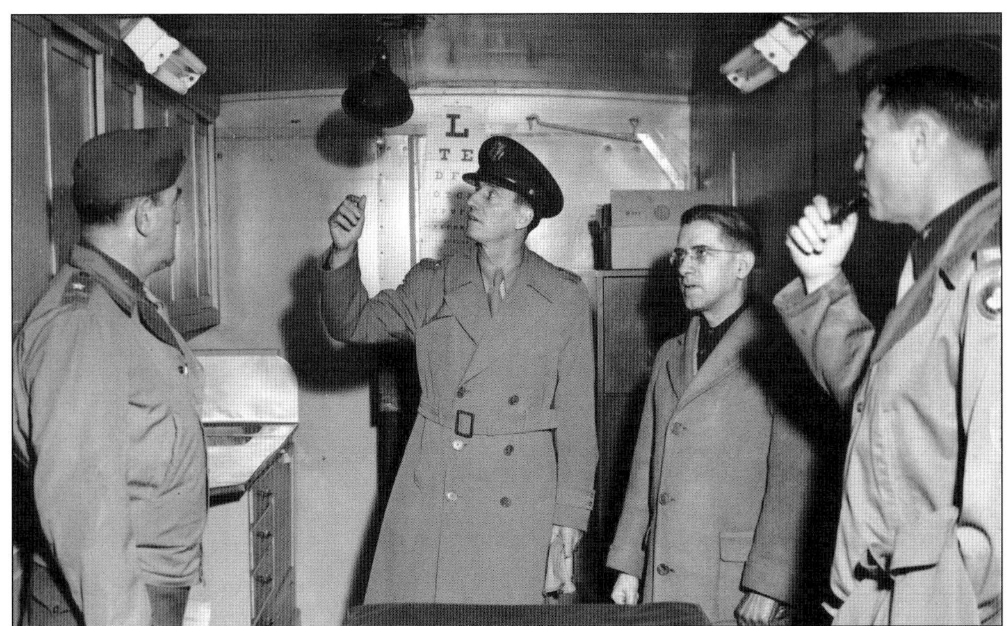

Prentice Cooper (second from the right) was an attorney; Tennessee state representative for Bedford, Coffee, and Moore Counties from 1936 to 1939; governor of Tennessee from 1939 to 1945; and US ambassador to Peru from 1946 to 1948. Under Cooper's leadership, Tennessee became the first state to establish a state defense council, a state guard, and a wartime food program for use by families. (Courtesy of MTSU.)

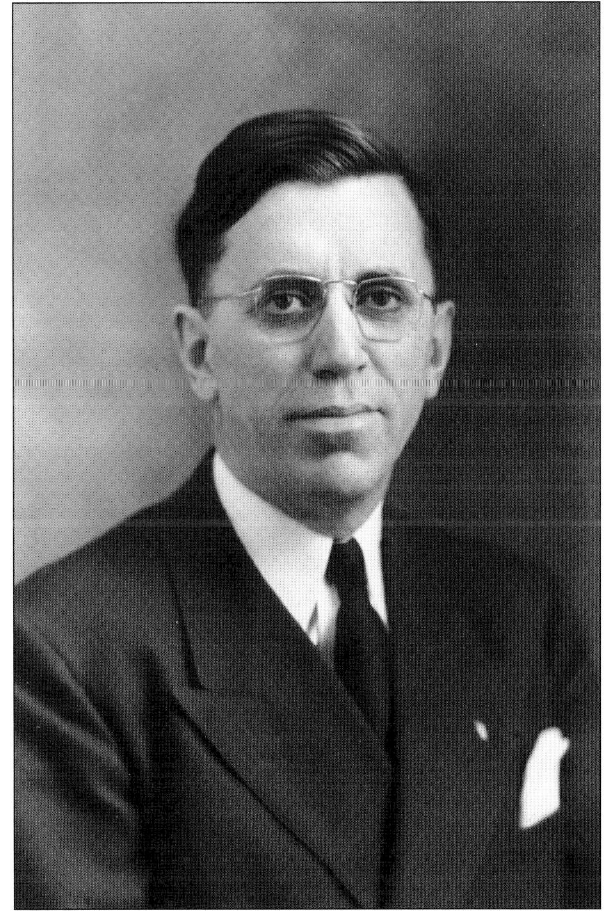

John W. Harton was a leader in community and state affairs in Tennessee. In his political career, he served as the mayor of Tullahoma for four terms and was Tennessee state treasurer from 1939 to 1943. His business interests were primarily in real estate, hotel management, and manufacturing. He served as either a trustee or board member for numerous local and state organizations, such as Tullahoma Rotary Club, Tullahoma Chamber of Commerce, Tullahoma School Board, Belmont College, and the Vocational School for Girls. (Courtesy of TSLA.)

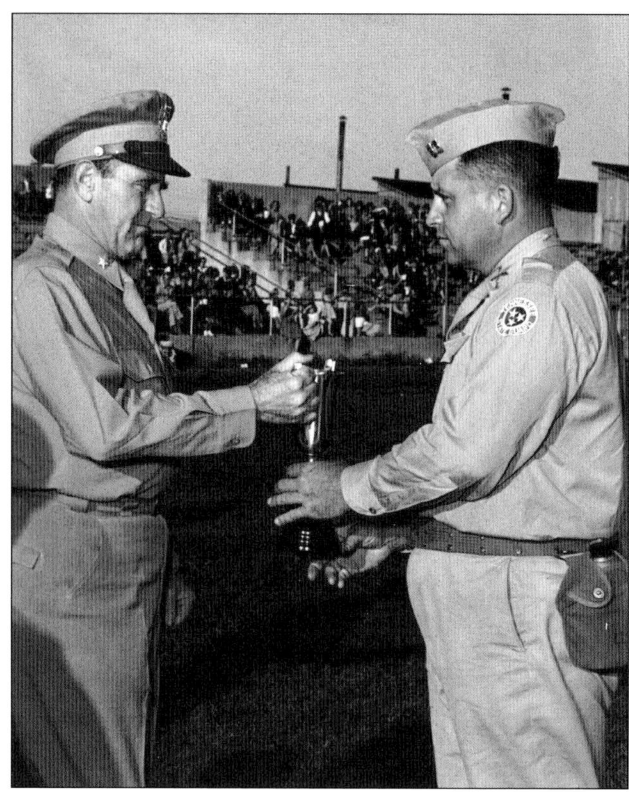

In August 1943, Gen. J.M. Dickinson presented the Maneuver Award cup to Capt. Sam Bone for best drilled platoon in the 7th Regiment competitive drill in the Tennessee State Guard maneuvers exercise. Most of the maneuvers took place on Capt. Joe Scott's farm and included simulated paratroop landings and Civilian Air Patrol planes. These exercises proved that the State Guard could handle a major defense problem. (Courtesy of TSLA.)

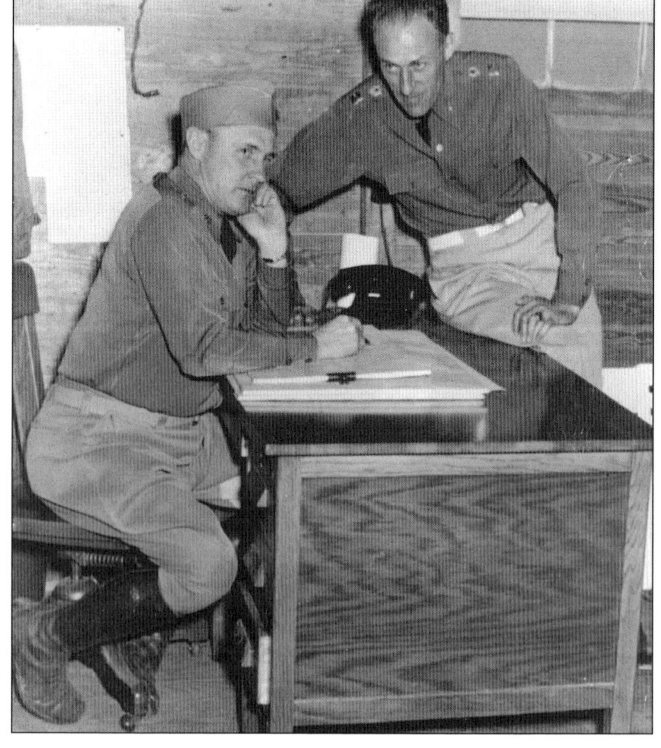

Tennessee native Maj. Carl H. Breitwieser (seated) oversaw all aspects of the construction of Camp Forrest until March 1941, when the US Army Corps of Engineers took over its project management. The Great War veteran and his aide, Capt. Robert C. Brown (Hibbing, Minnesota) were part of the Quartermaster Construction division. Breitwieser worked on several defense construction projects in Memphis, Tennessee, and Huntsville, Alabama, and received a promotion to lieutenant colonel in April 1942. (Courtesy of Hennepin County Library.)

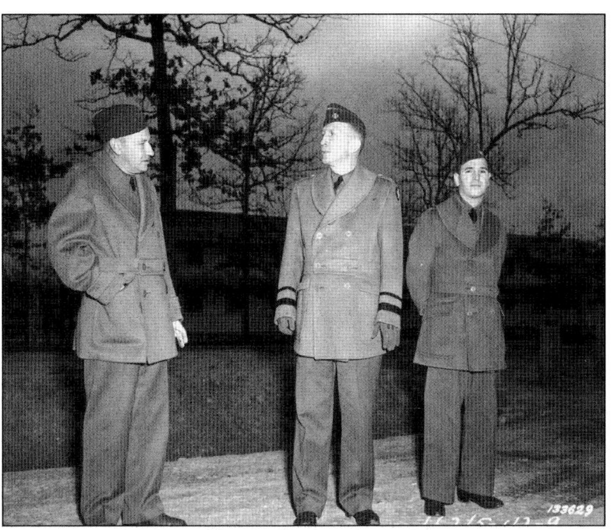

Pictured from left to right, Col. Horace E. Thornton, chief of staff, Maj. Gen. Samuel T. Lawton, 33rd Division commander, and Capt. Charles Barron, aide, reviewed the preparations for the movement of the 33rd Division to Fort McClellan, Alabama, where a cadre of its personnel formed the 633rd Tank Destroyer Battalion. Lawton was the third individual to serve as post commander of Camp Forrest. (Courtesy of NARA.)

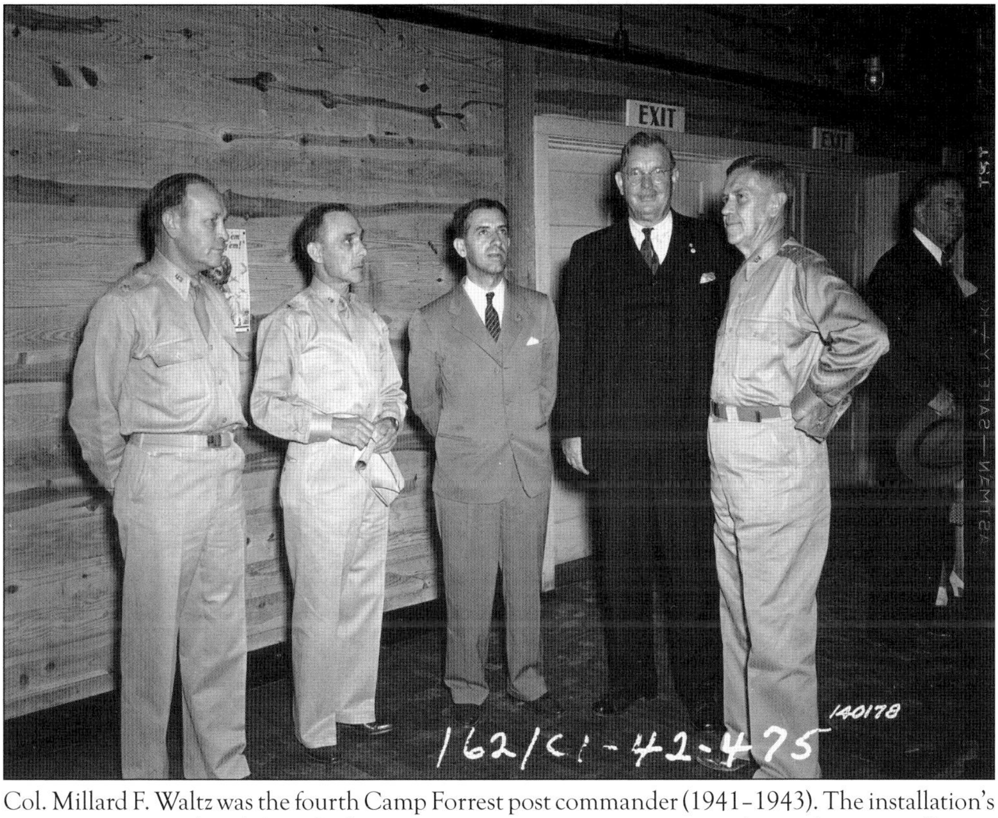

Col. Millard F. Waltz was the fourth Camp Forrest post commander (1941–1943). The installation's previous commanders left with their units upon reassignment to another military installation. When Lawton left for the Louisiana Maneuvers, the daily administrative functions of the base fell to a station complement. The station complement was concerned with the administrative functions of the camp and did not participate in war games. From left to right, Maj. W. Wimble (post special services officer), Col. M.F. Waltz (post commander), Gov. Prentice Cooper, Sgt. Alvin York, and Maj. Gen. Frank Mahin (33rd Division commander) pose for a photograph at a service club event. (Courtesy of NARA.)

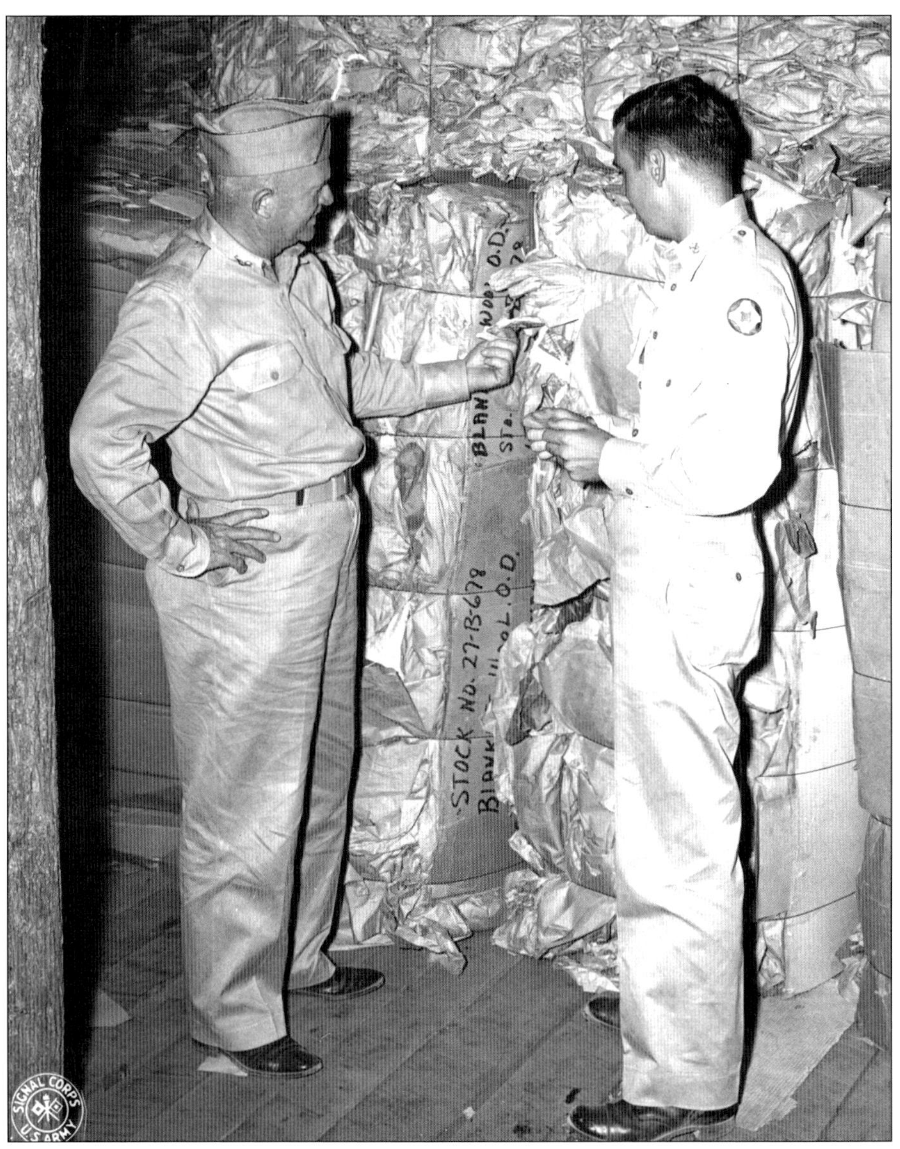

Col. Frank T. Addington (left) was the prisoner of war camp commander in Crossville, Tennessee, before his appointment as Camp Forrest post commander. He assumed command from Waltz, who was administratively retired because of the Army's mandatory age requirement. Addington was the post commander from October 1, 1943, until the federal government deactivated the installation in 1946. Seen here, Addington oversaw the base's salvage operations and examined part of the 29,000 pounds of wastepaper collected during a scrap drive. Lt. Augustus T. Naumann, post salvage officer (son of Fred and Estelle Naumann of Summit, New Jersey), explains the salvage process to him. Before the war, the United States imported raw materials from nations eventually aligned with the Axis Powers. These raw materials included natural rubber and tin. The disruption in trade forced the federal government to implement rationing and to ask citizens to "scrap" household items for the war effort. The federal government repurposed these items into war supplies, such as ammunition, airplanes, tanks, life rafts, ships, and gas masks. Military installations, civic organizations, and communities continually organized scrap drives for metal, rubber, and paper throughout the war. (Courtesy of USA HEC Military Museum.)

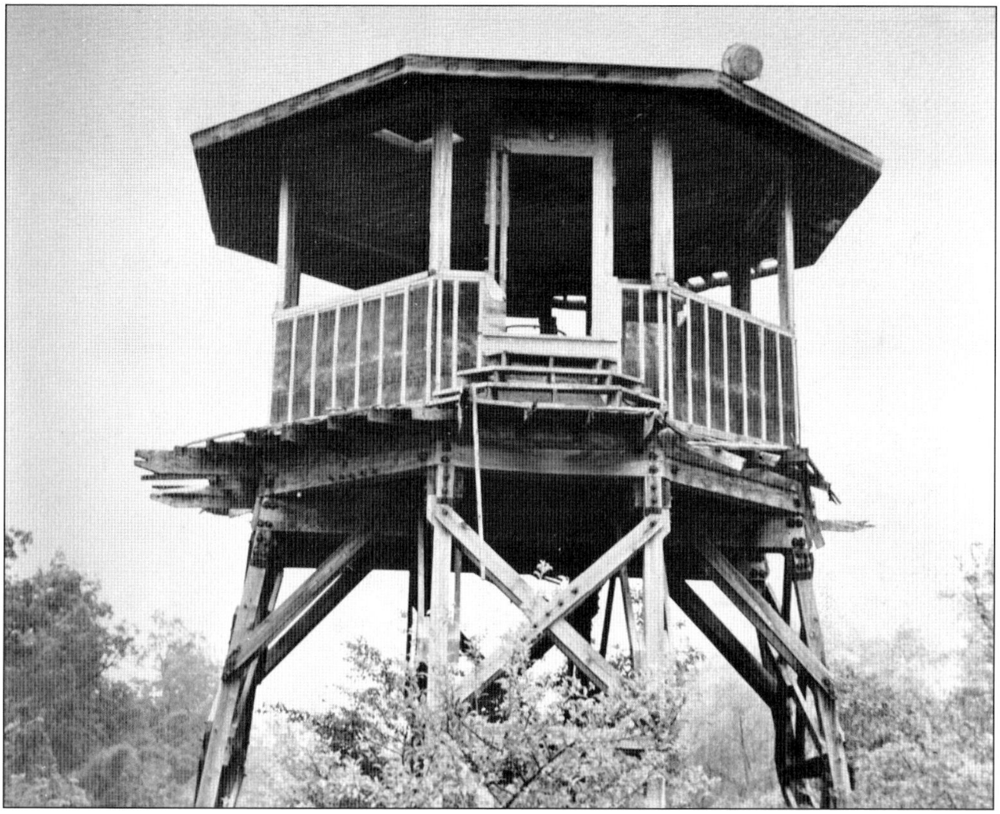

Camp Forrest transitioned to a prisoner of war (POW) facility in May 1943 and its commander also controlled numerous permanent and temporary branch camps in Tennessee, Alabama, Georgia, North Carolina, and South Carolina. During their free time, many POWs created drawings, paintings, ceramics, carvings, and jewelry from wood, metals, and paper. Many people remember the steadfast friendships with POWs who worked on the family farm. It was common for families to correspond with former POWs for decades after the war, despite the distance and language barriers. There were guard towers (above) around the Camp Forrest POW compound. The POW ceramic tile artwork (right) says, "I'm ready to go home." (Above, courtesy of TSLA; below, courtesy of CFF.)

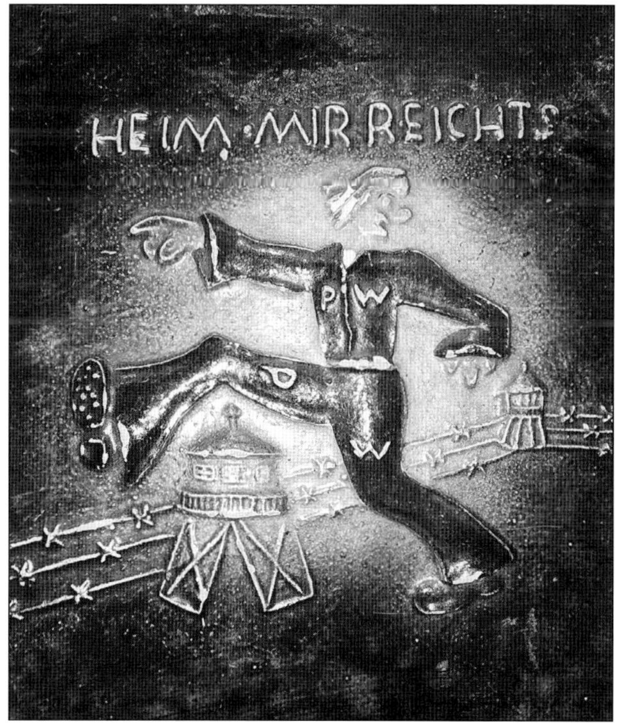

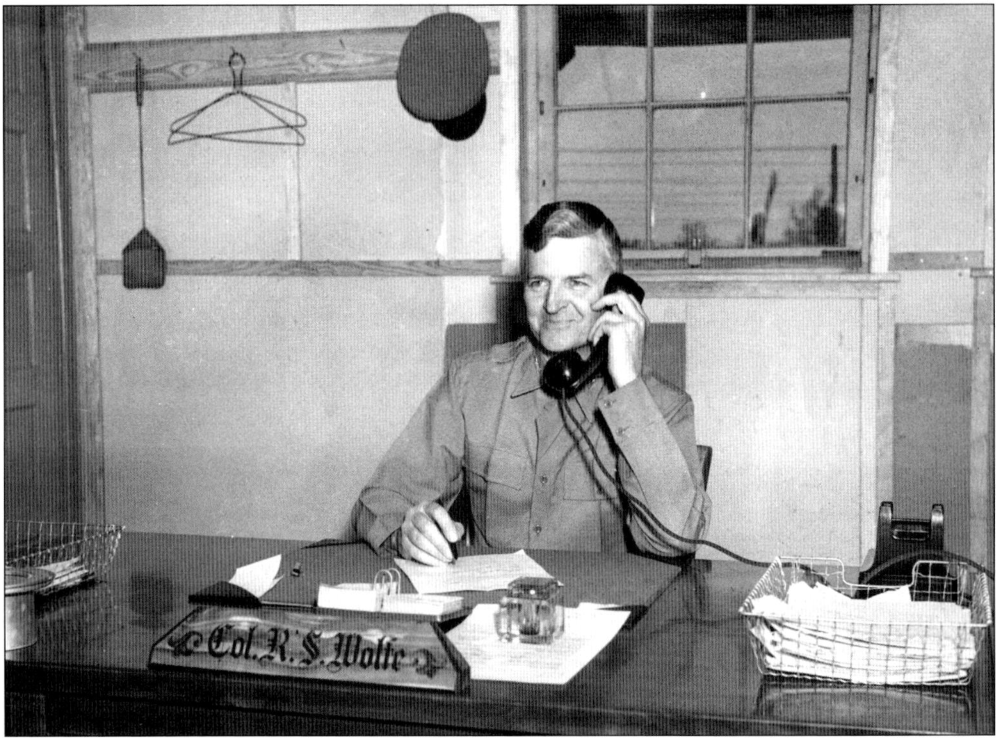

Clemson University alumnus Col. Russell S. Wolfe (class of 1911) commanded both the alien enemy internment camp and the prisoner of war (POW) camp. His military career began in the 2nd South Carolina Infantry, in which he served as an NCO during the Punitive Expedition. Commissioned as second lieutenant in 1917, he served in France during World War I with the 81st Infantry Division, as a platoon and company commander. Between the wars, he was a reserve officer in the 82nd Infantry Division serving in leadership positions including 327th Infantry regimental commander. He also led a regular army battalion during the Louisiana Maneuvers. In 1942, the War Department appointed Wolfe inspector and later commander of the detention facility. He oversaw its construction and transformation from an internment camp to a POW camp, including relocating internees, training staff, and transporting over 20,000 German and Italian POWs from North Africa. Camp administrators focused on identifying and segregating hardcore Nazis. After Camp Forrest and its branches were operational, Wolfe transferred to the War Department Manpower Board. (Courtesy of Col. Russell Wolfe Sr. family.)

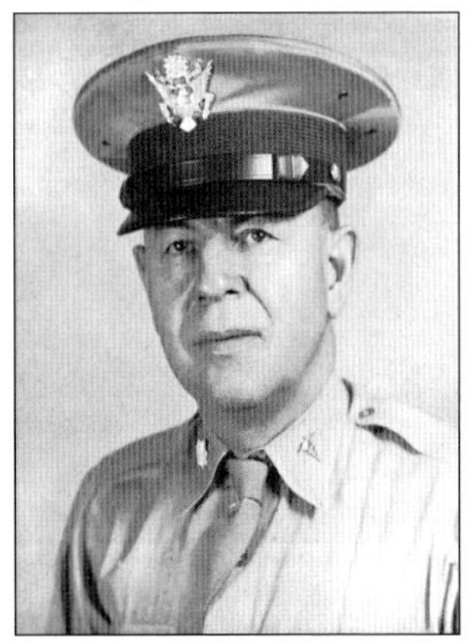

Lt. Col. F.T. Cavanor was the third camp surgeon and commanding officer of the station hospital. There were 118 soldiers in the permanent medical detachment, but many medical departments reported shortages in personnel and supplies. In April 1941, the hospital admitted 1,177 patients for treatment of respiratory issues primarily caused by climate changes and allergies. By June, all medical departments were fully operational. (Courtesy of CFF.)

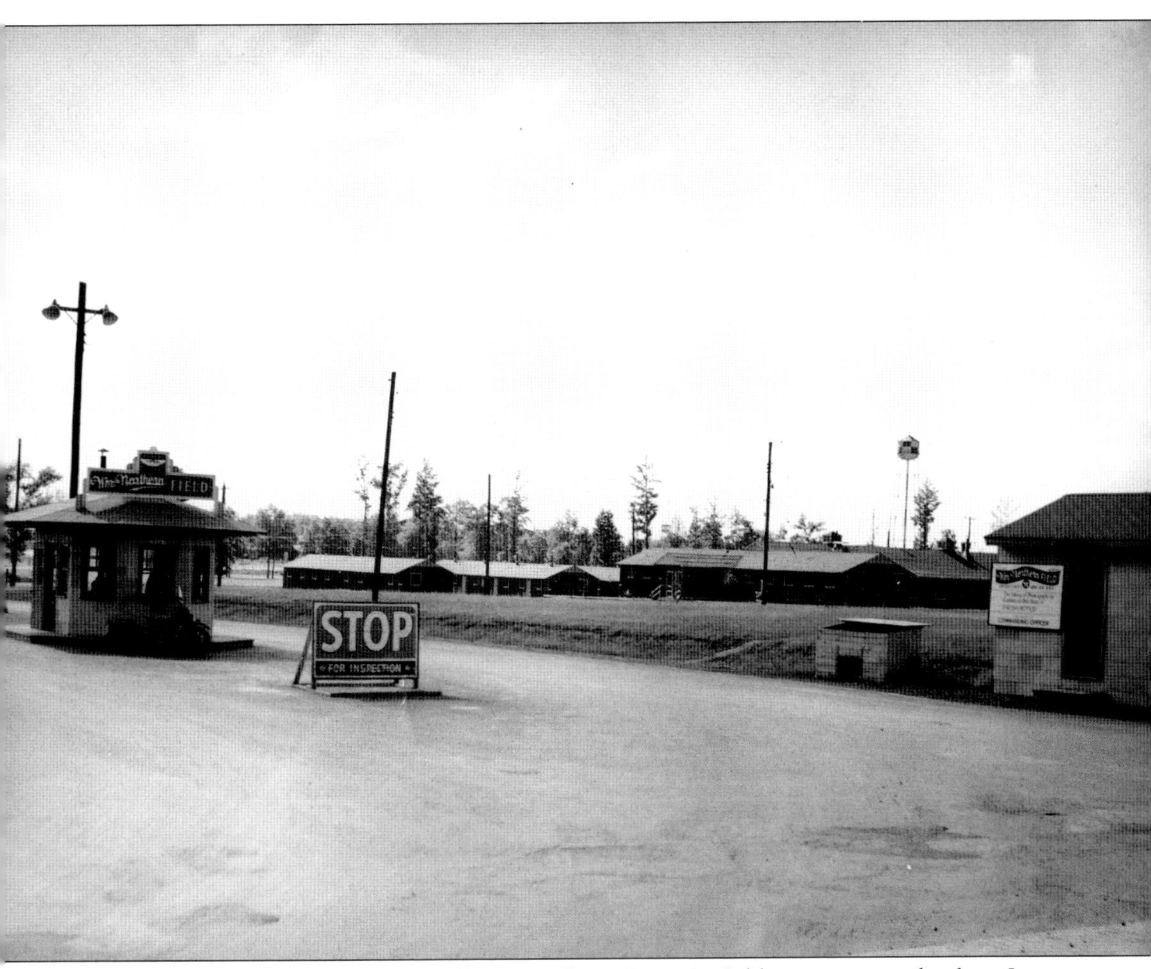

Col. Christopher C. Scott was the William Northern Army Airfield post commander from June 1942 to April 1944. Scott was a graduate of the Command and General Staff College, the Air Corps Tactical School, and had two decades of military aviation experience. Under Scott's leadership, the training activities of the field continually expanded to accommodate the intricate training needed to master problems of gunnery, navigation, precision bombing, and aerial observation. The installation was on 1,300 acres located a mile and a half from Camp Forrest. The advanced flight training facility had approximately 100 buildings and three 5,000-foot runways. The facility's name changed in November 1942 to William Northern Army Airfield to honor 2nd Lt. William L. Northern Jr., who was the first Tennessean killed in World War II. (Courtesy of Tullahoma Regional Airport.)

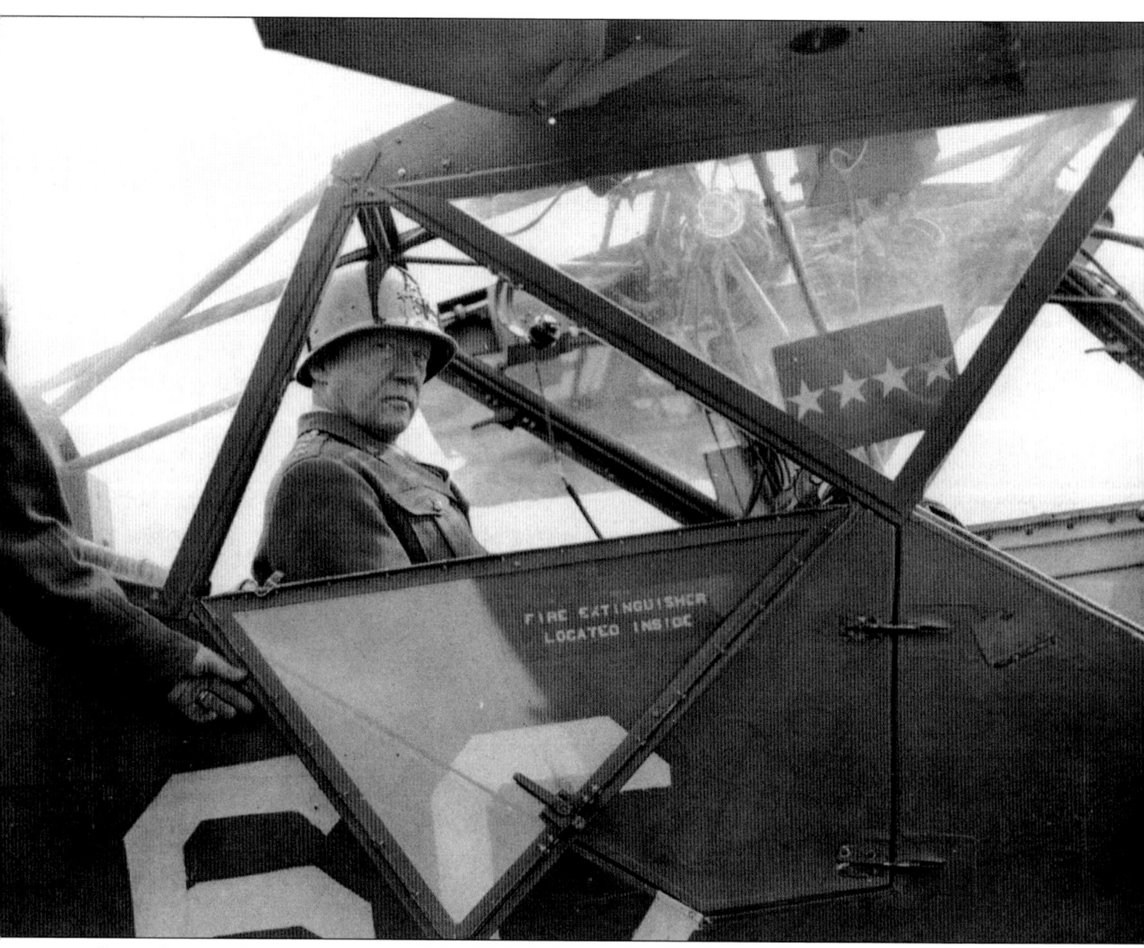

Gen. George S. Patton once stated, "All of the real heroes are not storybook combat fighters, either. Every single man in this Army plays a vital role. Don't ever let up. Don't ever think that your job is unimportant. Every man has a job to do, and he must do it. Every man is a vital link in the great chain." During World War II, Patton held numerous commands: 2nd Armored Division (stateside), US Tank School and led tanks into combat, Seventh Army in the Mediterranean, and Third Army in France and Germany (Allied invasion in Germany), and he played a key role in the Allied deception campaign during Operation Fortitude (predecessor to Operation Overlord). He died December 21, 1945, at the 130th Station Hospital in Heidelberg, Germany, from injuries sustained in a car accident. In this image, Patton is in a Piper Cub airplane. Tullahoma lore asserts Patton kept his Piper Cub plane on the outskirts of town during the 1941 Tennessee Maneuvers. He flew above the war games to monitor progress and quickly landed in the nearest open field if he saw troops that needed "further instructions." (Courtesy of CFF.)

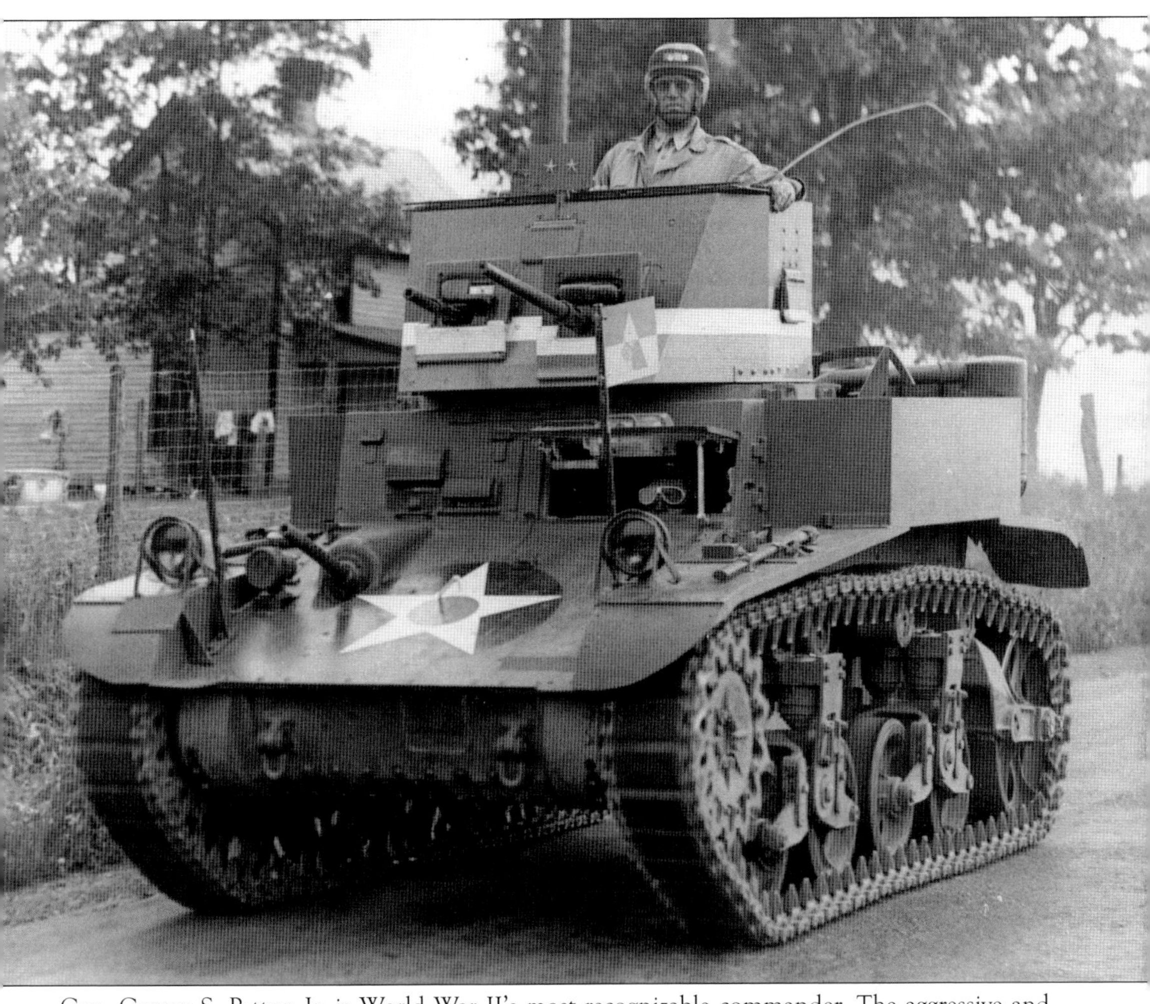

Gen. George S. Patton Jr. is World War II's most recognizable commander. The aggressive and often controversial general led troops from the front lines and inspired his men to continue fighting even when the odds appeared bleak. During the Great War, he served as Gen. John J. Pershing's aide and was the first man assigned to the Tank Corps. During the interwar years, he continued working on the development of the armored command doctrine, wrote a tank operations manual, and lobbied others that tanks should be an independent fighting force rather than serving as a support division. Patton competed in the modern Pentathlon in the 1912 Olympics and finished in fifth place. Following the Olympics, he studied fencing at the Cavalry School in Saumur, France, under Monsieur l'Adjutant Charles Clery, a French master swordsman. Upon his return to the States, Patton updated the Cavalry's saber combat doctrine and designed a new sword, the M1913 Saber (the Patton Saber). The innovative design modified the weapon to a thrusting rather than a slashing saber. In this image, Patton is on recon in the Tennessee countryside. (Courtesy of CFF.)

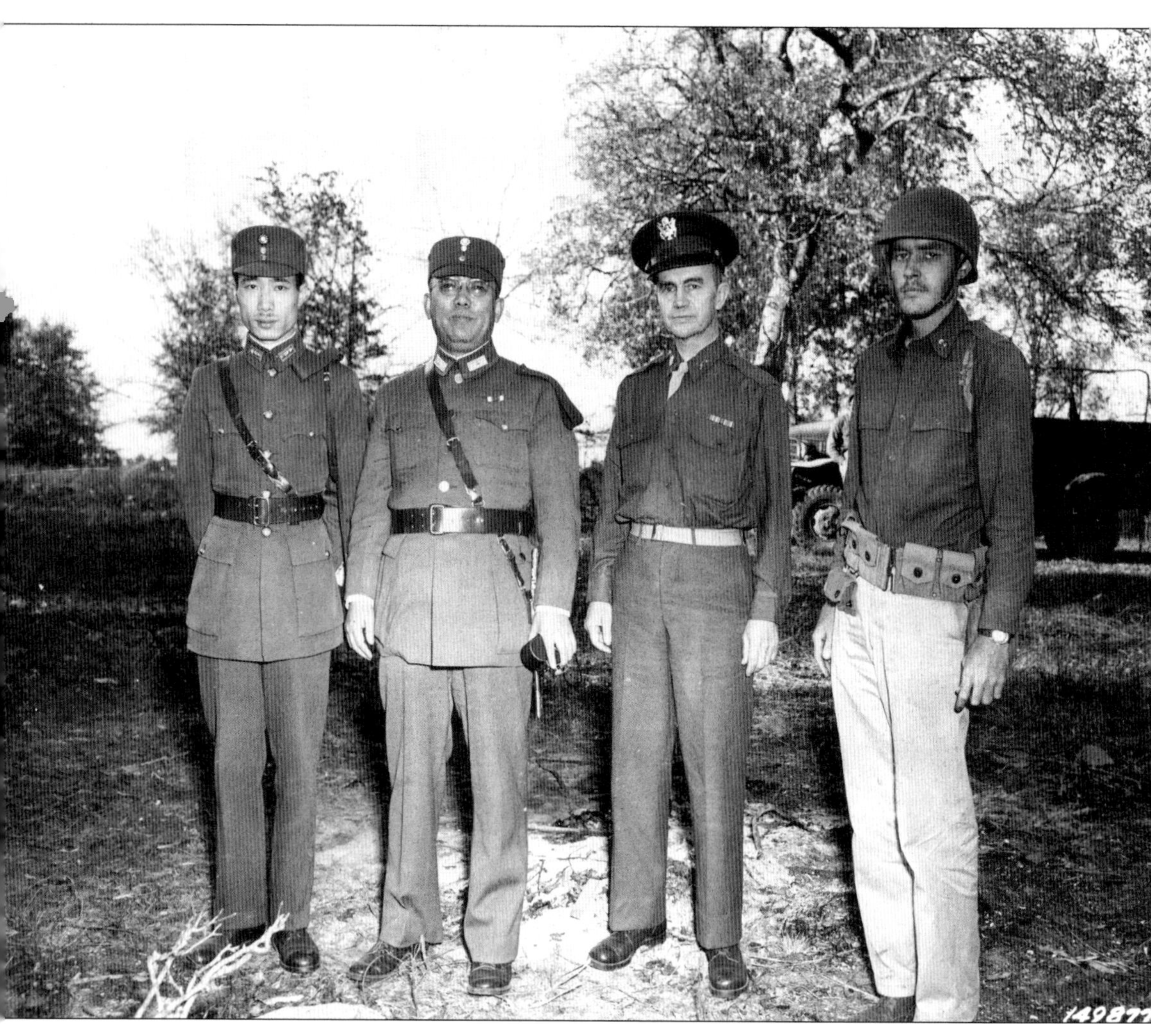

In the fall of 1942, China sent a military mission to meet with FDR to plead for more military support. Generalissimo Chiang Kai-shek recalled the mission after learning that the United States was sending India the war materials originally destined for China. From left to right are Capt. Ping-Tsuan Ho, Maj. Gen. Dai-Fung King, members of the Chinese Military Mission to the United States, Maj. Benjamin Muse, War Department, and Capt. Frank Haskell, Ordnance, Camp Forrest. (Courtesy of MTSU.)

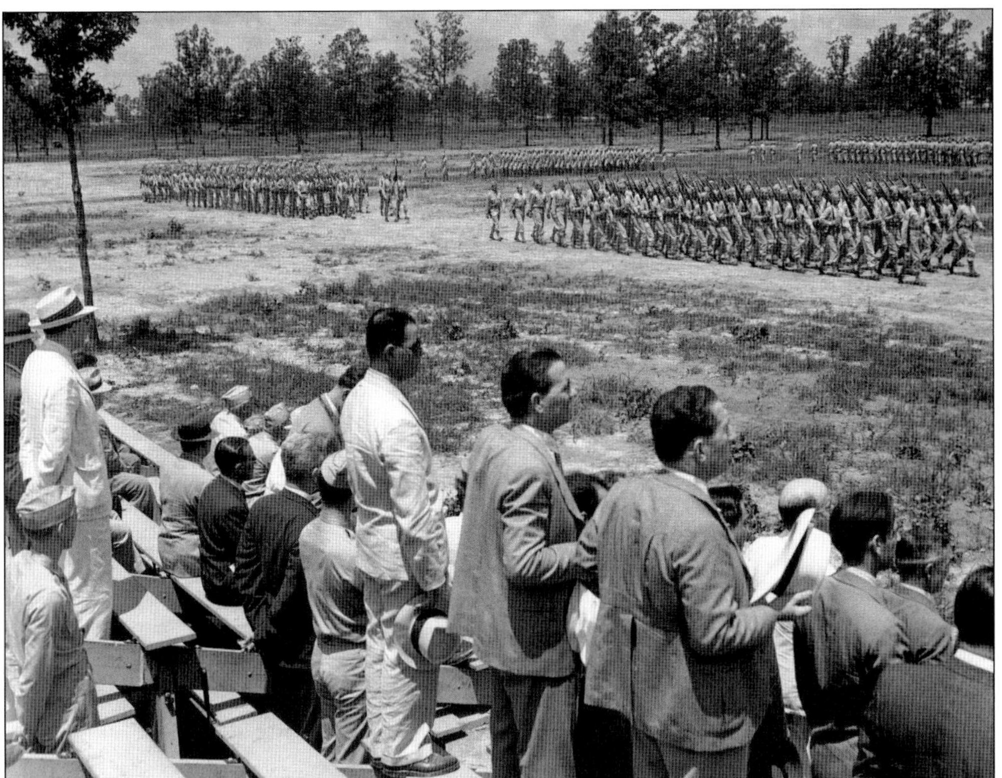

On July 15, 1941, Camp Forrest hosted leaders from 13 Latin American nations as part of a tour of defense industries and military installations in Tennessee. Maj. Gen. Samuel Lawton, 33rd Division commander, served as the mission's tour guide. The tour included a review of base facilities, a weapons demonstration by the 123rd Field Artillery, and a troop review on the parade grounds. Visitors were Latin American diplomats, naval and military officers, and representatives from the State Department, the Army Air Corps, and the Tennessee Valley Authority. The event highlighted hemispheric cooperation on the eve of America's entry into World War II, reflecting the importance of military diplomacy and shared defense efforts across the Americas. (Courtesy of CFF.)

Maj. Gen. Eurico Gasper Dutra, Brazilian minister of war, is pictured somewhere in Tennessee during his 1943 inspection visit of the maneuver exercises. He was a guest of Lt. Gen. Lloyd B. Fredendall, commander of the Second Army. Numerous high-ranking Brazilian officers accompanied Major General Dutra on the trip. He pledged Brazilian support to Allied Powers for the duration of the war. (Courtesy of CFF.)

SGT. ALVIN YORK

The Hon. Gov. Prentiss Cooper
Mr. John W. Harton
AND THE
State College A. & I. Coral Group
Will Appear at the

SPORTS ARENA

CAMP FORREST, TENN.
FRIDAY, MAY 15th, 8:00 p. m.

FREE!

Post Special Services Office

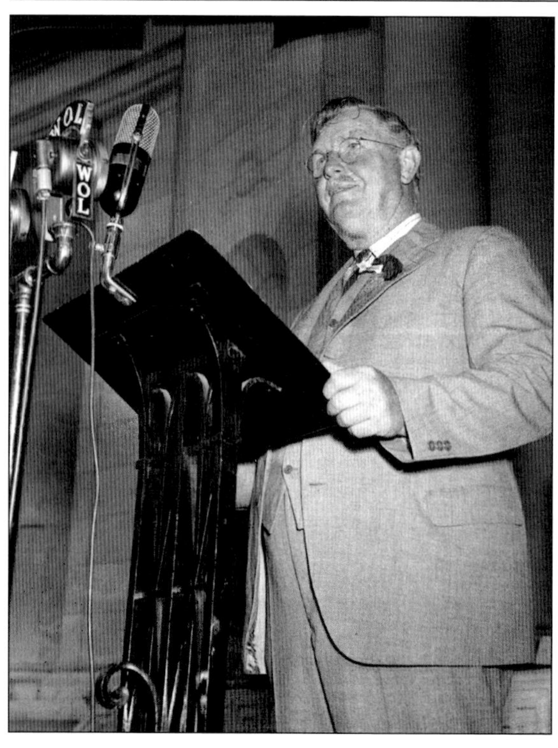

Sgt. Alvin York, a hero of the Great War, was from Tennessee. Following the bombing of Pearl Harbor, York stated that the attack was the "worst affront the United States has ever received—far worse than what the Germans did in 1917." York worked tirelessly throughout World War II, meeting with military and civilian leaders to boost morale and patriotism and giving presentations at the Camp Forrest Sports Arena. On July 30, 1941, York and several Tennessee leaders visited FDR in the White House before the premiere of the motion picture named after him. (Above, courtesy of Harton Family Partners, Joe Lester, general manager; left, courtesy of CFF.)

Two

Fighting for Victory

Combat Units at Camp Forrest

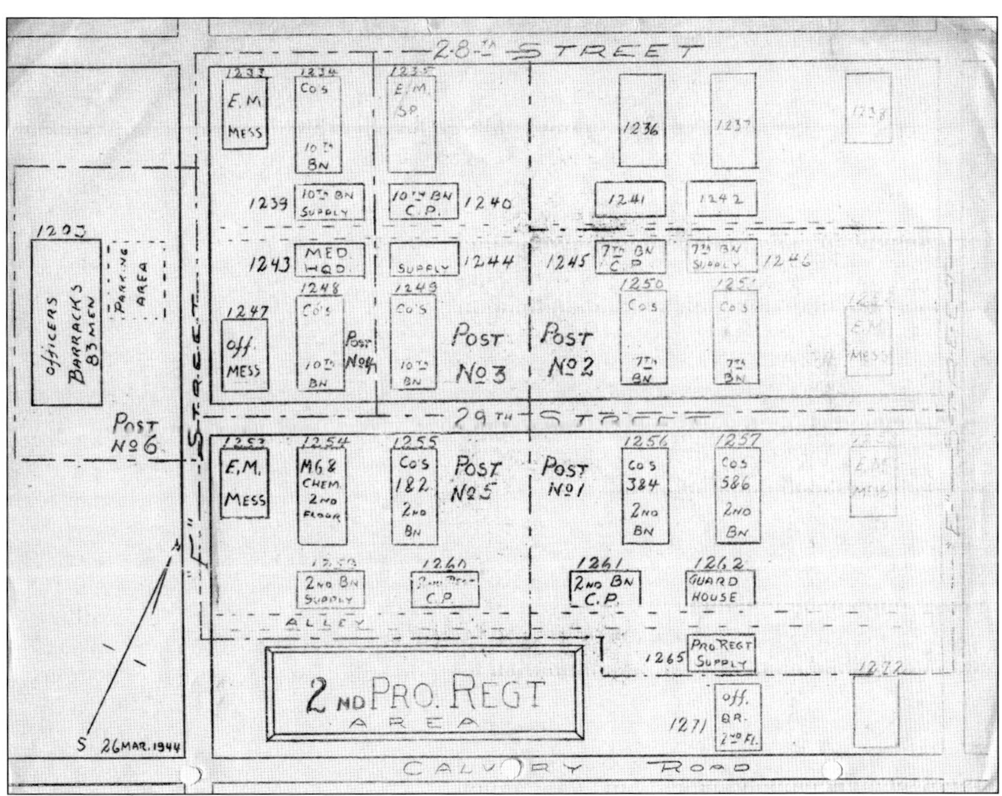

Over 80 years have passed since the sounds of jeeps, tanks, and planes echoed throughout Camp Forrest. As the fifth largest city in Tennessee, it was home to over 70,000 soldiers training in infantry, artillery, armor, engineer, airborne, combat support, and combat service support divisions. Throughout the Tennessee Maneuvers, Camp Forrest hosted the Quartermaster and Ordnance Depots, a main railhead, and bivouac areas for troops. (Courtesy of TSLA.)

THIRTY-THIRD, or PRAIRIE DIVISION

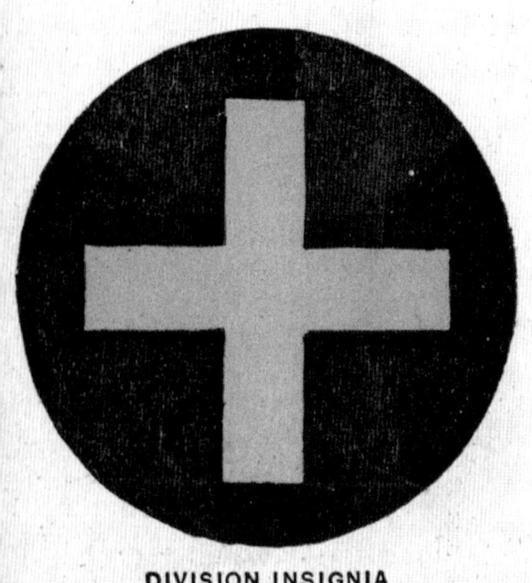

DIVISION INSIGNIA

Quotations from History, issued by 33rd Division Headquarters while in Luxembourg

"FIRST American Division to hold portion of front line on Verdun Sector." "Only American Division having men decorated by King of England in person." "Only American Division which fought with British, French and American Armies." Captured 3,924 German Prisoners. Engaged at Hamel, St. Mihiel, Chippilly Ridge, Gressaire Wood, Meuse-Argonne, Bois de Forges, Bois de Dannevoux, Bois de la Cote Lemont, Bois de Chaume, Bois Du Plat Chene, Consenvoye, Bois d'Harville St. Hilaire, Chateau D'Aulnois, Riaville Marcheville, Mont. Sec. Very, Gesnes to Pouilly and Stenay, ARMY OF OCCUPATION.

Medals awarded		Casualties		
American	118	Killed	227	
British	52	Wounded	8,098	7,
French	47	Captured	18	
Belgian	1	Missing	4	
Total	218	Total	8,347	8,

In 1923, the 33rd Infantry Division (Illinois National Guard) reformed and began training intensively, and in the interwar years participated in several maneuver exercises. Col. George C. Marshall was the division's head instructor from 1933 to 1936. As a result of this training, the division was well prepared when war in Europe broke out in 1939. The first cadre of soldiers, equipment, and vehicles arrived at Camp Forrest a week after induction into federal service. Amid the rain, snow, and mud, it took approximately three weeks for the entire division to move to Camp Forrest. The 13 weeks of basic training started in April 1941, and in the fall the division participated in the Arkansas-Louisiana Maneuvers. Following Pearl Harbor, military leaders assigned troops from the division to guard defense-related installations throughout Tennessee against sabotage. A month later, the War Department recalled the troops to Camp Forrest. The 33rd Division departed for Fort Lewis in September of 1942. (Courtesy of CFF.)

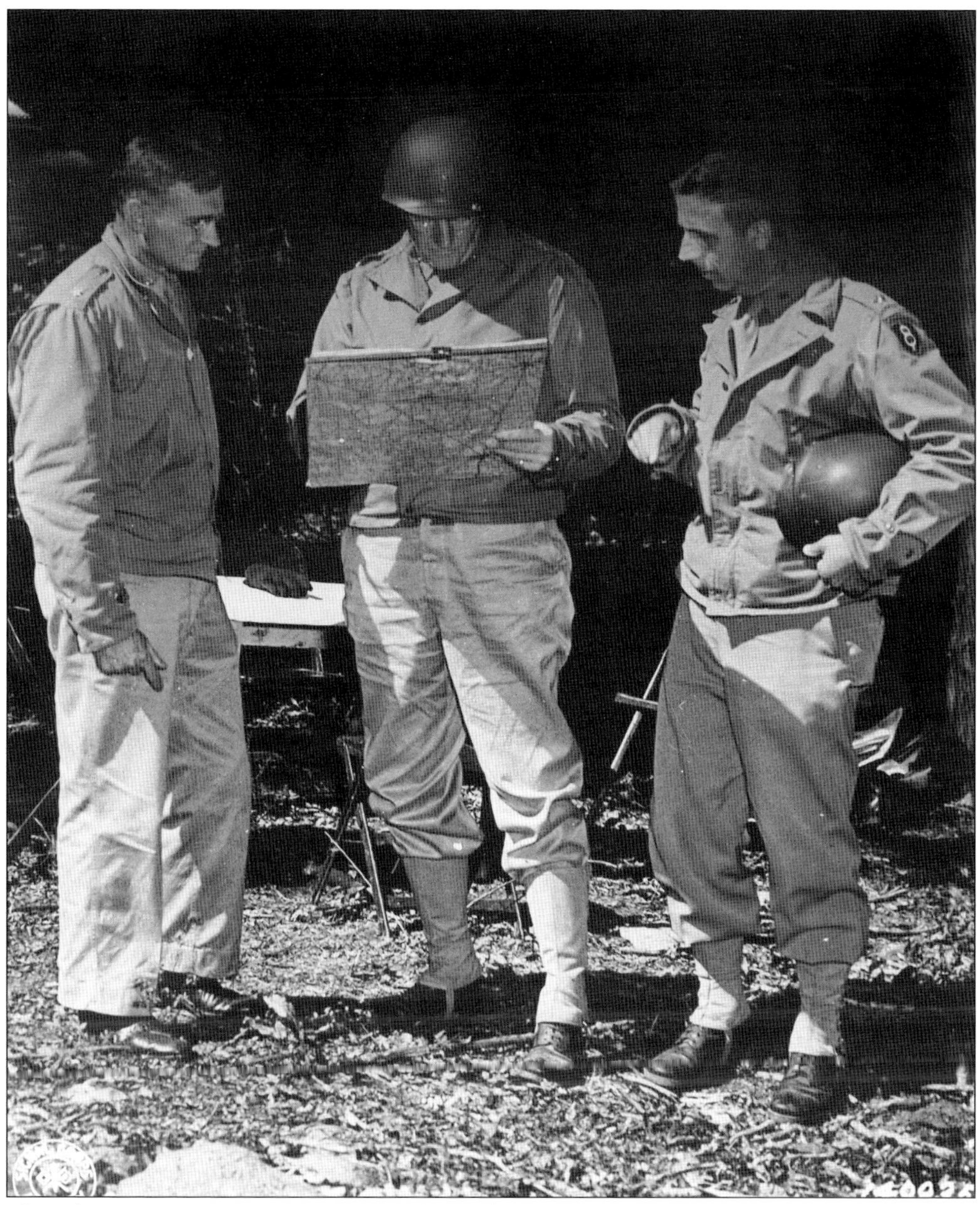

The 8th Infantry Division was reactivated on July 1, 1940, when the Army began building up its military forces. The Great War ended before the division saw combat. In World War II, the 8th Infantry stormed Omaha Beach and advanced through France, overtaking several key parts of the country. After participating in the 1943 Tennessee Maneuvers, the Division bivouacked at Camp Forrest until its departure for Europe in December 1943. In the interim, soldiers spent time training and perfecting infantry tactics and advancing small arms and artillery skills. In this September 28, 1942, photograph, Maj. Gen. Paul Peabody (left), Brig. Gen. James Pickering, and Brig. Gen. John McKee confer at 8th Division Headquarters during a maneuvers exercise. (Courtesy of NARA.)

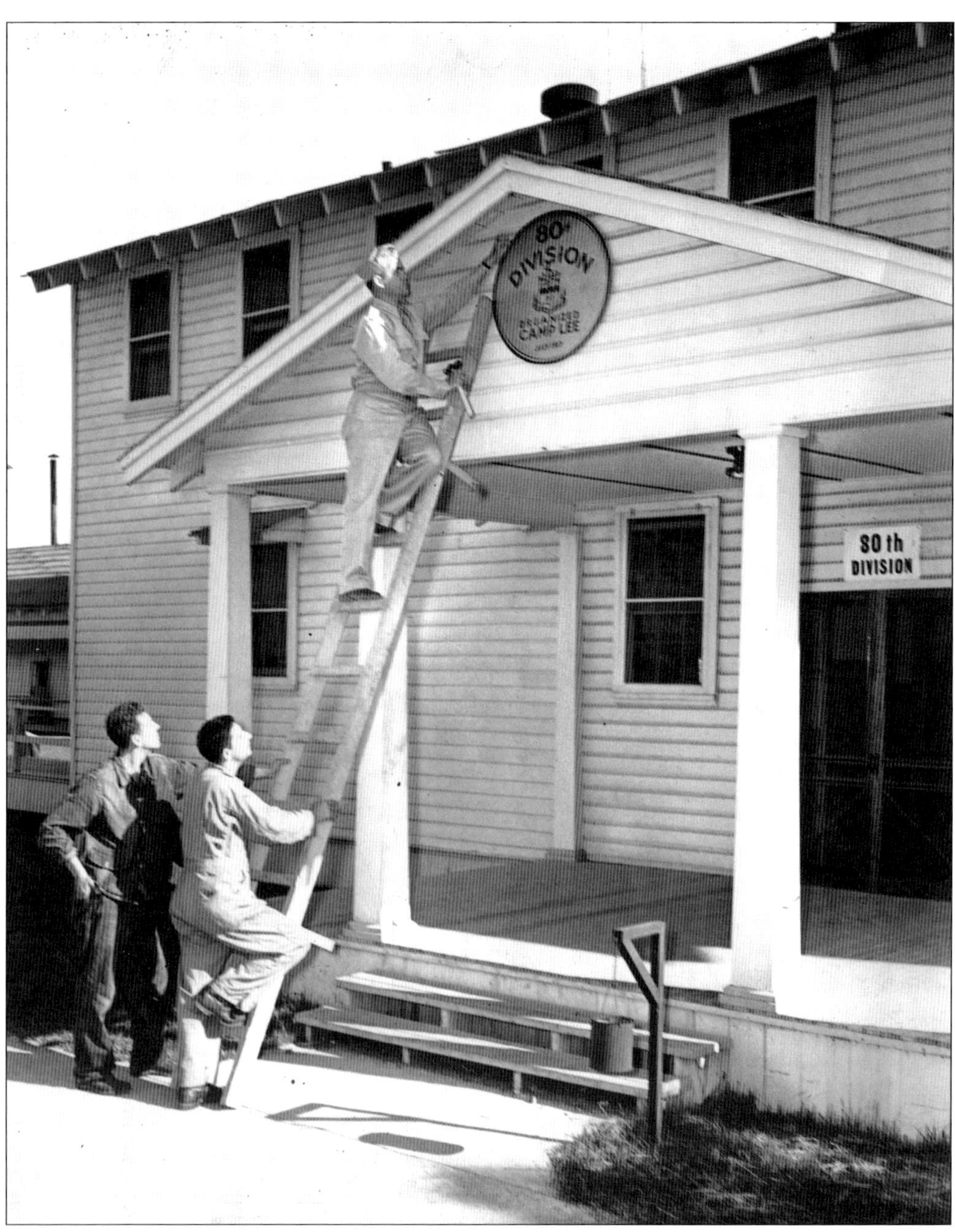

The 80th Infantry Division was activated at Camp Forrest on July 15, 1942. In April 1943, the presidential inspection tour of the South featured a review of the 80th Division soldiers, and their equipment and weapons. The post band played "The Star-Spangled Banner" while the infantry provided a 21-gun salute. Here, Maj. Joseph O. Matthews Jr. fastens the 80th Division sign to the Headquarters building at Camp Forrest while Privates Sullivan and Gidio look on. (Courtesy of MTSU.)

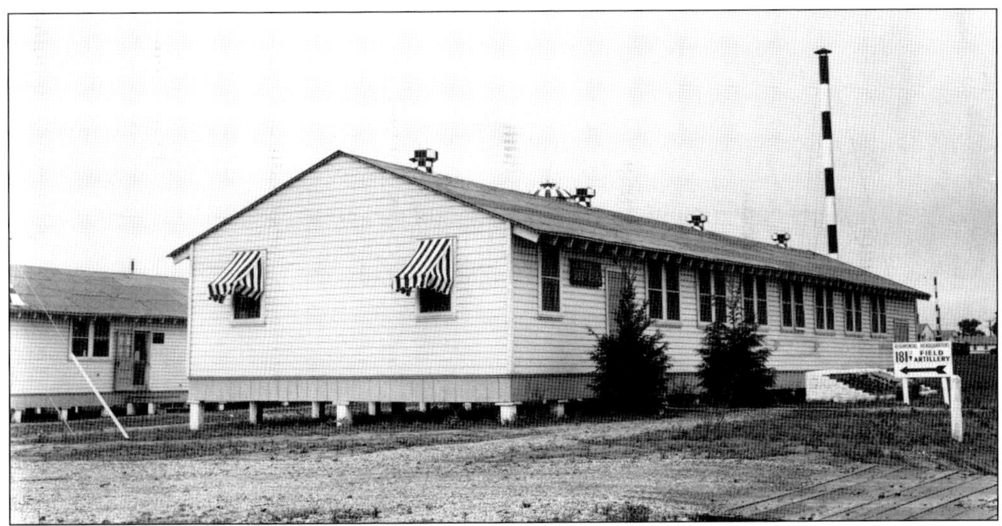

The 181st Field Artillery Regiment was a Tennessee National Guard unit until FDR enacted the Protective Mobilization Plan on August 31, 1940. This order gave the president congressional authority to order the National Guard and the Organized Reserves into active federal service for a year. Col. Ira Summers commanded this regiment until he was administratively retired based on age limitations. The young-at-heart Summers then enlisted in the Tennessee State Guard. (Courtesy of NARA.)

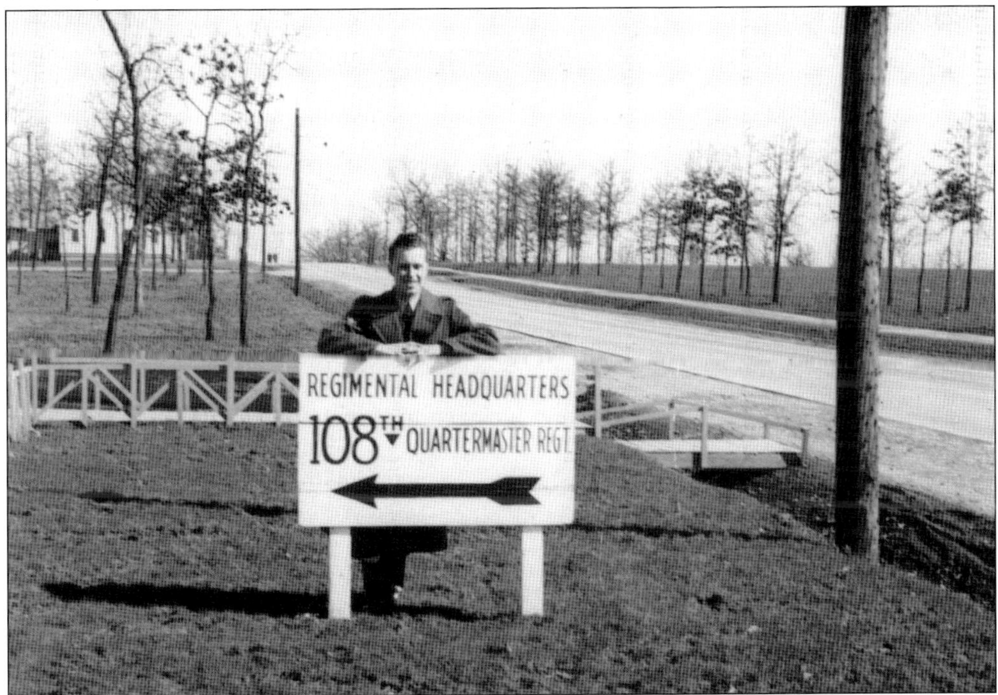

The Quartermaster Corps supplied every item that the soldier and division needed in the field. With the depth and breadth of supplies and equipment used by the Army, quartermaster personnel became supply area specialists. For example, the soldiers distributing clothing supplies may not know about distributing vehicle supplies. Seen here is the regimental headquarters for the 108th Quartermaster Regiment, 33rd Infantry Division. (Courtesy of MTSU.)

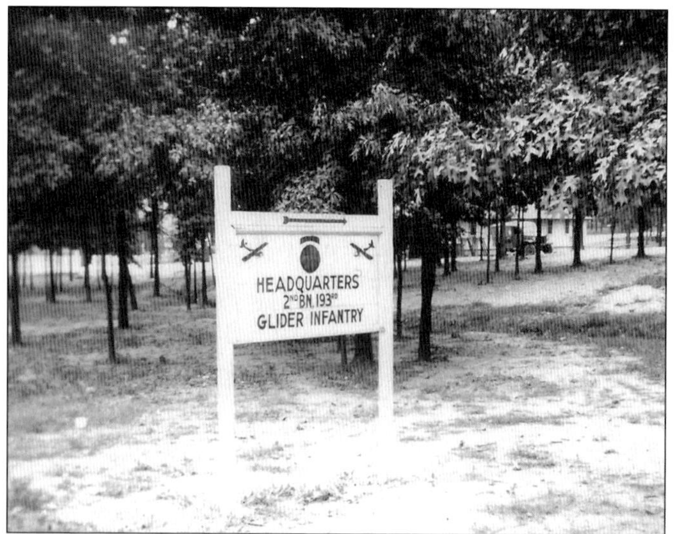

The 193rd Glider Infantry Regiment was attached to the 17th Airborne Division. The regiment activated on April 15, 1943, under the command of Col. Maurice Stubbs and was stationed at Camp Forrest from February 7 to March 24, 1944. The 193rd Glider Infantry Regiment fought during the Battle of the Bulge and sustained heavy casualties. After World War II, the Army discontinued gliders based on unreliability and safety concerns. (Courtesy of CFF.)

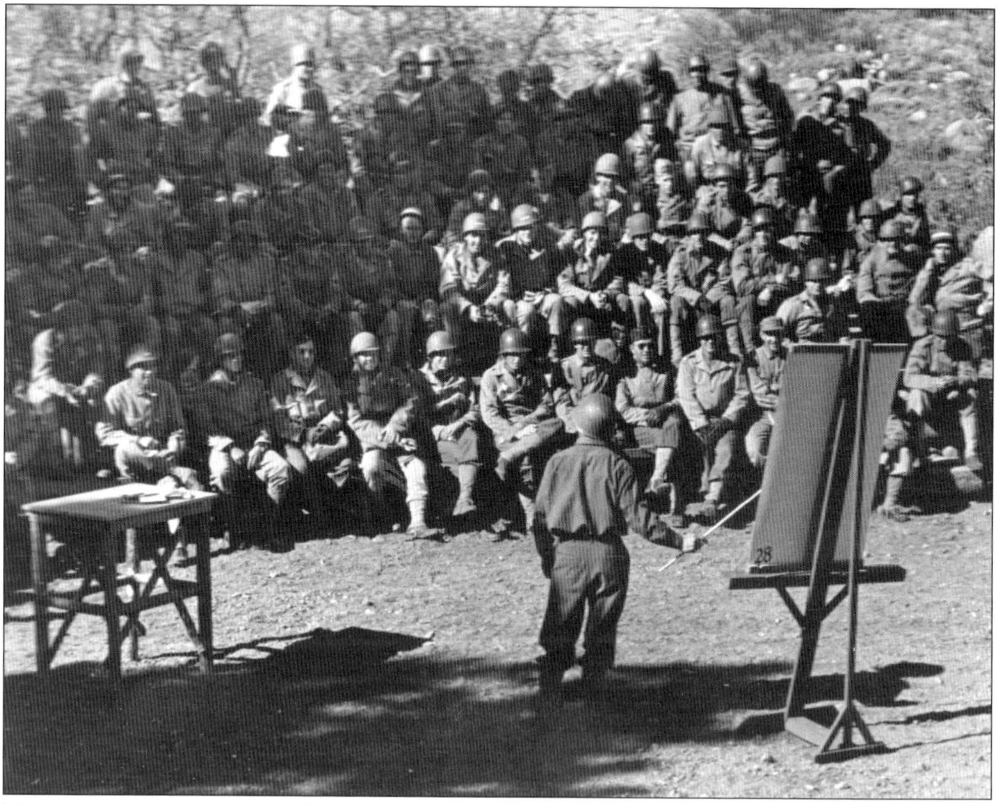

Troops began arriving in March 1941, making the base a hub of activity with over 20,000 enlisted men and 1,100 officers. The Army's task of turning civilians into soldiers began by teaching geography, economics, drills, exercises, and demonstrating proficiency in firing weapons at one of the base ranges. During weapons training, soldiers learned the mechanics of weapons from manuals, books, training films, oversized training aids, and simulated ammunition that demonstrated bullet mechanics. They also learned how to thoroughly clean and store a weapon, and to load a magazine. (Courtesy of CFF.)

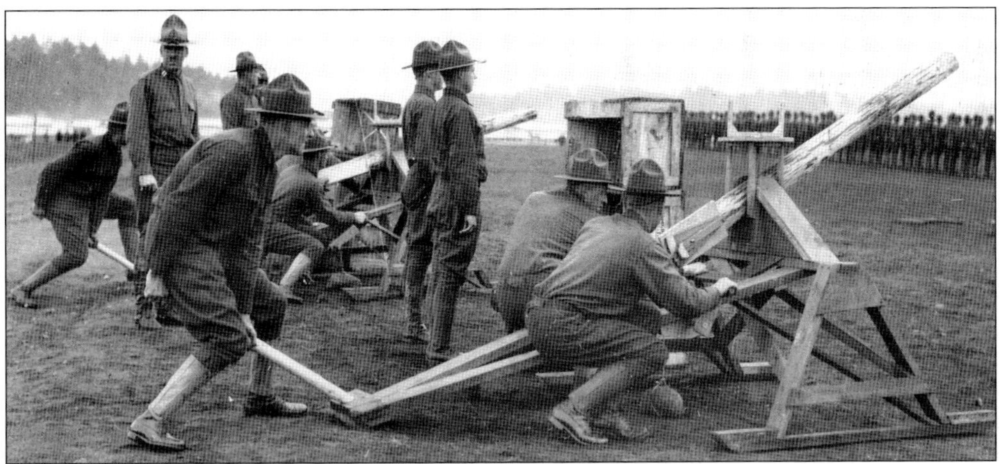

Despite a lack of equipment and weapons, training schedules did not alter, as time was of the essence. Learning to improvise amid war was a hallmark of the US Army. Makeshift supplies and equipment constructed from available materials, such as wood, tin cans, or stovepipes, were substitutes until equipment was issued. Soldiers threw rocks and flour-filled cans to simulate bombs. In the photograph, soldiers during the Great War temporarily trained using a wooden antiaircraft gun. (Courtesy of CFF.)

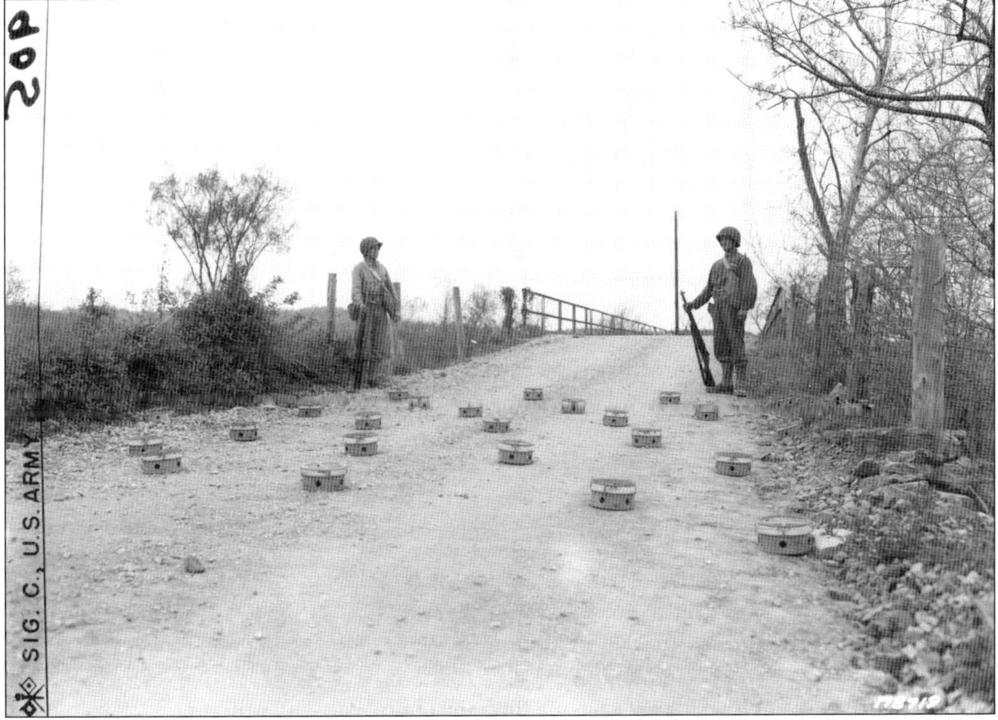

Pvt. Francis J. Trabert (Dighton, Kansas), at left, and Pvt. John Stalder (Dearborn, Missouri) guard the mined approach on the bridge over the Stones River two miles west of Lofton, Tennessee. Practice mines spewed red smoke when detonated, indicating the soldiers were "dead." There were several versions of the anti-tank practice mine. One of the earliest versions of the anti-tank mine used two boards that sandwiched a liquid-filled glass bottle. Pressure applied to its exterior boards would break the bottle and produce a cloud of smoke. (Courtesy of NARA.)

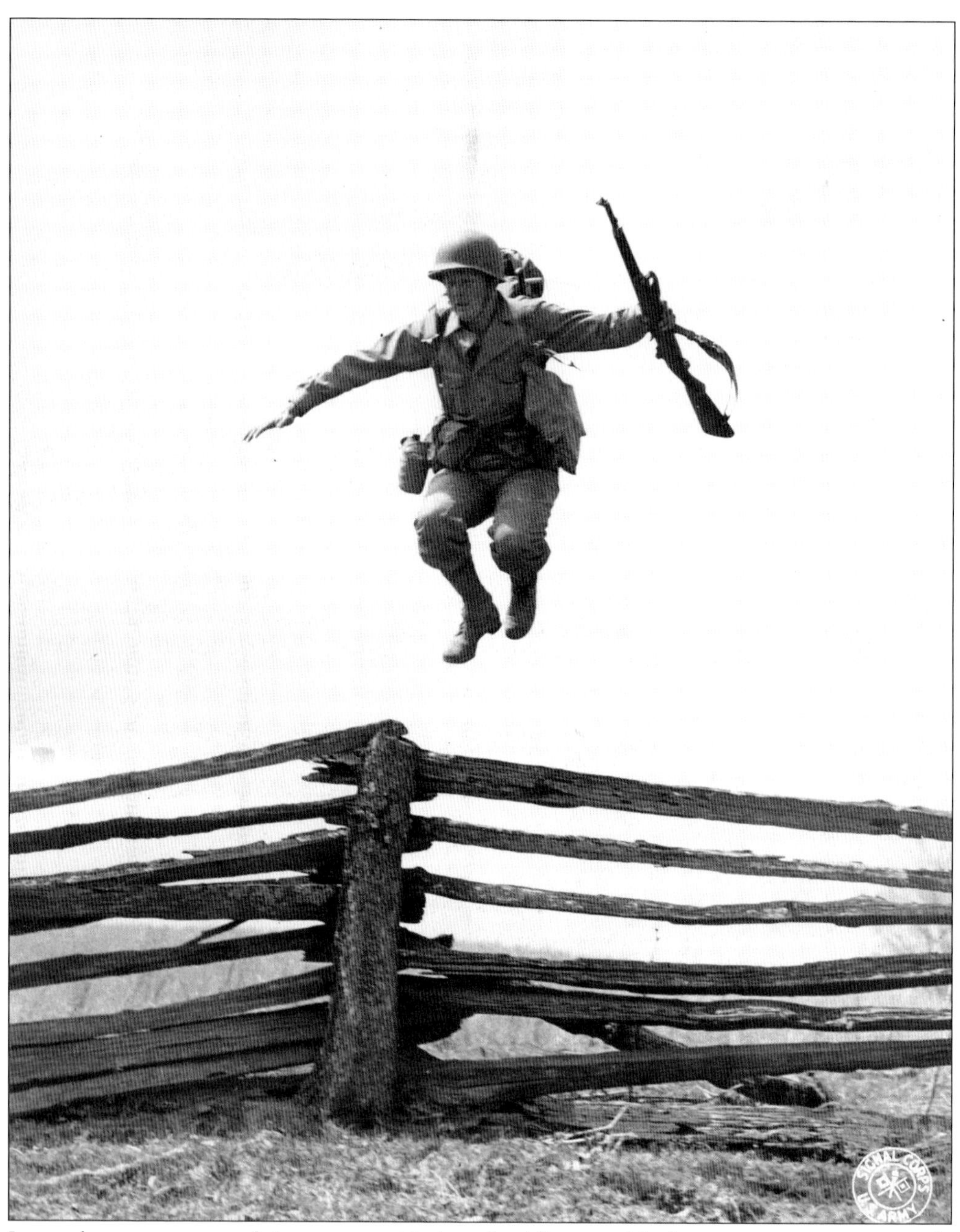

In combat, weapons proficiency was critical, and soldiers qualified on numerous weapons. At Camp Forrest, weapons training focused on small arms, grenades, and artillery. Proficiency levels ranged from marksman (lowest), sharpshooter, and expert (highest). Here, Pvt. Edward Wiggins (Robbinsville, North Carolina) of Company C, 315th Infantry, leaped over a rail fence with his M1 Garand to make a swift getaway. (Courtesy of CFF.)

The 155 mm howitzers of the 123rd Field Artillery used live ammunition during a Tennessee Maneuvers exercise on June 12, 1941. The 155 mm Howitzers threw a 95-pound shell approximately 12,800 yards (7.3 miles), but their effective range was from 7,000 yards (4 miles) to 10,000 yards (5.7 miles). (Courtesy of CFF.)

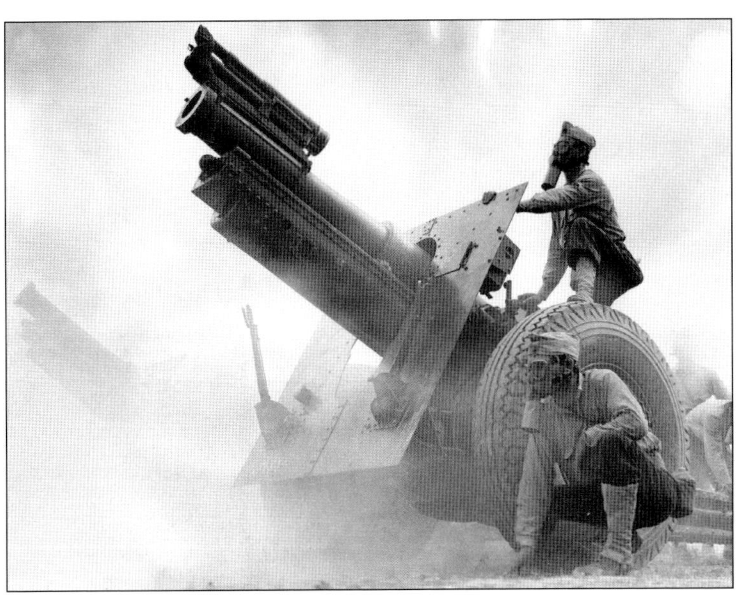

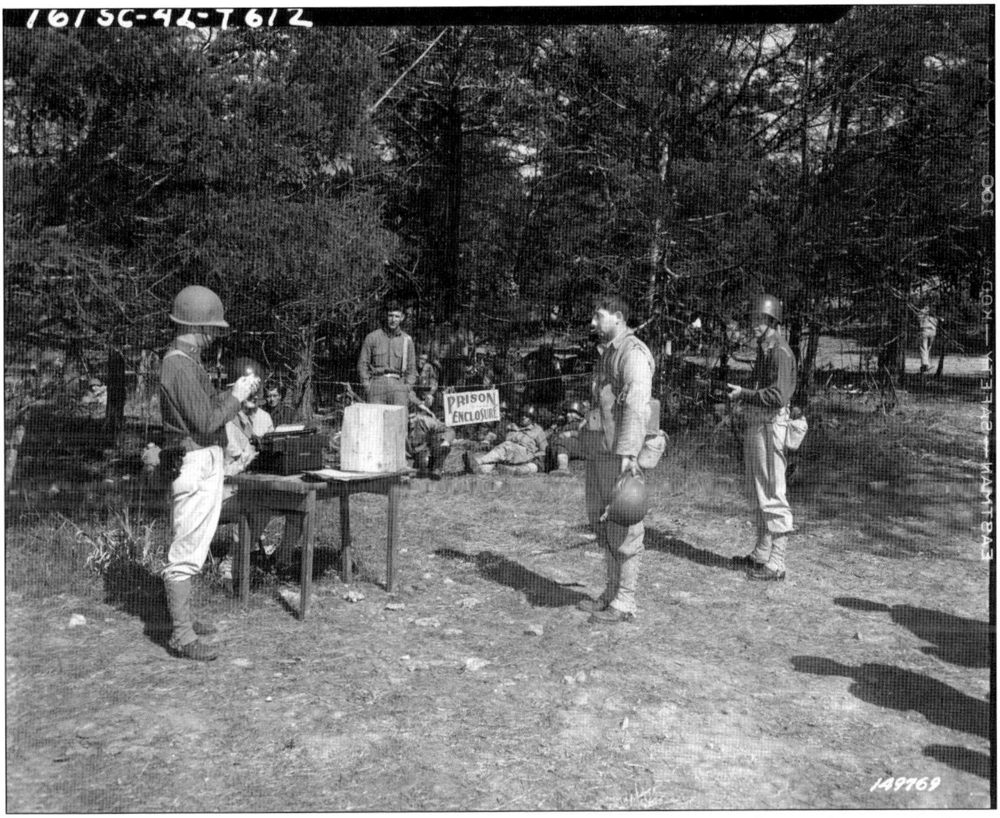

During maneuvers, captured soldiers were POWs and "detained" behind a single strand of wire and one guard, which made escapes easy. In later maneuvers, large trucks encased in screens made of heavy wire were used as encampment areas, and intelligence officers questioned POWs. Some POWs complained about the inadequate food and shelter during their capture. (Courtesy of NARA.)

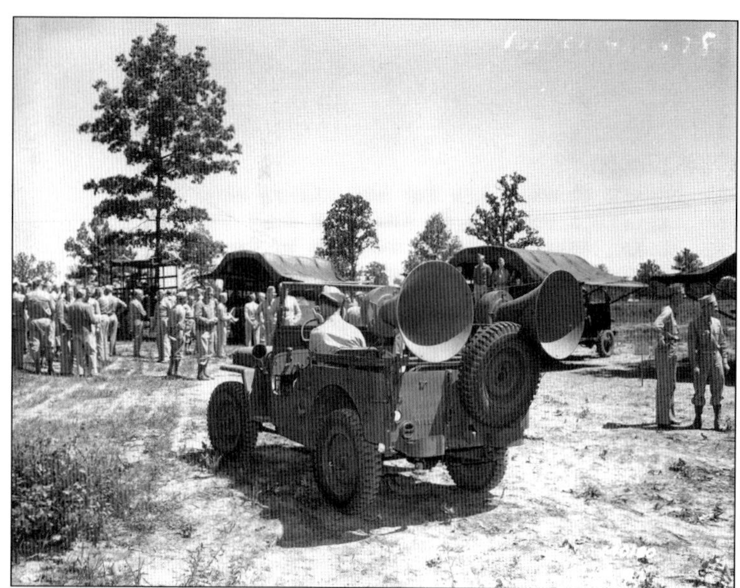

By May 1942, training activities at Camp Forrest were underway. The vastness of the training areas and the considerable number of soldiers made it necessary to develop mobile sound systems to ensure orders and commands were audible. Divisions outfitted a quarter-ton Willys jeep with loudspeakers mounted on the rear seat to direct men and machines. (Courtesy of NARA.)

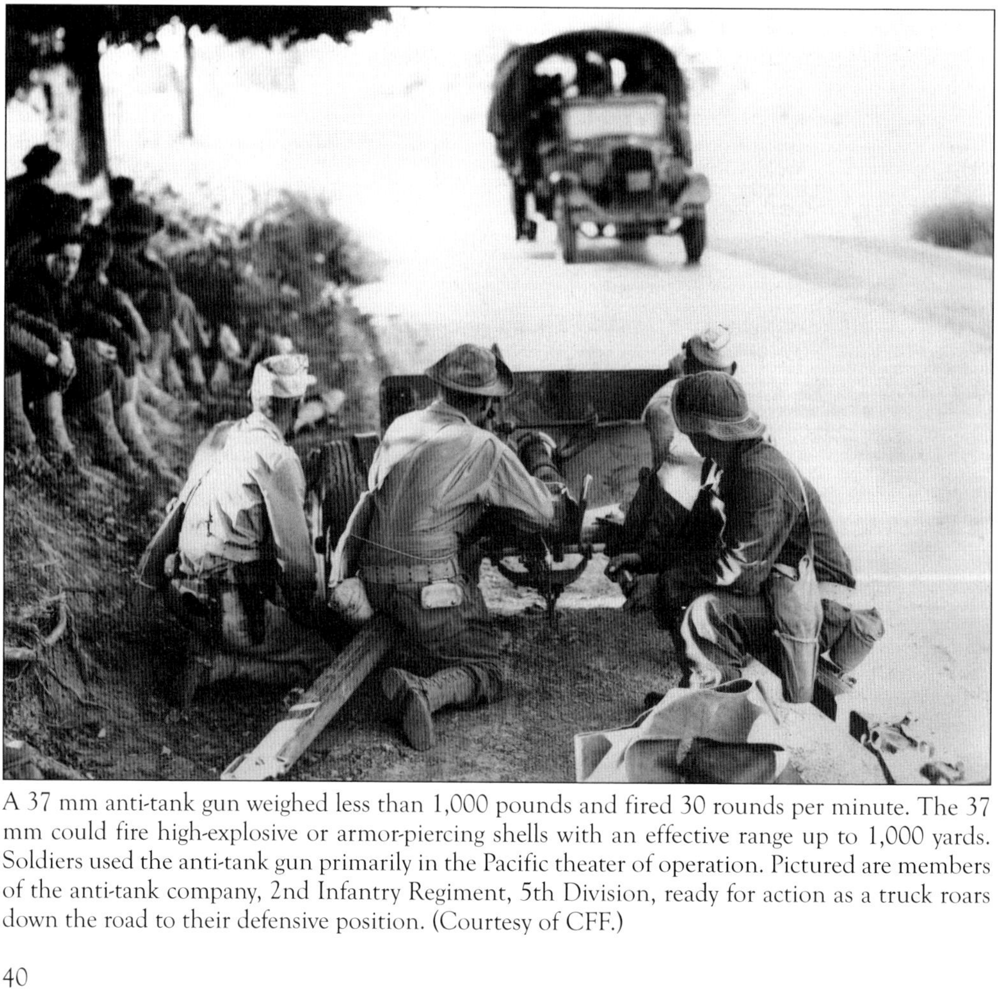

A 37 mm anti-tank gun weighed less than 1,000 pounds and fired 30 rounds per minute. The 37 mm could fire high-explosive or armor-piercing shells with an effective range up to 1,000 yards. Soldiers used the anti-tank gun primarily in the Pacific theater of operation. Pictured are members of the anti-tank company, 2nd Infantry Regiment, 5th Division, ready for action as a truck roars down the road to their defensive position. (Courtesy of CFF.)

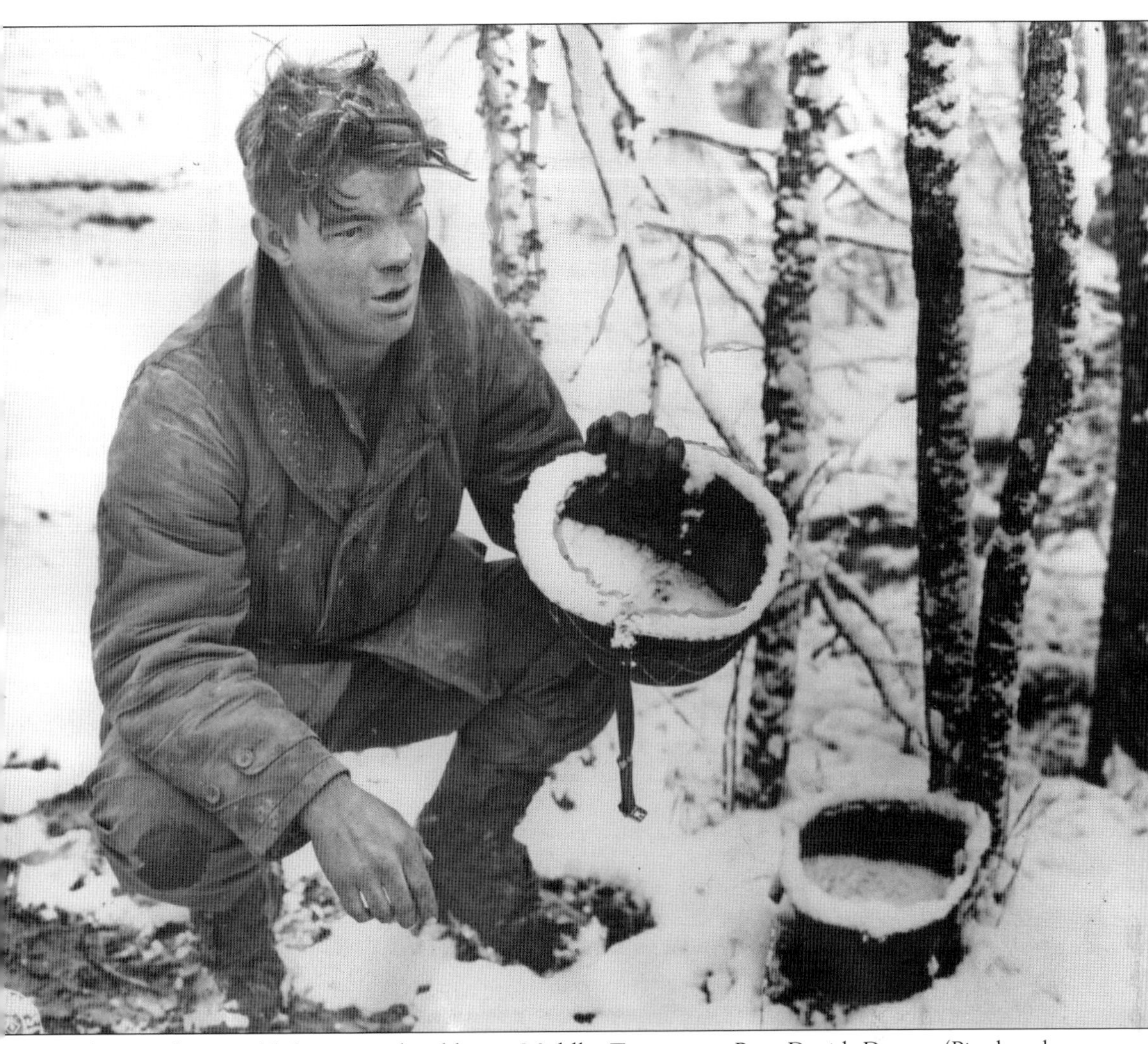

The weather could be unpredictable in Middle Tennessee. Pvt. David Dugan (Pittsburgh, Pennsylvania) crawled from his pup tent to find the area covered in snow. He and other members of his ordnance battalion were engaged in winter maneuvers in the Tennessee countryside. During the construction of Camp Forrest, crews continued working despite the area having one of the coldest winters on record. Accurate weather forecasts required data on barometric pressure, temperature, and wind velocity. With this data, issuing weather predictions within a 72-hour window was possible. Temperatures might plummet to subzero in winter, and sweltering temperatures above 100 degrees were normal throughout the summer months. High daytime temperatures could quickly drop after sunset. Rains caused muddy quagmires that could instantly halt advancing men and machines. In addition to the temperatures, men had to be aware of the potential for tornadoes, floods, and lightning. (Courtesy of CFF.)

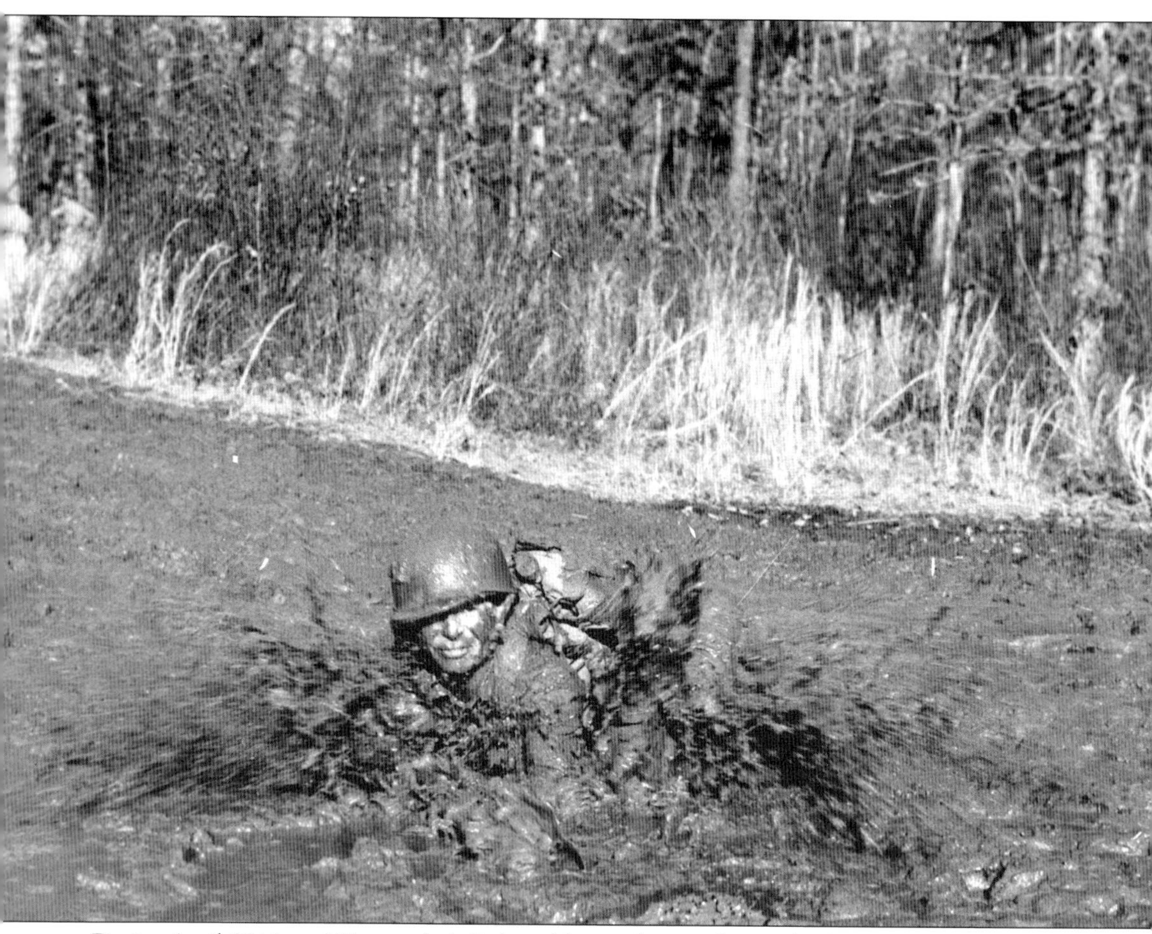

During April 1944, an F-2 tornado killed a soldier and injured several others. Sudden downpours caused flooding and washed away supplies and equipment. The 118th Infantry Regiment, 30th Infantry Division, fell victim to a torrential downpour that caused a small earthen dam to fail. Much of their supplies and equipment washed downstream. Men scrambled in the knee-high rushing water to grab equipment before heading to higher ground. Throughout the war years, numerous soldiers were struck or killed by lightning. While on duty in a guardhouse, two officers were knocked onto the floor after lightning struck the building. Although shaken, the officers were unharmed. Throughout the winter, snow and ice could make road conditions treacherous, and freezing temperatures were unbearable to the bivouacking soldiers. Weather conditions were to blame for colds, upper respiratory infections, pneumonia, trench foot, and frostbite. Rain and fog grounded planes due to low visibility. As pictured, soldiers learned to fight in any environment. (Courtesy of CFF.)

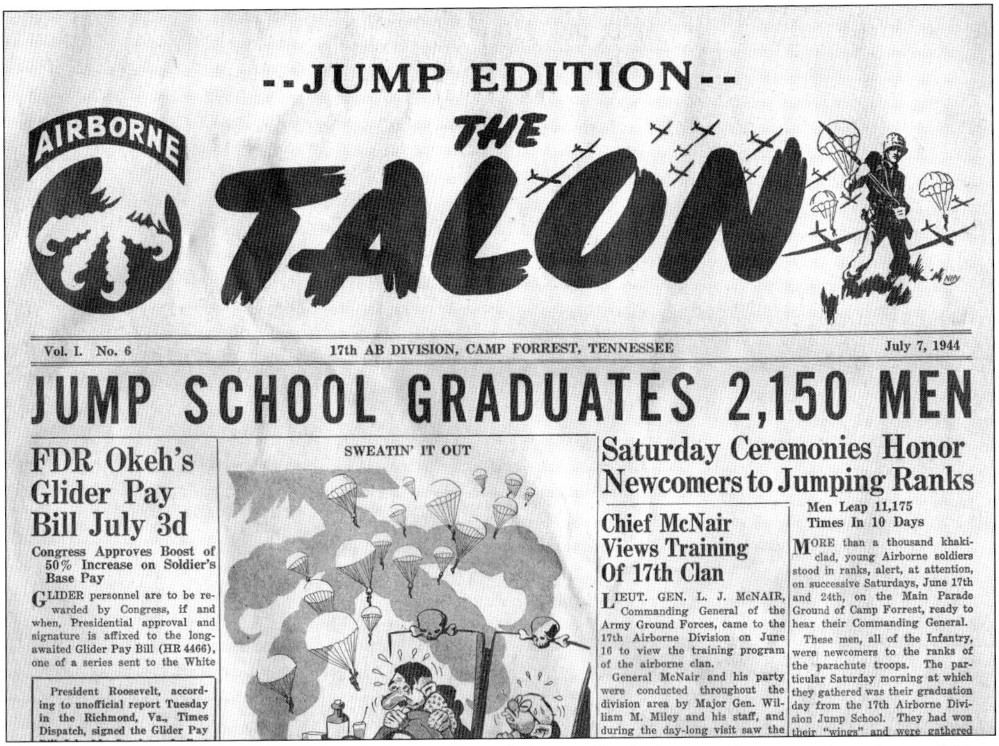

--JUMP EDITION--

AIRBORNE

THE TALON

Vol. I. No. 6 | 17th AB DIVISION, CAMP FORREST, TENNESSEE | July 7, 1944

JUMP SCHOOL GRADUATES 2,150 MEN

FDR Okeh's Glider Pay Bill July 3d

Congress Approves Boost of 50% Increase on Soldier's Base Pay

GLIDER personnel are to be rewarded by Congress, if and when, Presidential approval and signature is affixed to the long-awaited Glider Pay Bill (HR 4466), one of a series sent to the White

President Roosevelt, according to unofficial report Tuesday in the Richmond, Va., Times Dispatch, signed the Glider Pay

SWEATIN' IT OUT

Saturday Ceremonies Honor Newcomers to Jumping Ranks

Chief McNair Views Training Of 17th Clan

LIEUT. GEN. L. J. McNAIR, Commanding General of the Army Ground Forces, came to the 17th Airborne Division on June 16 to view the training program of the airborne clan.

General McNair and his party were conducted throughout the division area by Major Gen. William M. Miley and his staff, and during the day-long visit saw the

Men Leap 11,175 Times In 10 Days

MORE than a thousand khaki-clad, young Airborne soldiers stood in ranks, alert, at attention, on successive Saturdays, June 17th and 24th, on the Main Parade Ground of Camp Forrest, ready to hear their Commanding General.

These men, all of the Infantry, were newcomers to the ranks of the parachute troops. The particular Saturday morning at which they gathered was their graduation day from the 17th Airborne Division Jump School. They had won

The Talon served as the divisional newsletter of the 17th Airborne Division, keeping soldiers informed and connected during training and deployment. Under the command of Maj. Gen. William Miley, the division included four key regiments: the 513th Parachute Infantry, the 193rd Glider Infantry, the 507th Parachute Infantry, and the 194th Glider Infantry. Like many unit publications, *The Talon* blended official announcements with stories, humor, and reflections of daily life in the airborne. It offered soldiers both practical information and a sense of camaraderie while also preserving a record of the division's activities during World War II. (Courtesy of CFF.)

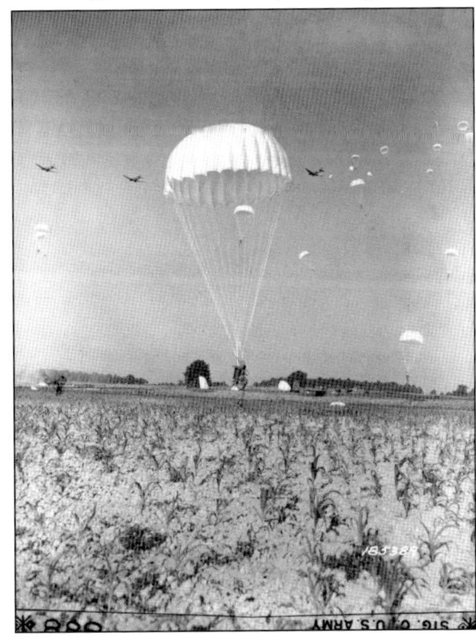

The Tennessee Maneuvers in June 1943 marked the first extensive use of paratroopers in large-scale Army training. Near Lafayette, Tennessee, airborne troops practiced repeated jumps and landings, honing skills essential for future combat operations. Each exercise emphasized precision, since even a small mistake on landing could result in a sprain, fracture, or a more serious injury. Perfecting these techniques under maneuver conditions prepared paratroopers for the demands of battlefield drops overseas, where success often depended on the ability to land quickly, regroup, and move into action. These exercises in Middle Tennessee represented a critical step in developing the Army's airborne forces during World War II. (Courtesy of MTSU.)

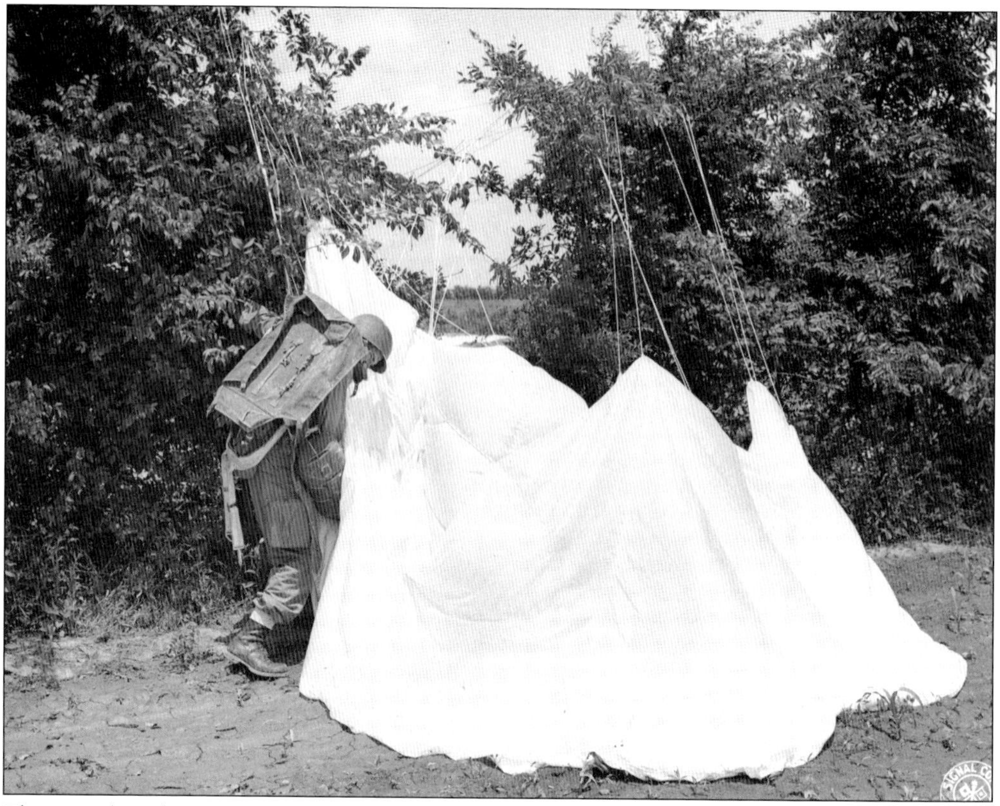

This parachute became entangled in a bush when the paratrooper landed. Once the paratroopers landed in the drop zone, they worked quickly to gather and secure their parachutes. An improperly secured parachute could reflect a light source or blow across a field. Either scenario might alert the enemy that paratroopers were in the area. (Courtesy of John Allan.)

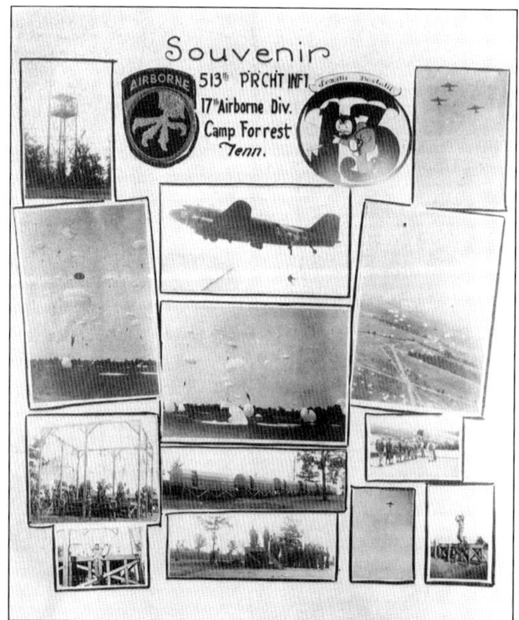

In March 1944, while stationed at Camp Forrest, the 513th Parachute Infantry Regiment participated in the Tennessee Maneuvers. Riggers packed, repaired, and maintained parachutes. The riggers used sewing machines, webbing, canvas, and fasteners for repairs. Riggers were infantry positions but became a quartermaster specialty postwar. (Courtesy of John Allan.)

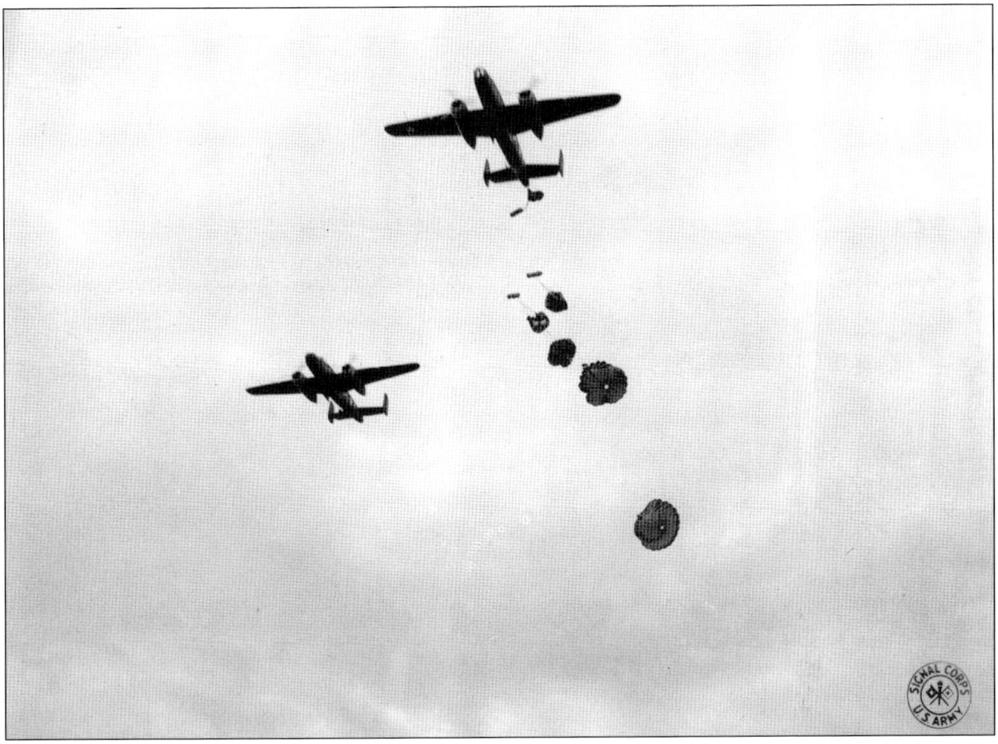

Quartermaster units packed supplies into crates and attached them to parachutes for deployment from Army planes. For each supply drop, the parachute color denoted the type of supplies so units could quickly identify the contents of the crate. For the D-Day operations, the red parachute was ammunition or weapons, the yellow was medical equipment, the blue was food, the green was radios, and the white was other equipment. To confuse the enemy, parachute colors would change each time planes airdropped supplies to ground forces. (Courtesy of John Allan.)

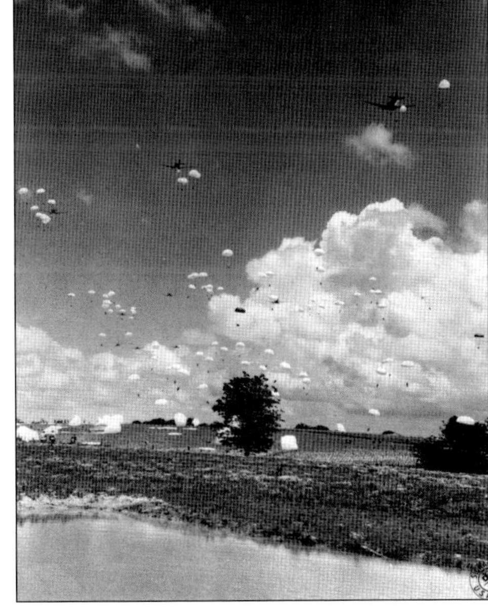

In the 1943 Tennessee Maneuvers, the Second Army's "Blue Army" cascaded, like tiny white mushrooms, behind the "Red Army" lines. More than 85 chutes were still in the air while other paratroopers, already freed from their harnesses, were running toward their assembly area. Soldiers used the white chutes, and the colored ones were supplies. (Courtesy of John Allan.)

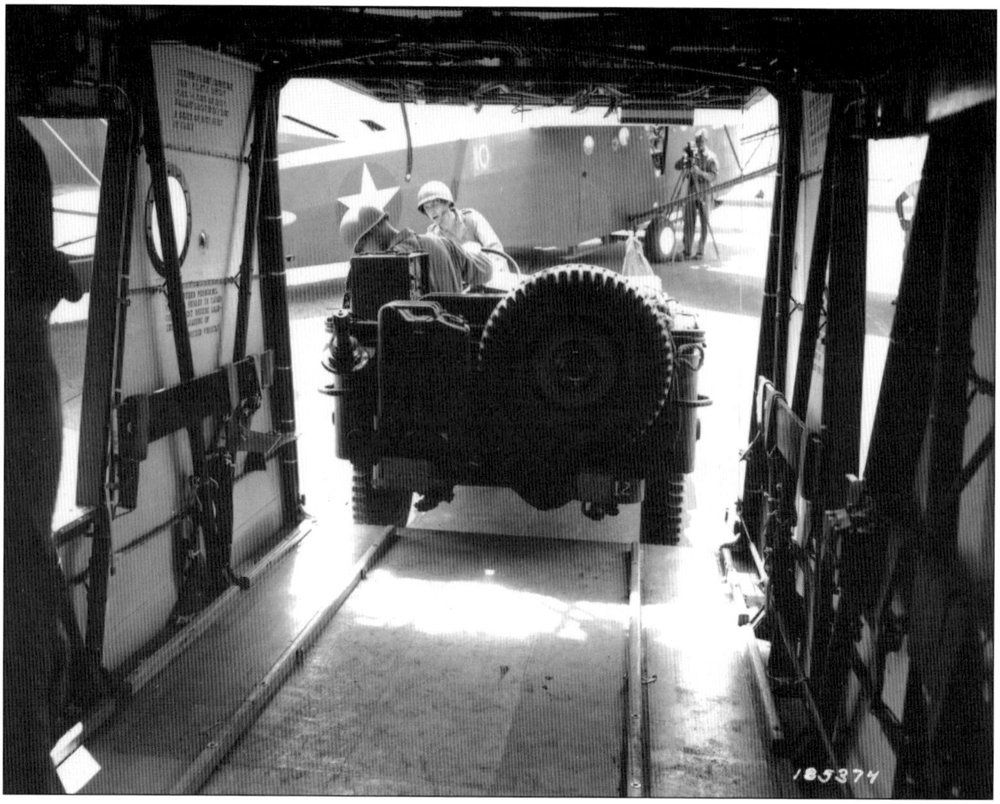

During World War II, military gliders were designed by the Weaver Aircraft Company (WACO) and made from steel, wood, and canvas. They were the lightest and quietest flying machines in the war. The gliders did not require fuel, could transport equipment and personnel, could land in small areas, and it was not a requirement for pilots to attend advanced flight training programs. The glider attached to the towing aircraft by a cable, which released the flying machine near the landing zone. Numerous glider accidents occurred when the towing cable either broke or became tangled. High winds could damage the glider or alter its destination. The above photograph shows the inside of a glider. Equipment and soldiers unloaded from the glider's nose, which lifted. Below, an Army glider is visible beneath the wing of a second glider. (Both, courtesy of NARA.)

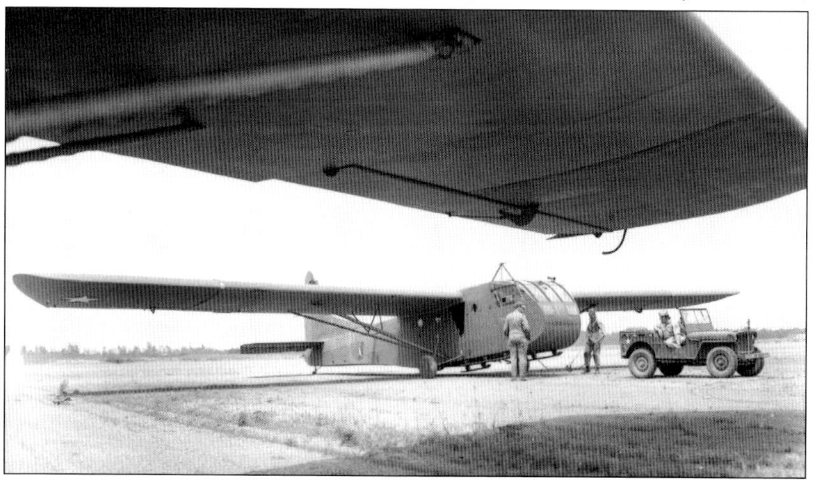

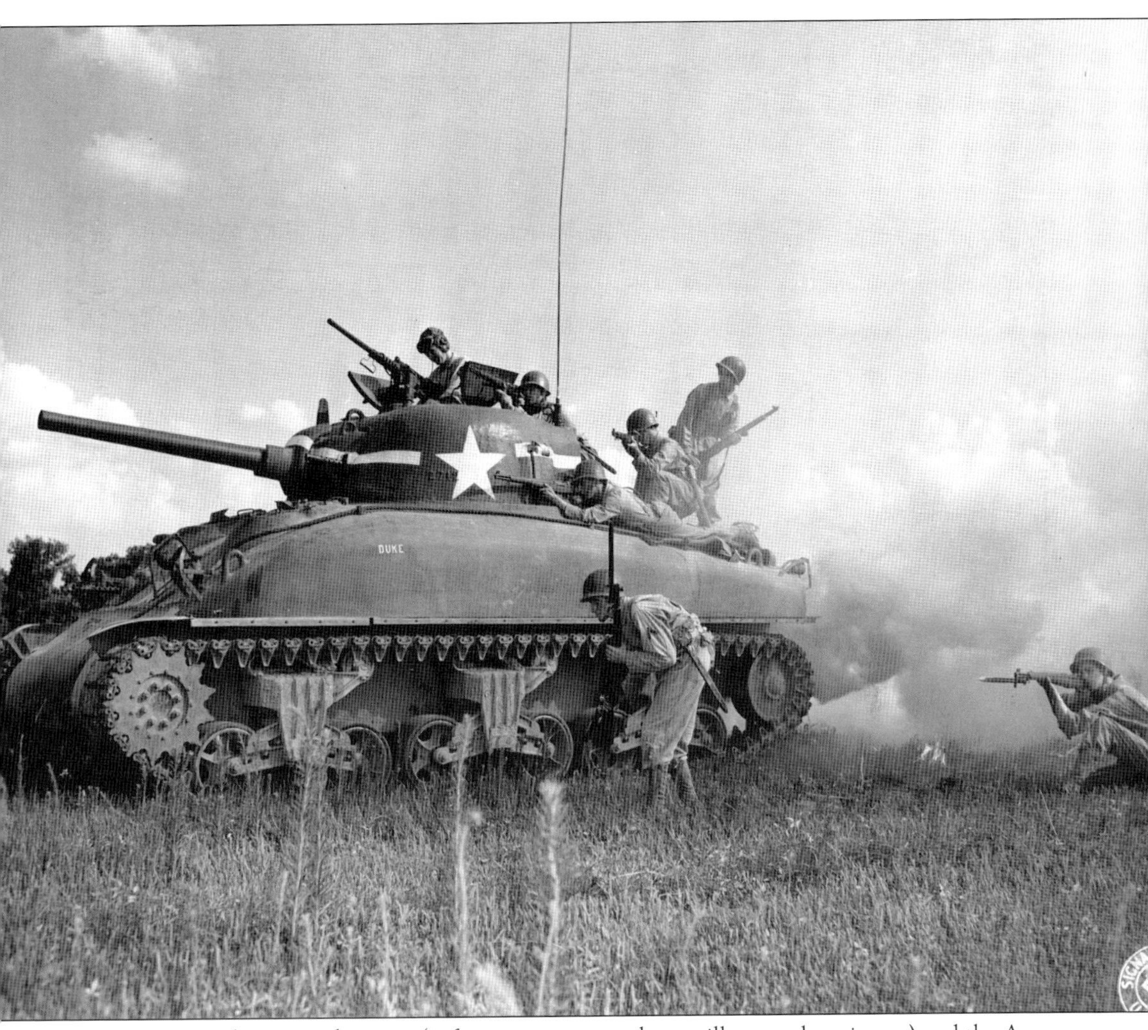

Ninety-two combat arms elements (infantry, armor, cavalry, artillery, and engineers) and the Army Air Corps learned to fight as a team while on maneuvers. Of the US Army's 92 divisions, 25 trained in Tennessee. Of these divisions, 21 went to Europe, three went to the Pacific, and one went to occupy Japan. The armored division was composed of tank units, armored infantry, self-propelled artillery, armored engineers, and signal, medical, ordnance, and quartermaster units. Additional support for the division was provided by aviation reconnaissance and bombardment. With such a complement of resources, the 2nd Armored Division was a small army. In this photograph, the tank and hitchhiking infantry have emerged from a smoke cloud almost at the enemy lines, and the soldiers scramble off the top to deploy and strike a quick blow. (Courtesy of John Allan.)

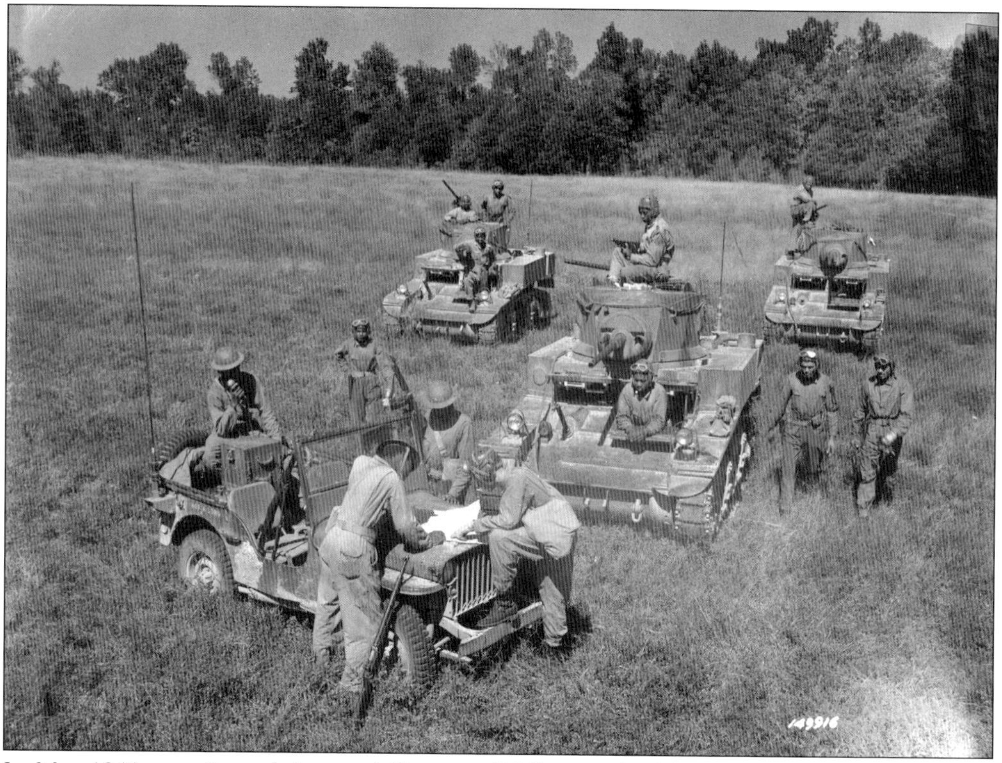

In May 1941, two Second Armored Division "Hell on Wheels" crews under the direction of Lieutenant Allard provided a group of 12 generals and 20 colonels from both the Second Army and the VII Corps with a demonstration of the versatility of the new tanks. The 67th Armored Regiment (medium tanks) and the 66th Armored Regiment (light tanks) showed diverse types of maneuvers each tank could perform and the ease with which each one could traverse difficult terrain. Pictured above in September 1942, three light tanks pause in a pasture to receive directions to their new bivouac area. The 758th Tank Battalion (pictured below) participated in the 1942 Tennessee Maneuvers, practicing blitzkrieg tactics similar to those used by German forces. These training exercises proved soldiers could stop opposing forces quickly in their tracks. (Above, courtesy of NARA; below, courtesy of John Allan.)

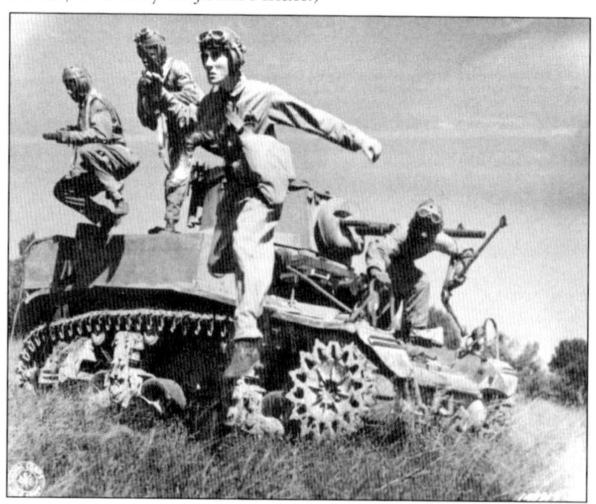

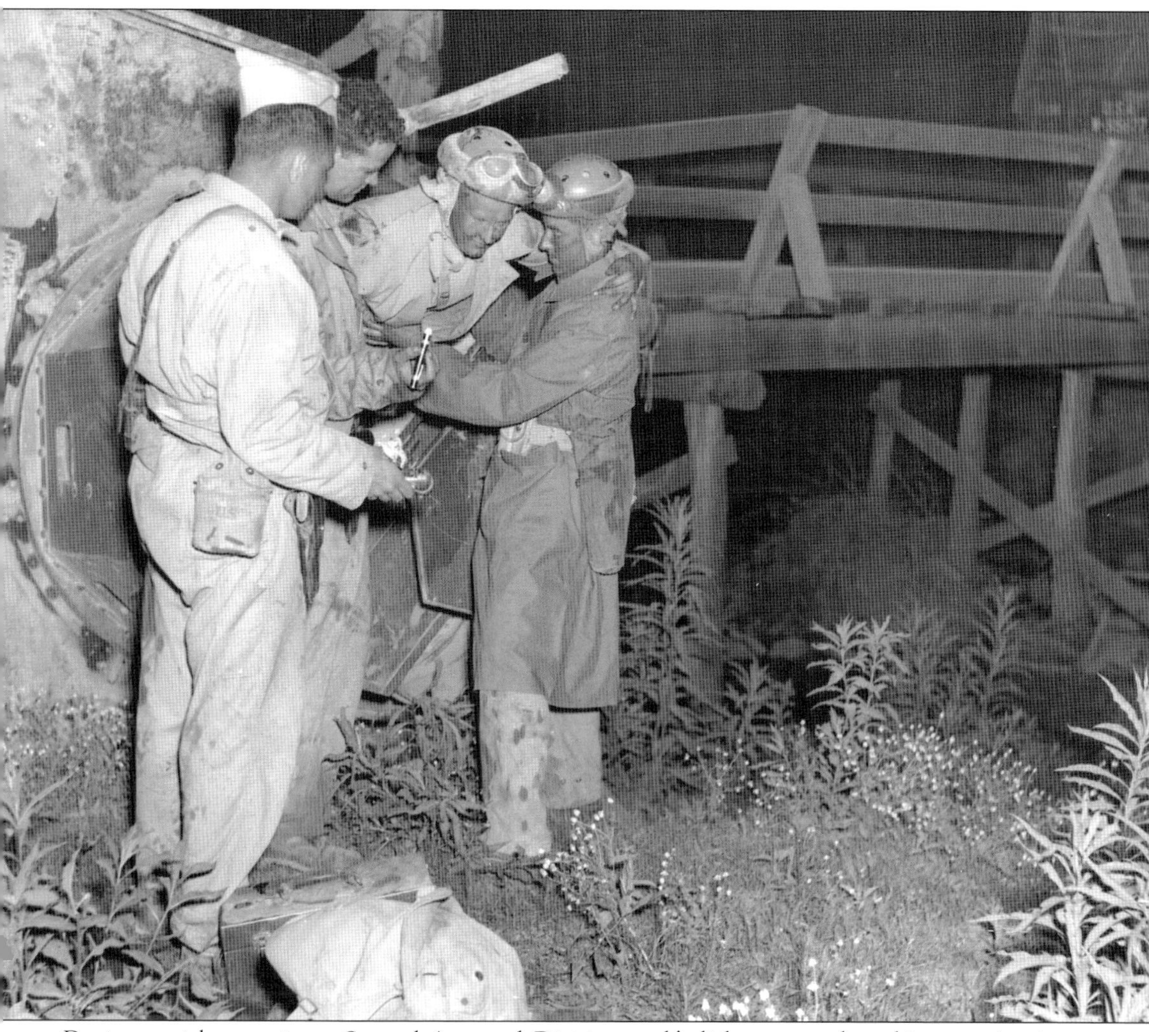

During a night exercise, a Second Armored Division tank's lights stopped working, causing it to plunge through the railing of the wooden bridge. Luckily, no one inside the tank sustained injuries, but two large wreckers were necessary to retrieve the wrecked 28-ton medium tank. The soldiers at the accident were from Company H, 66th Armored Regiment, and were (left to right) 1st Lt. Joe Moore, Pfc. Daumont Valentine, Pvt. Gene McKessy, and Pvt. Pat Nice. (Courtesy of John Allan.)

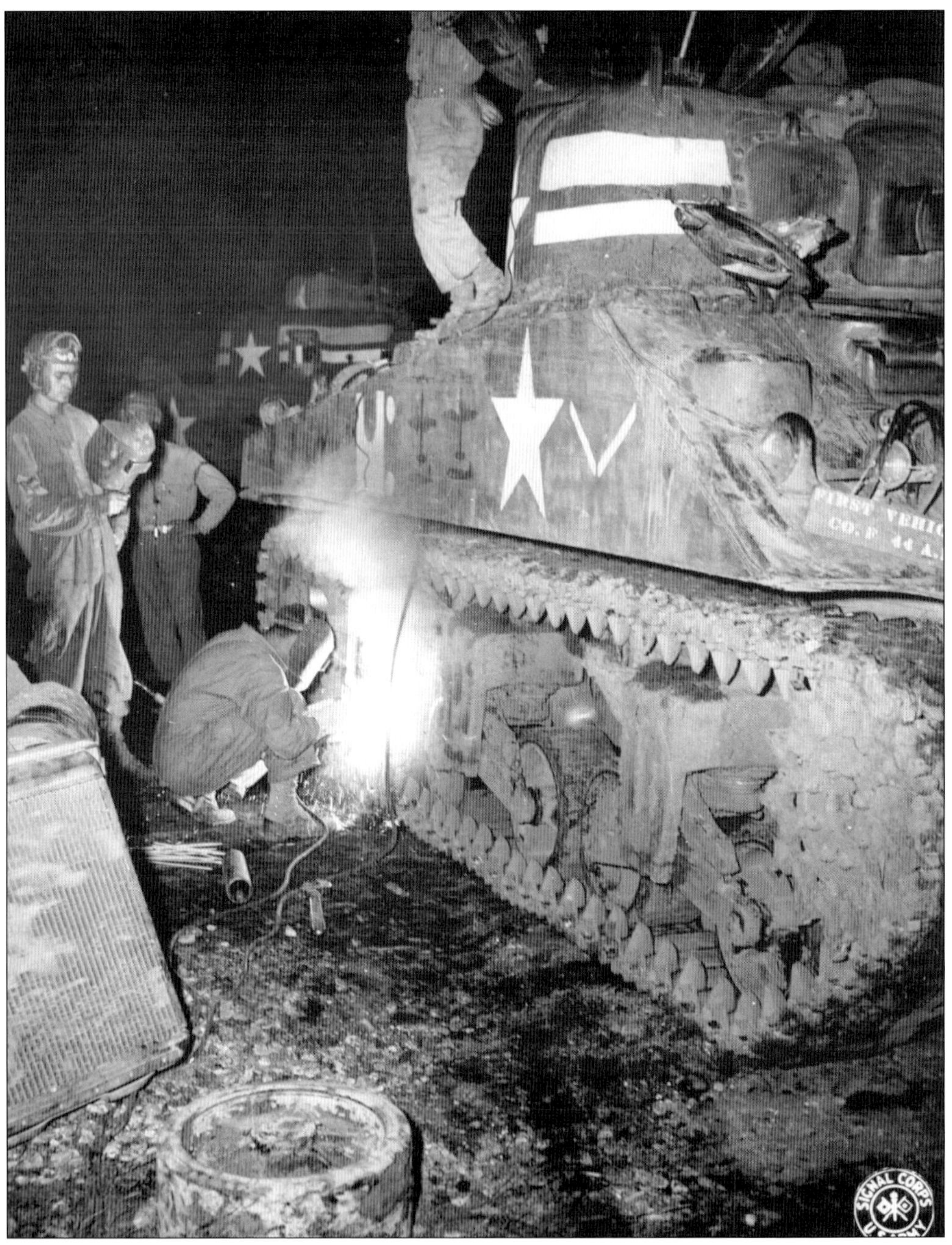

During maneuvers, the military enforced blackout restrictions as strictly as in real combat, but even total darkness gave way to urgent repairs. At Norene, Tennessee, soldiers risked enemy observation to have their medium tank battle-ready by morning. Atop the tank (left to right): Sgt. T.P. Shaw; Cpl. P.T. Hood; Cpl. G.T. Montgomery; and Pvt. L. Wigdon. (Courtesy of John Allan.)

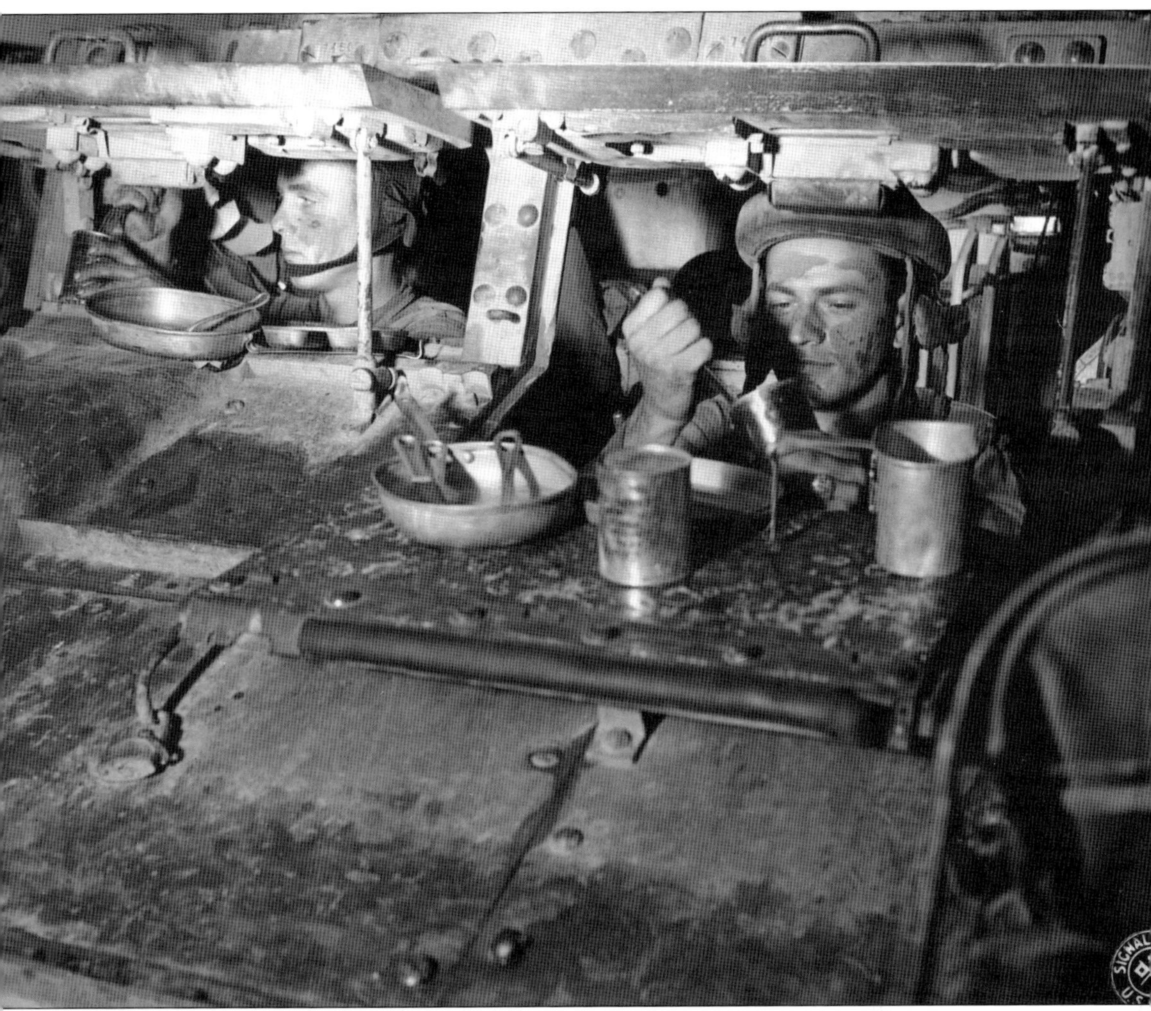

The 2nd Armored Division trained in large-scale maneuvers across Louisiana, Tennessee, and the Carolinas, where tanks repeatedly proved their value as modern war machines. Even in heavy rain, the tank driver and his assistant driver could work from a sheltered table without leaving their seats. Pictured are Pvt. Ray Profitt, assistant driver, and Cpl. Marvin P. Allen, driver. (Courtesy of CFF.)

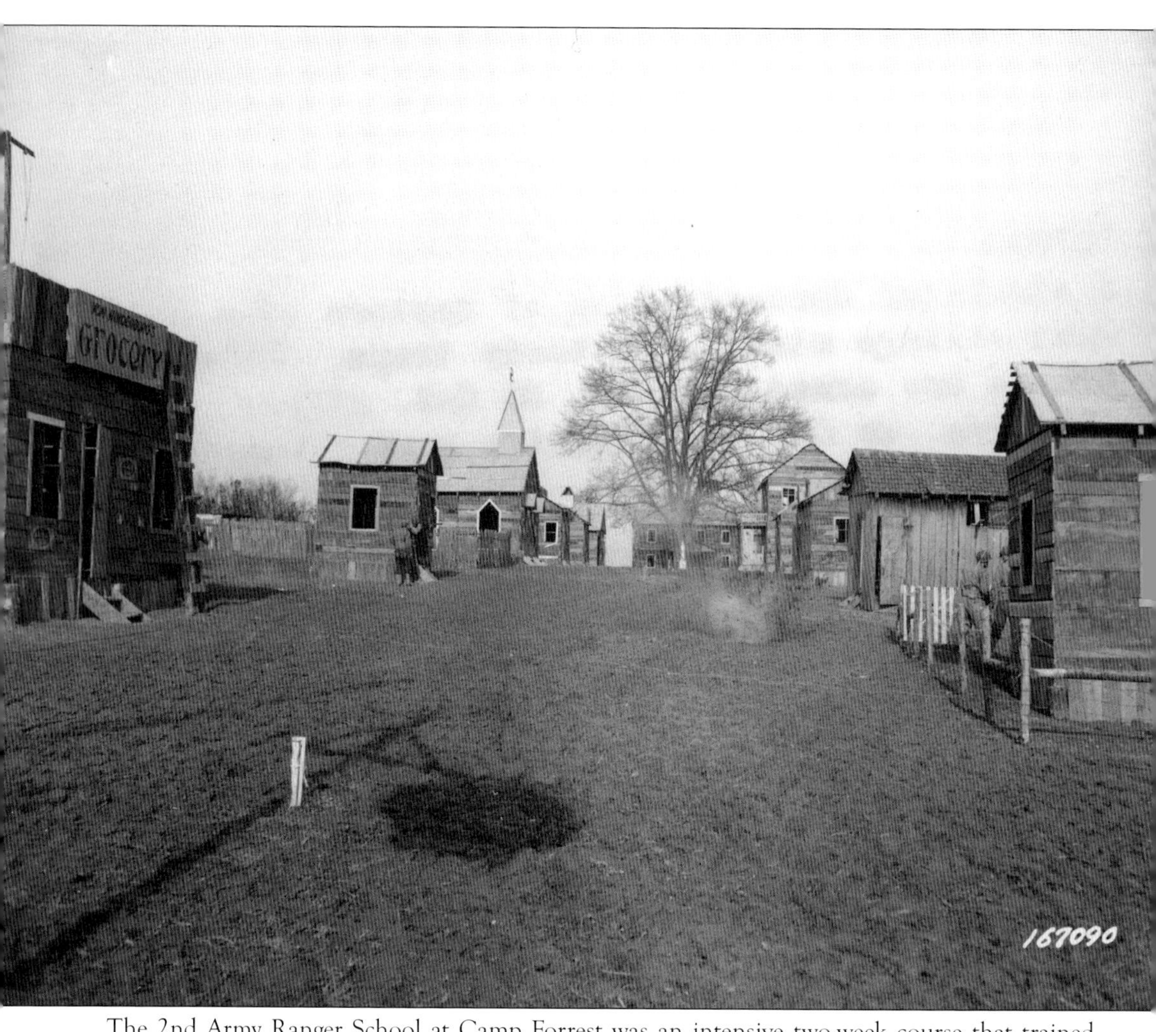

The 2nd Army Ranger School at Camp Forrest was an intensive two-week course that trained soldiers to incapacitate or kill the enemy swiftly, without reliance on weapons or adherence to the rules of fair play. The first cadre of 600 men graduated in January 1943. Their graduation exercise served as a public demonstration of the skills mastered during the course. Amid live fire and explosions, the soldiers proved to assembled commanders and members of the press that they were prepared to win any fight. This photograph shows the intersection of Yabostrasse and Lindenstrasse in the model Nazi village known as the Town of Feuhrerville. (Courtesy of NARA.)

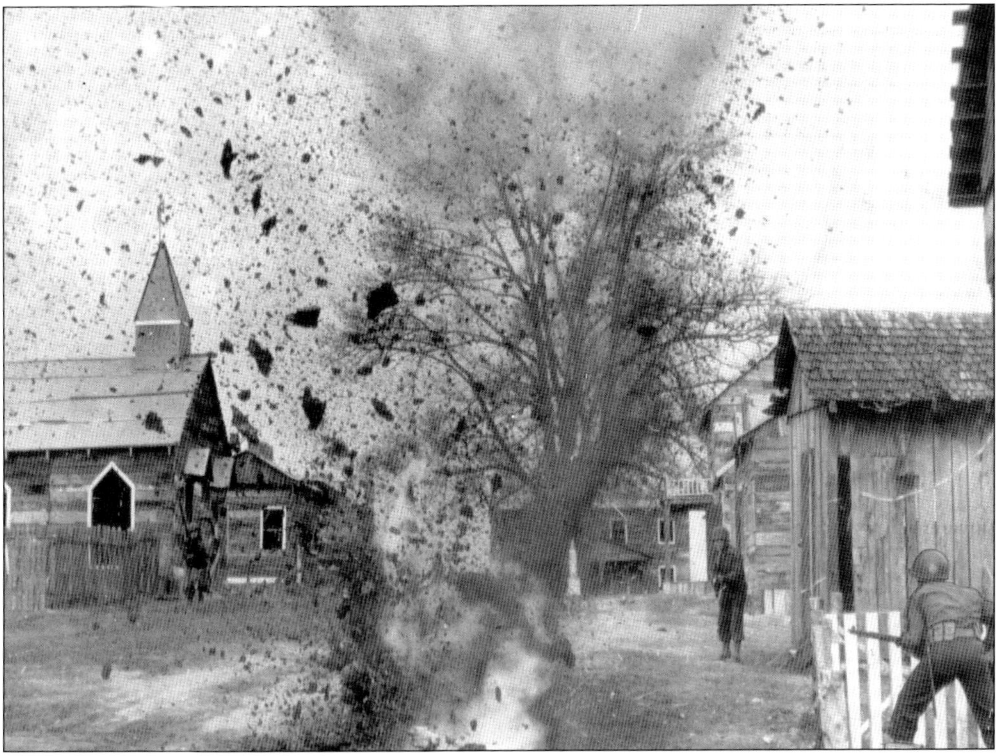

In March 1943, reporter Norman Bradley described the methods soldiers used to identify, disarm, and construct explosive devices. His account noted demonstrations of numerous types of booby traps as well as the mechanics of detonation. Fortunately, the blasts used in training stunned onlookers rather than caused injury. Such demonstrations reminded soldiers to remain doubly cautious when moving through an enemy bivouac. In this image, simulated artillery shell explosions detonate throughout the model Nazi village, providing a realistic training environment. (Courtesy of John Allan.)

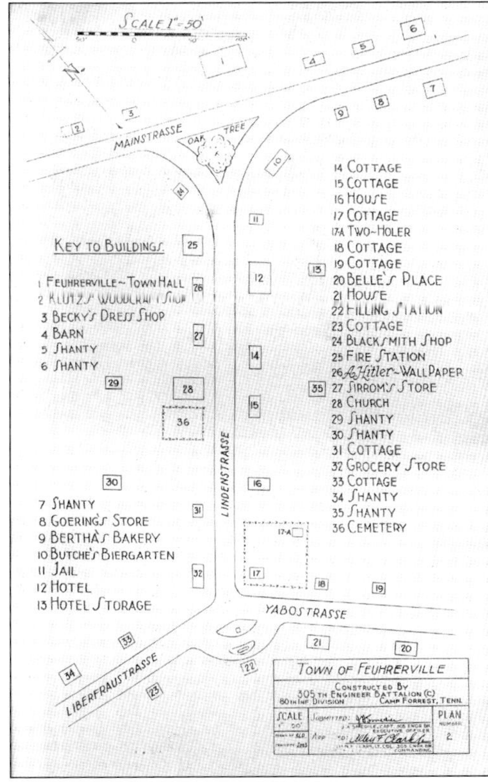

The Town of Feuhrerville resembled the German villages in the European Theater of Operations. This realistic model was a new military training aid, designed to familiarize all of a soldier's senses with that type of environment. Company C of the 505th Engineer Battalion, 80th Infantry Division, constructed the village's wooden structures. (Courtesy of CFF.)

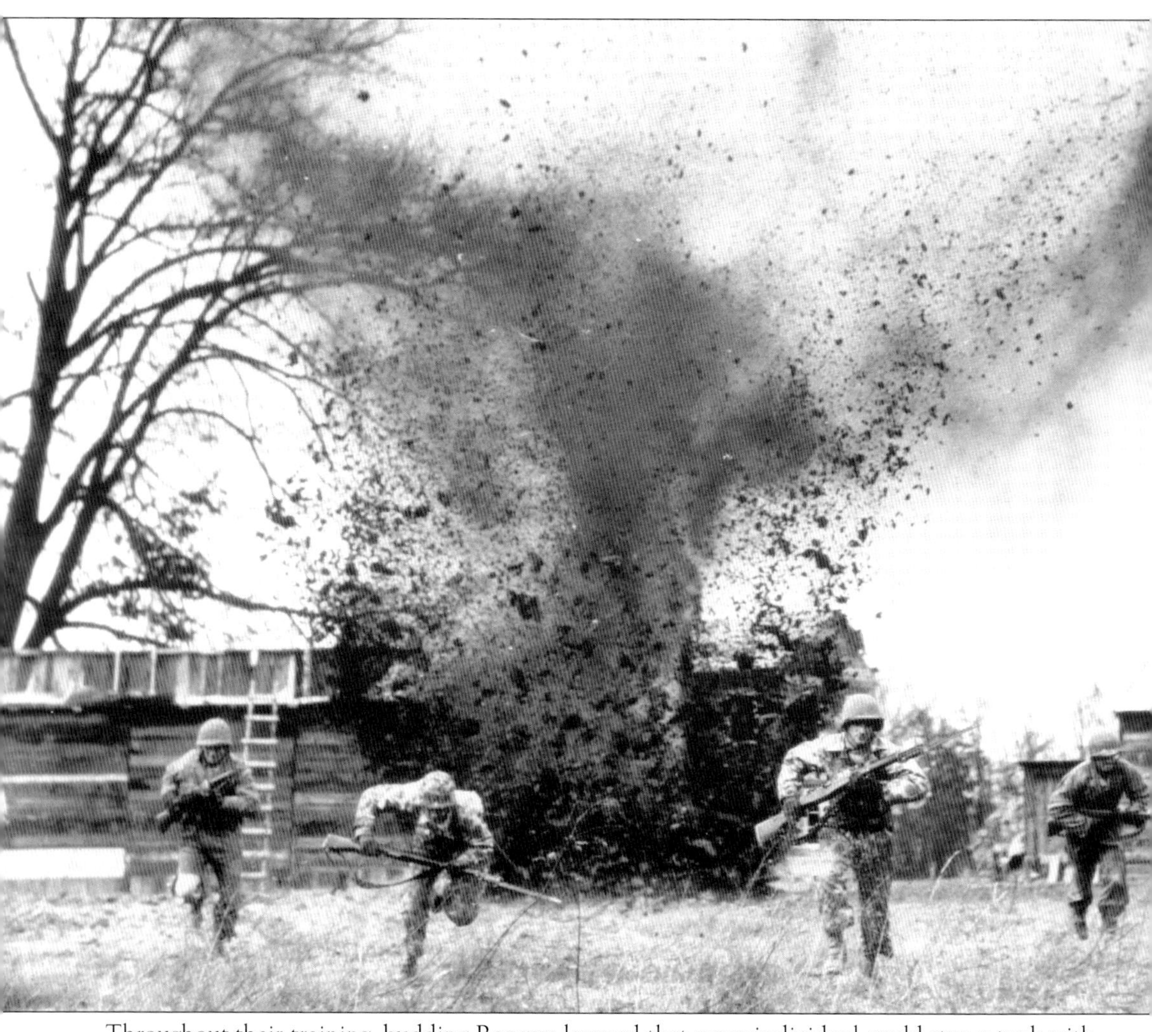

Throughout their training, budding Rangers learned that every individual could stop a tank with a few simple materials if trained to do the job. On the battlefield, these soldiers maintained a mentality of kill or be killed. Rangers charge through the Nazi village amid the explosives bursting around them. Rangers fired live ammunition at mock targets and used bayonets on German soldier figures in exercises at the model Nazi village. (Courtesy of CFF.)

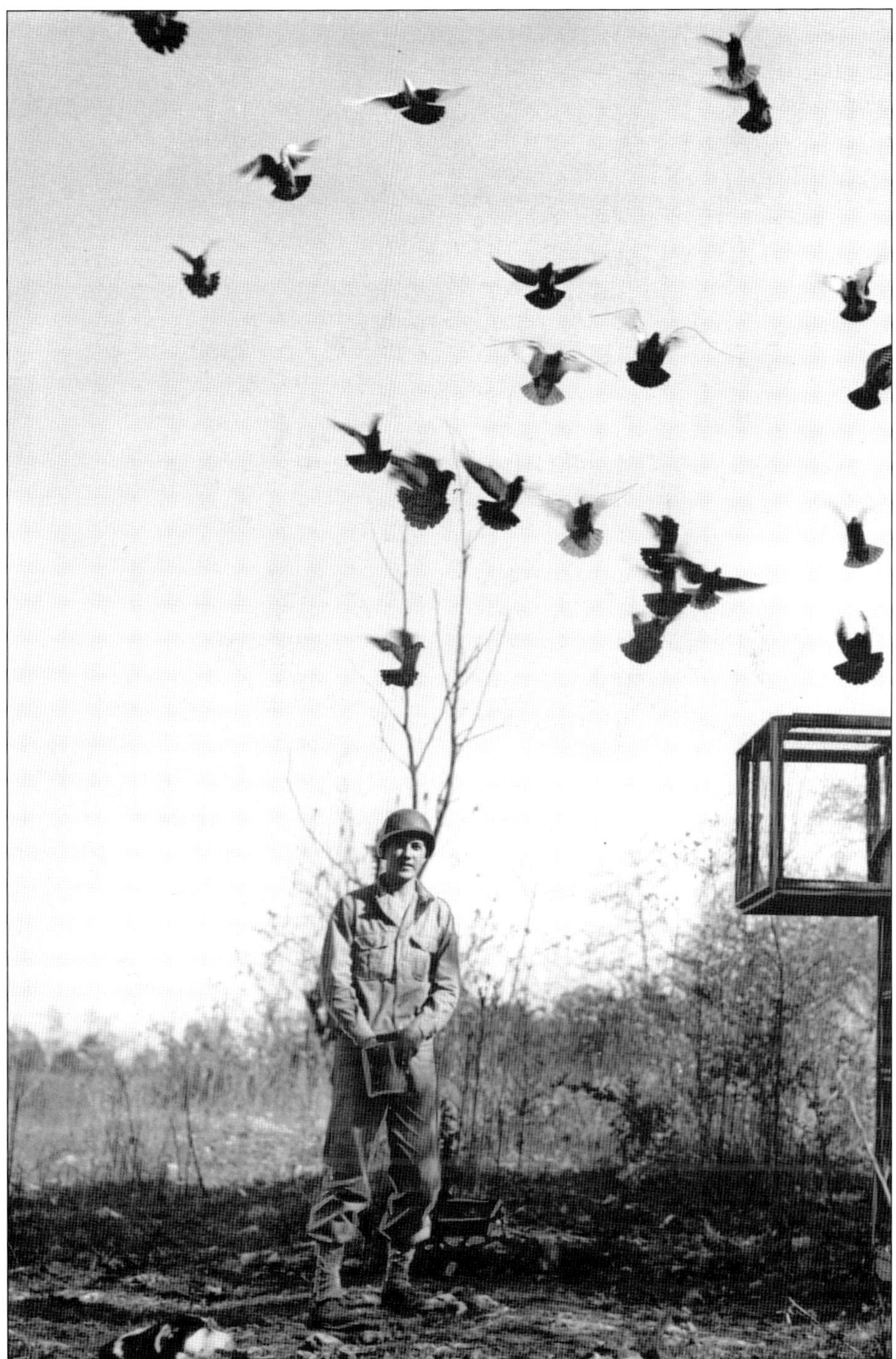

Soldiers with wings return to their mobile pigeon loft after a training flight. Pigeoneer T/4 William Dolin trained the birds for combat. Pigeons were valuable messengers with the ability to fly home over 400 miles at a speed of 50 mph. Pvt. James Lang raced pigeons at the Buffalo racing club for 10 years. Lt. Randolph C. Lang was the unit's commanding officer. (Courtesy of John Allan.)

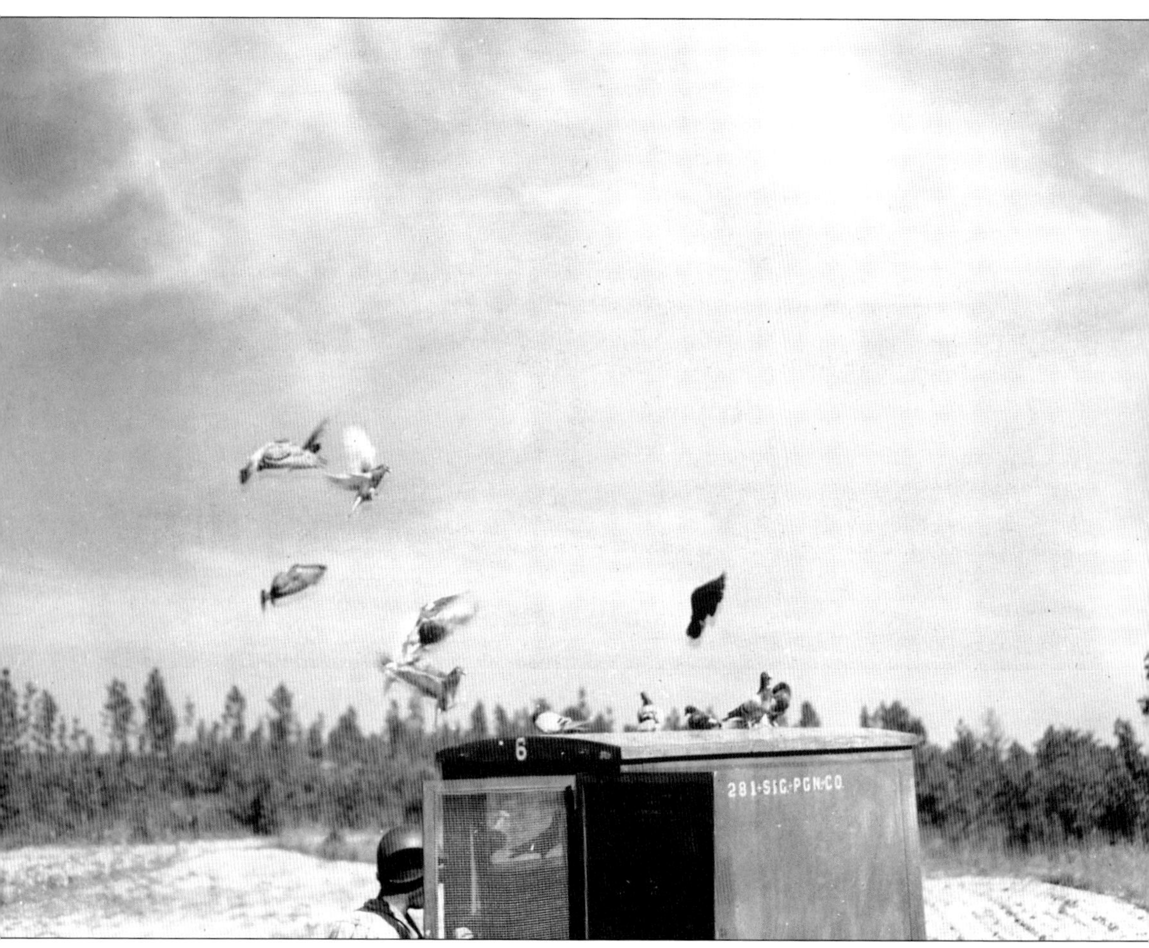

On D-Day, these winged messengers served as spies for Allied Forces. The handler placed the pigeon in a felt-lined cage that attached to the paratrooper's rigging. The cage helped absorb the shocks from a paratrooper's jump behind enemy lines. The handler placed the coded messages in a tube attached to the pigeon's leg before it flew approximately 150 miles to Commanders, headquartered in Britain. Axis forces intercepted messages by either capturing or destroying pigeons with gunfire. (Courtesy of NARA.)

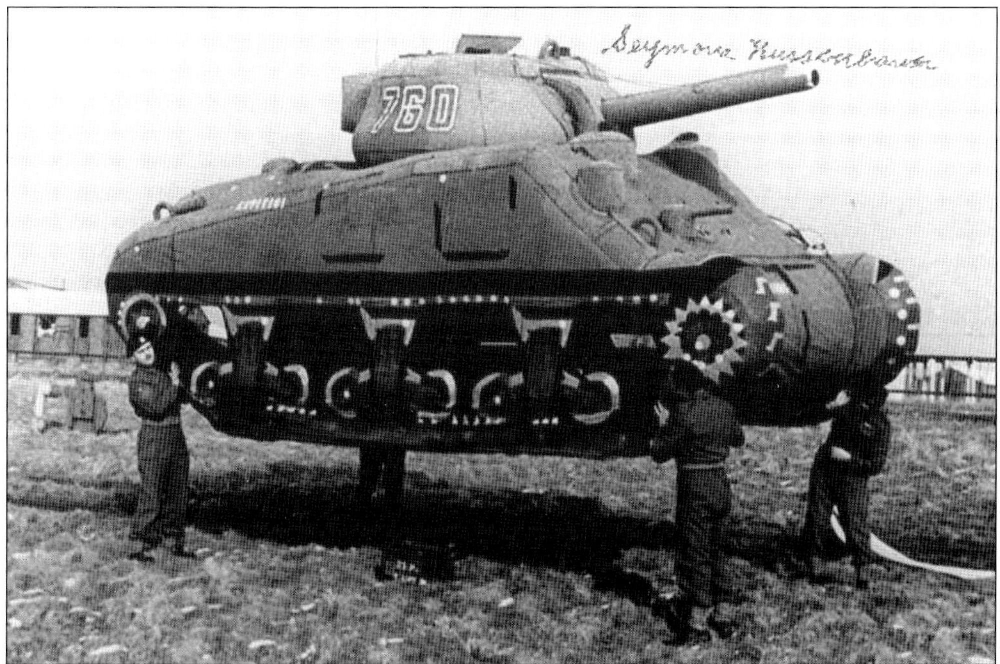

The 23rd Headquarters Special Troops, known as the "Ghost Army," used deception techniques, such as inflatable tanks and trucks, fake radio transmissions, and recorded sound effects to simulate two divisions. The Ghost Army was activated on January 20, 1944, at Camp Forrest and was composed of the 406th Combat Engineers and the 23rd Headquarters Special Troops. The three units in the 23rd Headquarters Special Troops were the 603rd Engineer Camouflage (379 men in charge of physical deception), the 3132nd Signal Service Company (145 men in charge of sonic deception), and Signal Company (296 men in charge of radio deception). The Deception Corps soldiers were artists, actors, and sound technicians. The 406th Combat Engineers provided security for the other divisions. The Ghost Army participated in 22 major deception operations in Europe. Reports estimate the unit saved over 30,000 lives based on their ability to divert the enemy's attention. (Above, courtesy of CFF; below, courtesy of MTSU.)

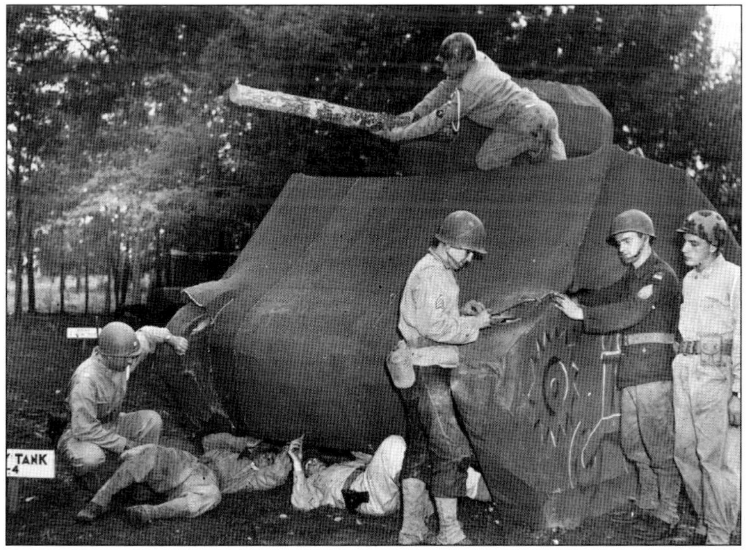

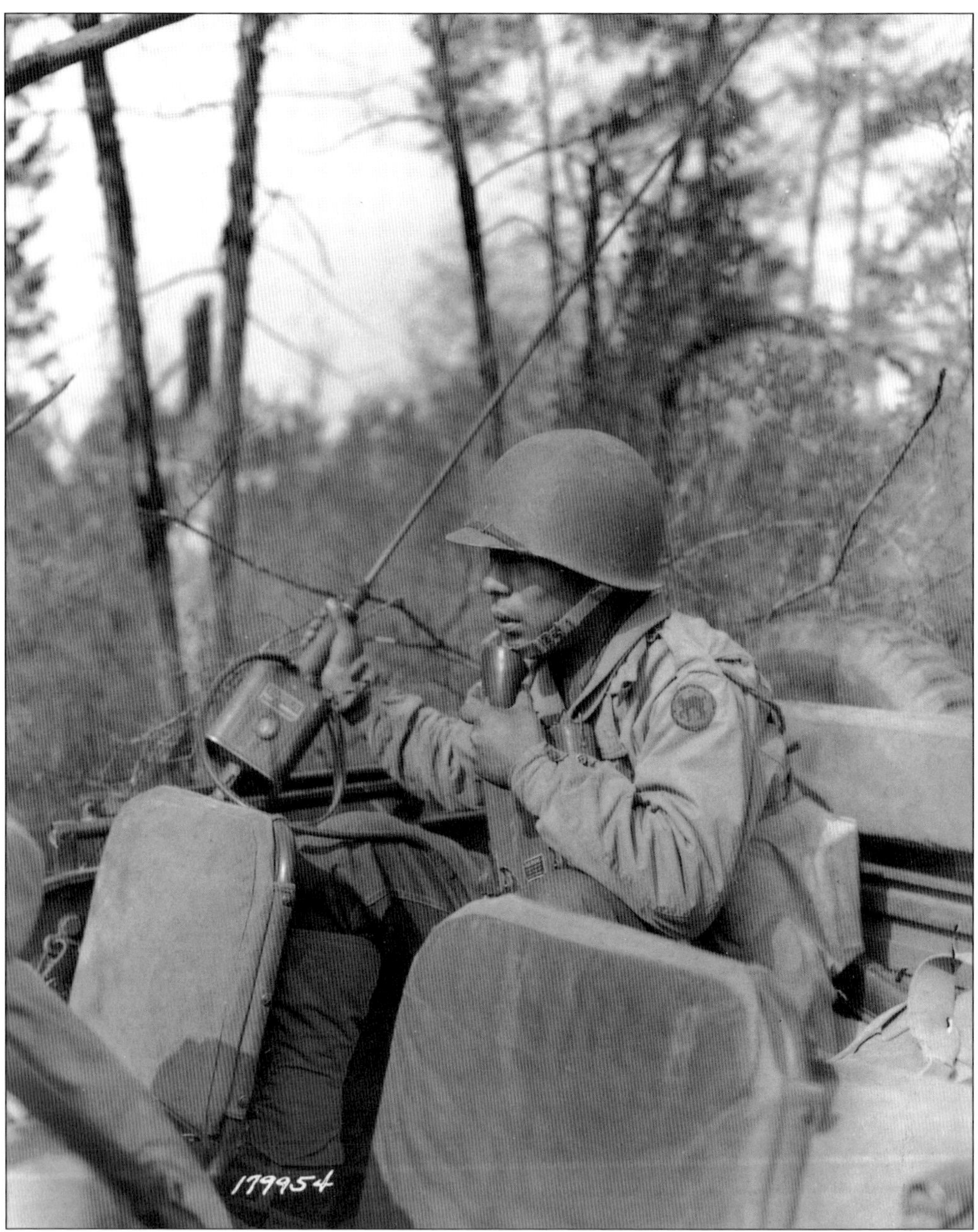

Pvt. Floyd Dann, a Hopi Indian from Tuba City, Arizona, used the Hopi Indian Network to converse with the seven other tribe members during the 1943 Tennessee Maneuvers. These soldiers devised an unbreakable code for radio transmissions that was based on their native language. Their conversation baffled interceptions not only during the maneuvers but also on the battlefront. Floyd Dann's Hopi Indian name was Loma Tuchyoma. (Courtesy of John Allan.)

Three

SUPPORT FOR VICTORY

COMBAT SERVICE AND SUPPORT UNITS AT CAMP FORREST

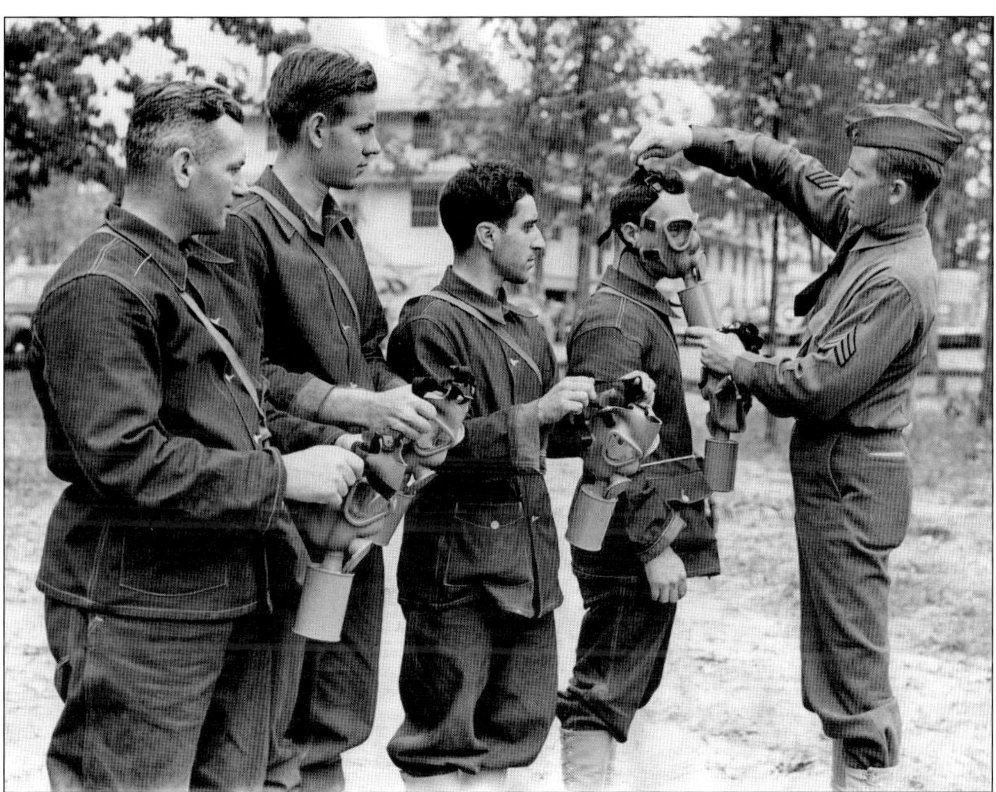

The often-forgotten combat service and combat service support units (MPs, engineers, firefighters, nurses, doctors, lawyers, cooks, and bakers—just to name a few) received basic and advanced training in their respective specialties. The unsung heroes of the Combat Service and Combat Service Support units ensured the front lines had supplies and medical equipment. Without bullets, equipment, and supplies, soldiers could not advance toward the enemy, and many more may have perished. In this image, soldiers received instructions on the proper use of gas masks. (Courtesy of CFF.)

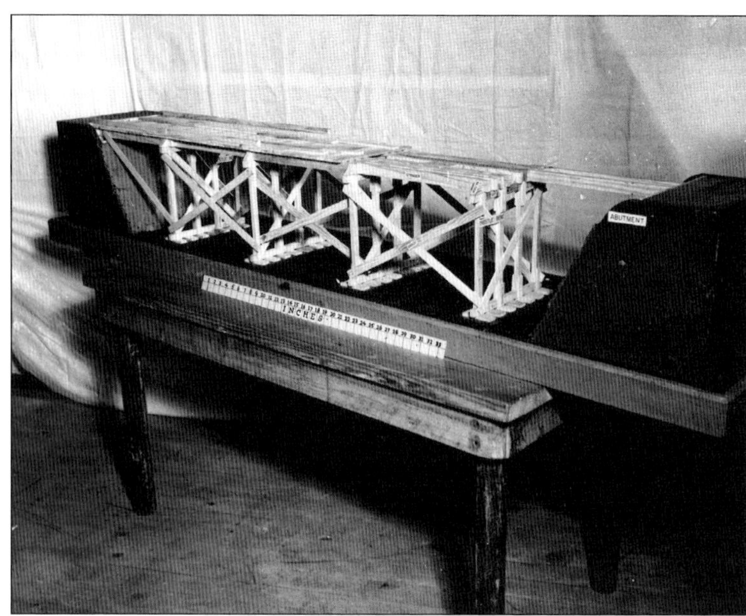

Models were used extensively as training aides to teach men the theory and methods of bridge design, construction, and destruction. The models helped visualize information presented in the classroom. 2nd Lt. R.W. Meyer supervised the construction of the cross-timber bridge model (1 inch = 1 foot) pictured. (Courtesy of NARA.)

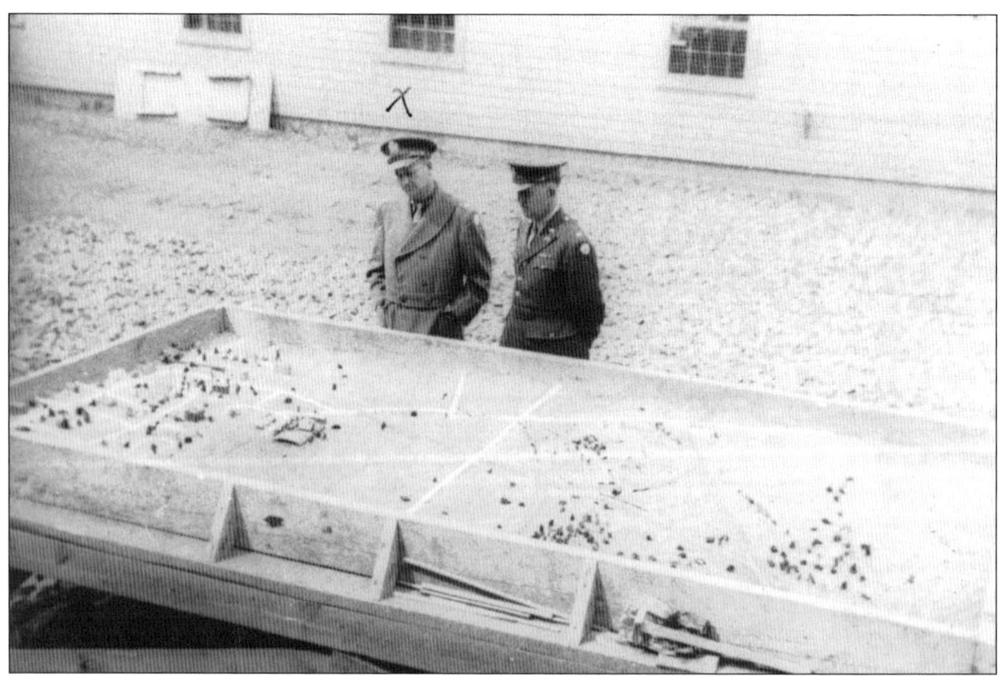

Sand or terrain tables were visual aids used in operational and tactical military planning. Use of both sand tables and area maps gave planners a multidimensional view of an operation. Tables could be simple or an elaborate model of an area and include permanent small objects showing terrain elevations, trees, buildings, or lakes. Moveable objects in the table represented troops so that planners could analyze strikes against enemy lines. (Courtesy of CFF.)

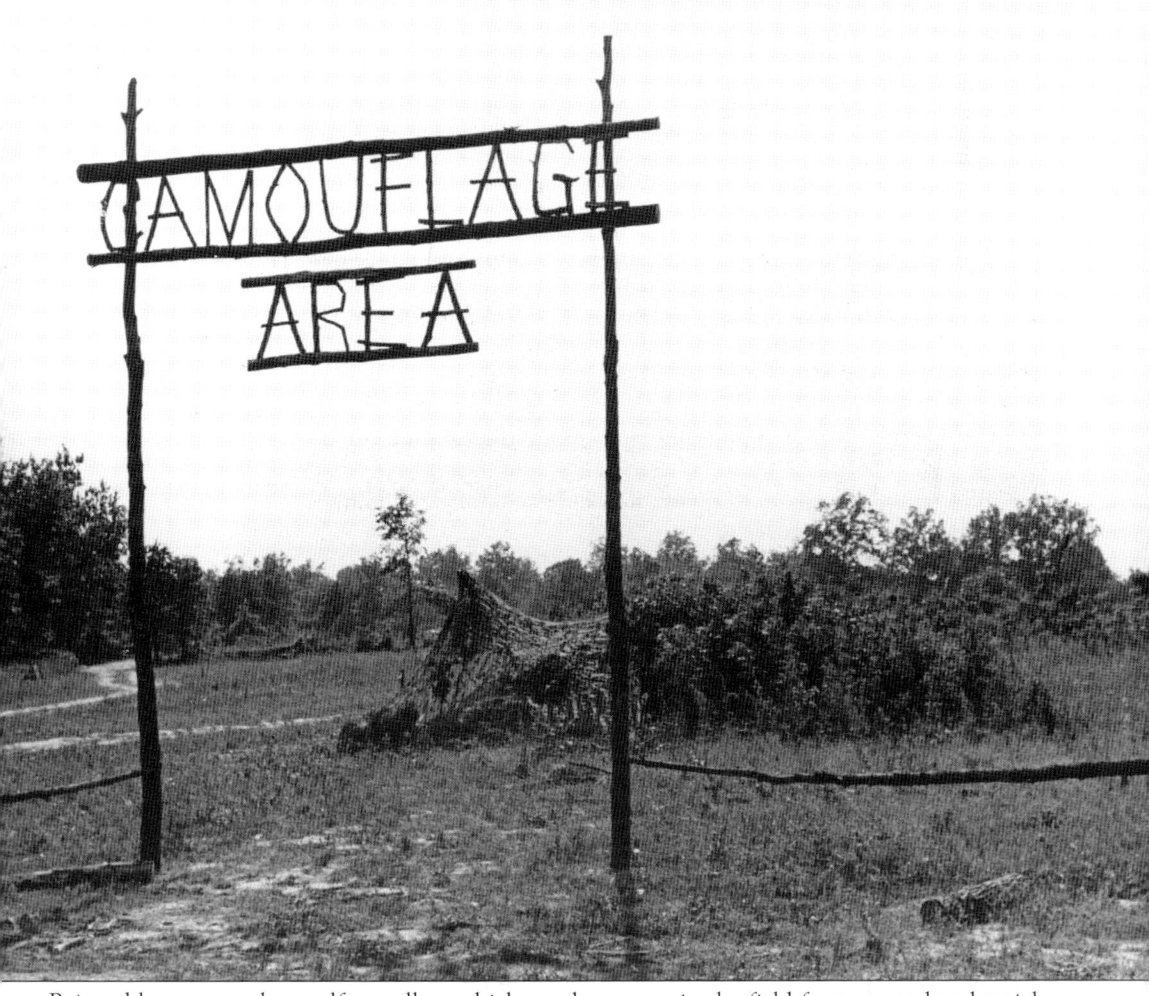

Being able to conceal oneself as well as vehicles and weapons in the field from ground and aerial attacks was an extremely important skill. The Corps of Engineers oversaw camouflage paintings on vehicles and taught soldiers how to hide in plain sight in combat zones. Soldiers needed to be camouflage conscious and know tactical methods of concealment and techniques that used natural surroundings to their advantage, and how to disguise themselves in individual camouflage suits. Strategic camouflage techniques helped conceal factories and airports from the air. (Courtesy of CFF.)

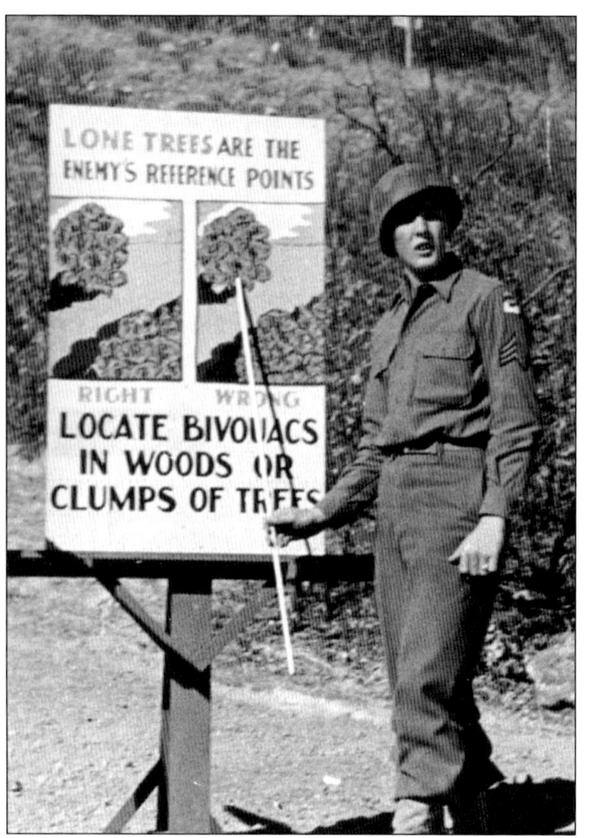

In addition to combat and construction responsibilities, the Corps of Engineers organized a Camouflage School to train soldiers in methods of concealment for personnel and equipment. Instruction covered layered painting to disguise objects, the use of natural and artificial materials, and adaptive methods for specific climates and terrain. Soldiers learned, for instance, that green netting offered little protection in desert environments. Other lessons included the application of mottled camouflage, sniper nets, artificial coverings for gun emplacements, and even the use of mud on skin to reduce reflection. (Both, courtesy of CFF.)

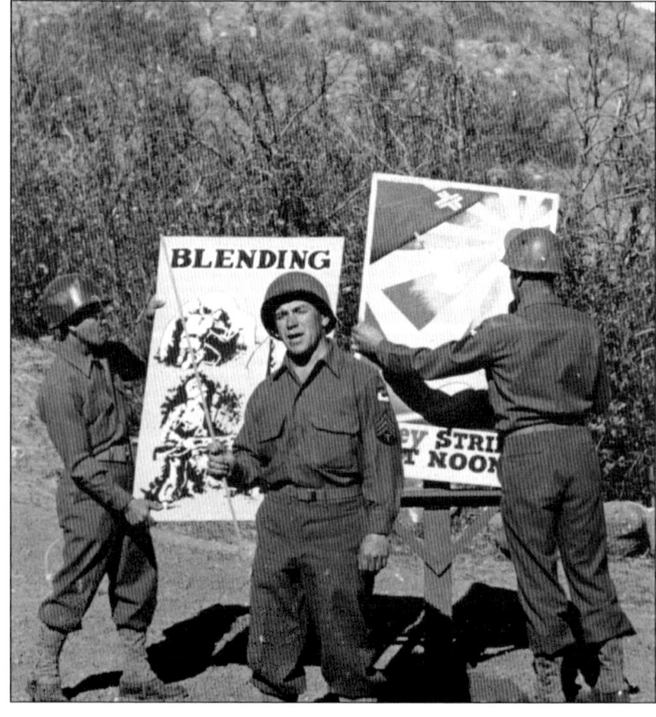

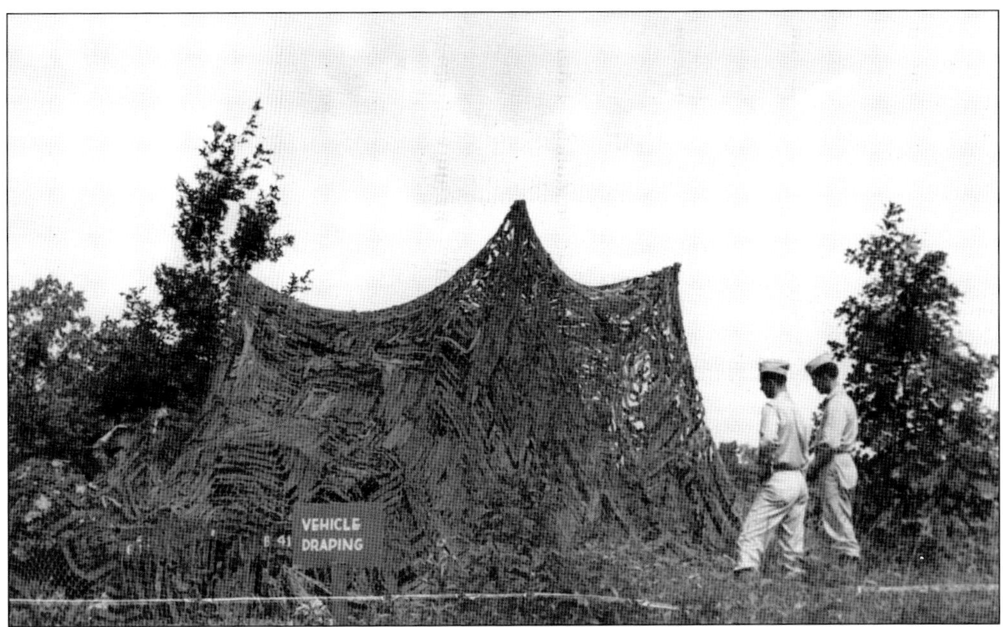

Camouflage School displays brought classroom instruction into practice, showing soldiers how to apply concealment methods to large equipment. In these photographs, soldiers concealed the plane (above) and tank (below) from planes flying overhead using techniques adapted to the terrain and environment. Such demonstrations reinforced the lectures, helping soldiers visualize how camouflage could protect both personnel and machinery in combat. (Both, courtesy of CFF.)

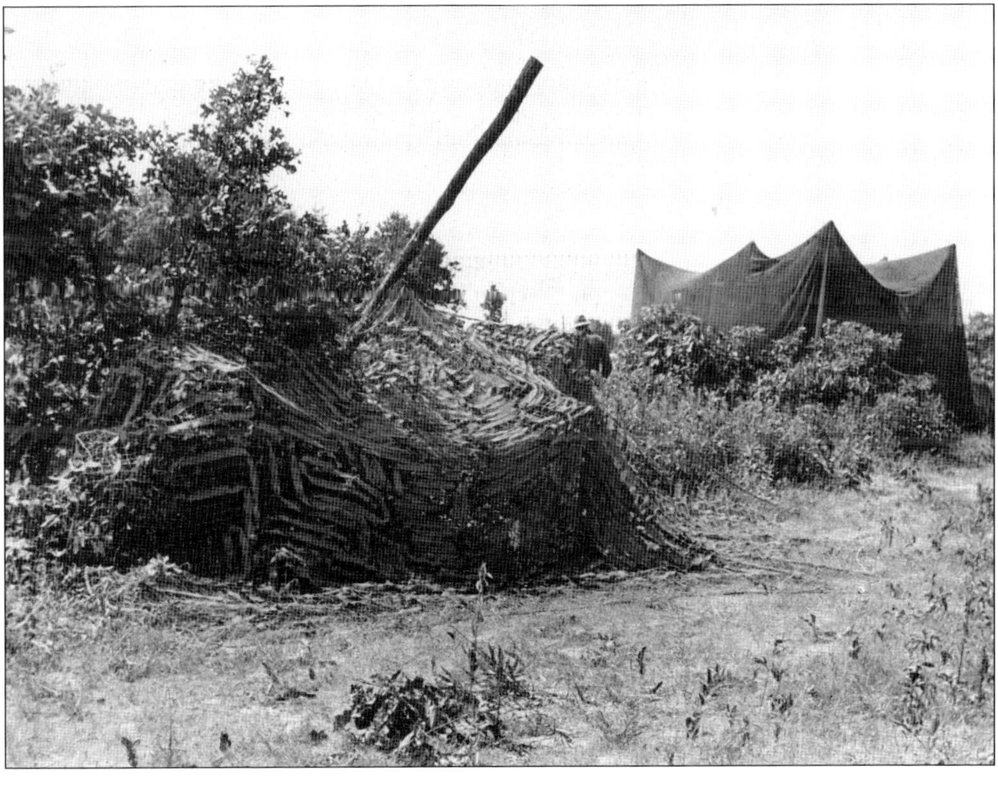

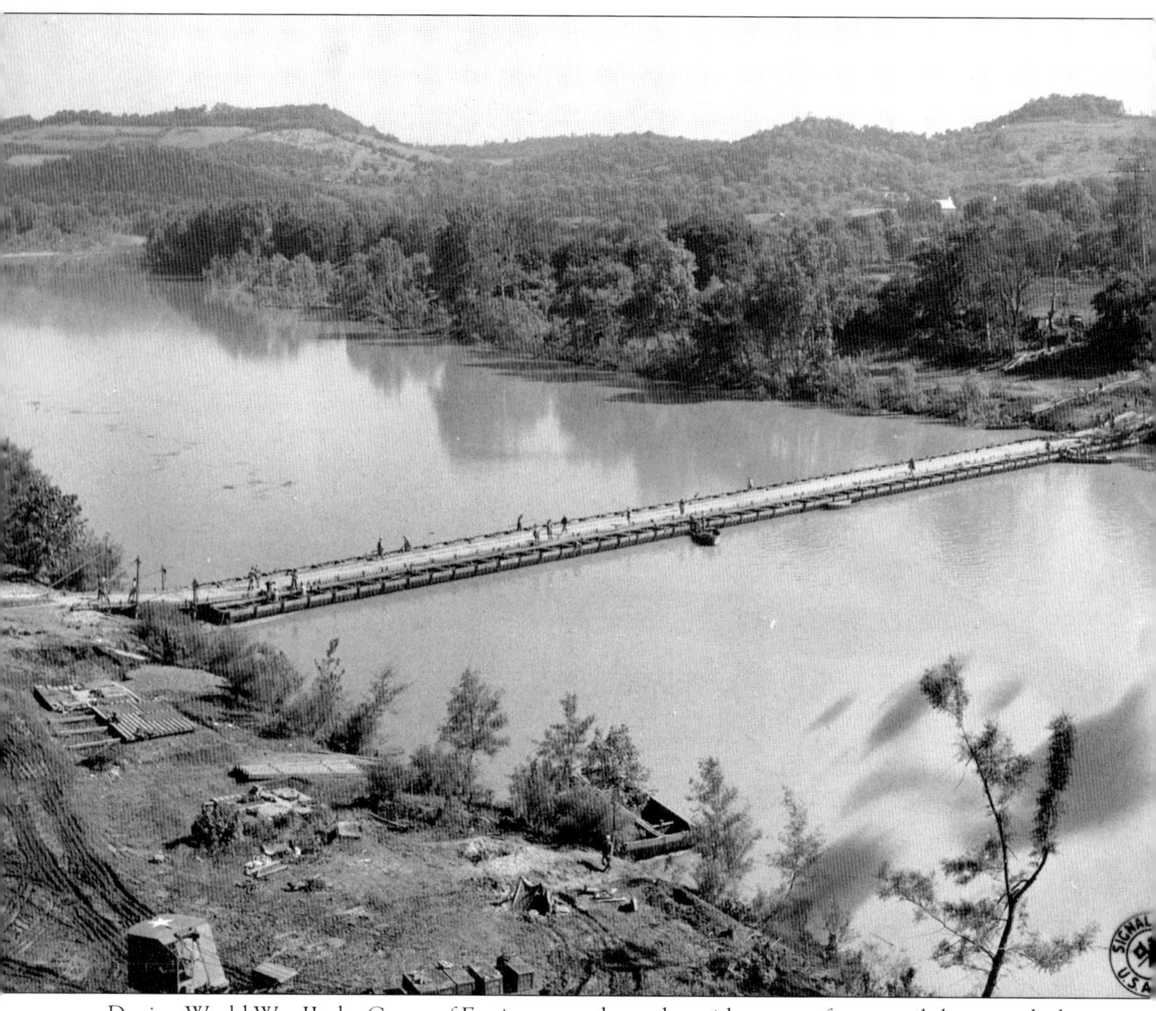

During World War II, the Corps of Engineers undertook a wide range of responsibilities, including road and bridge construction, training engineer troops, maintaining equipment, producing maps, collecting intelligence, managing waterways, and operating laboratories and specialty schools. At Lake Tullahoma, the 181st Heavy Ponton Battalion of the 33rd Division trained in bridge construction and in driving skills required to maneuver six-ton trucks and trailers across these structures. The ponton bridge shown here, built across the Cumberland River in Middle Tennessee, was strong enough to support the weight of 33-ton tanks. (Courtesy of John Allan.)

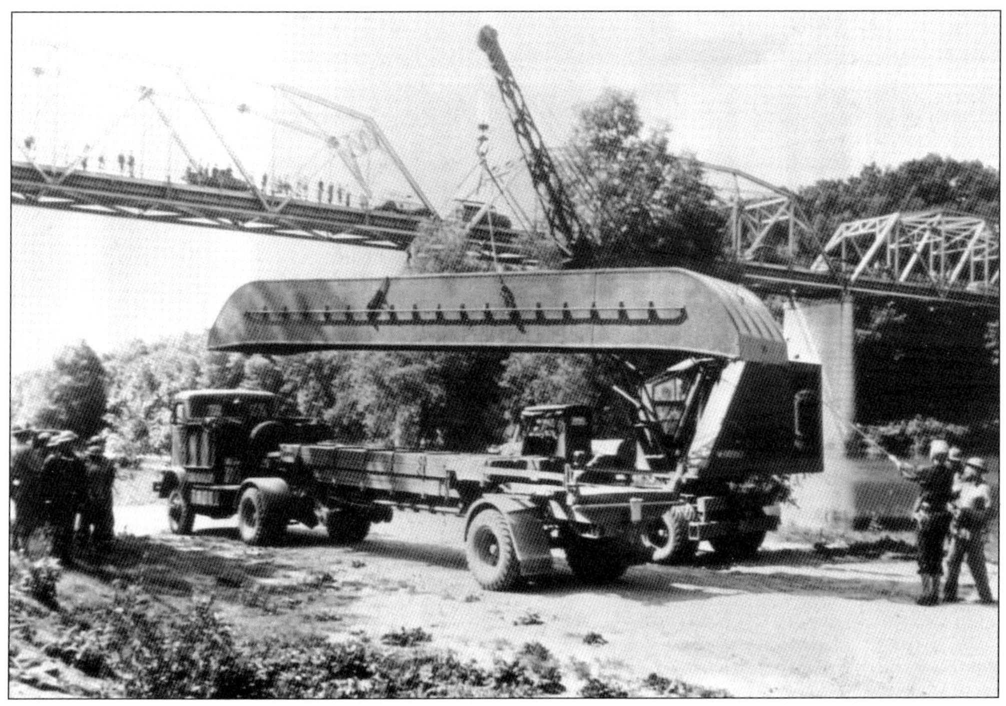

The 2nd Armored Division's 87th Engineer Battalion used cranes mounted on 10-ton trucks to hoist massive pontoons into place. Building a ponton bridge across the Barren Fork River in Tennessee formed one phase of a larger maneuver exercise that commanders assigned to the battalion to successfully complete within a specified time. (Courtesy of CFF.)

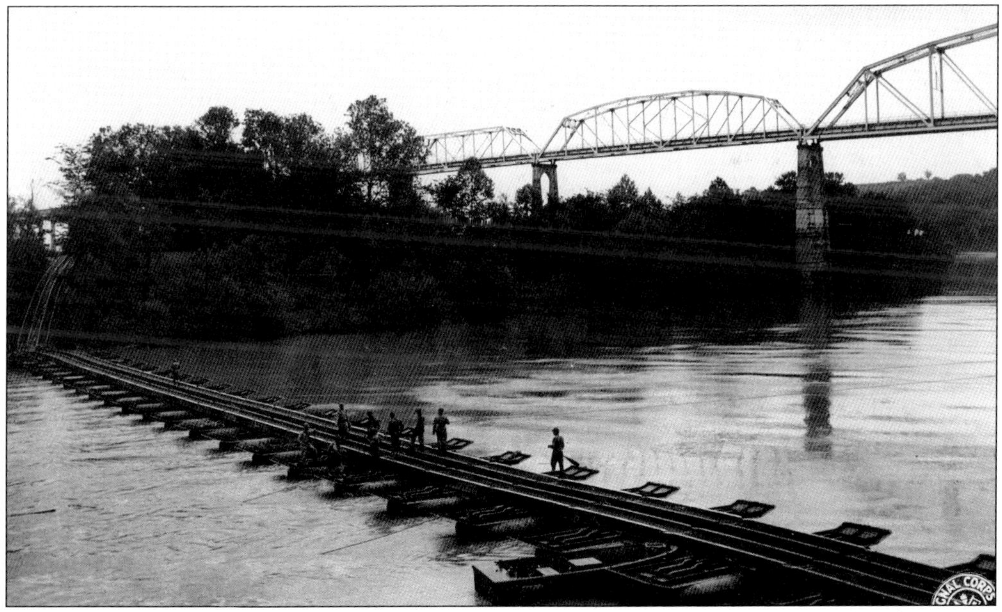

During the spring of 1943 Tennessee Maneuvers, Army engineers demonstrated speed and precision in constructing a treadway bridge supported by pneumatic pontoons across the Cumberland River. Within only a few hours, the soldiers completed a bridge strong enough to carry troop convoys. (Courtesy of CFF.)

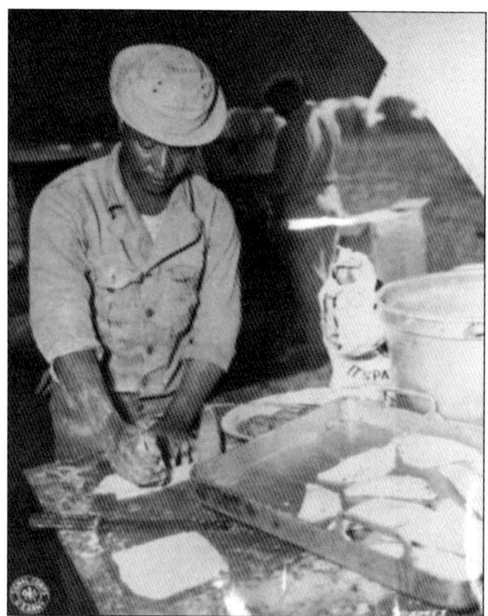

Cpl. Charles Stone, the company cook, makes the unit's favorite dessert—apple pie—at the Engineers Light Ponton Company mobile kitchen. The skilled Army bakers also prepared a half-pound of bread per day for each soldier on intensive training maneuvers. Trucks brought flour to one end of an assembly line; an hour and 20 minutes later, hot loaves were ready. Approximately 20,000 loaves of fresh bread were prepared daily. (Courtesy of NARA.)

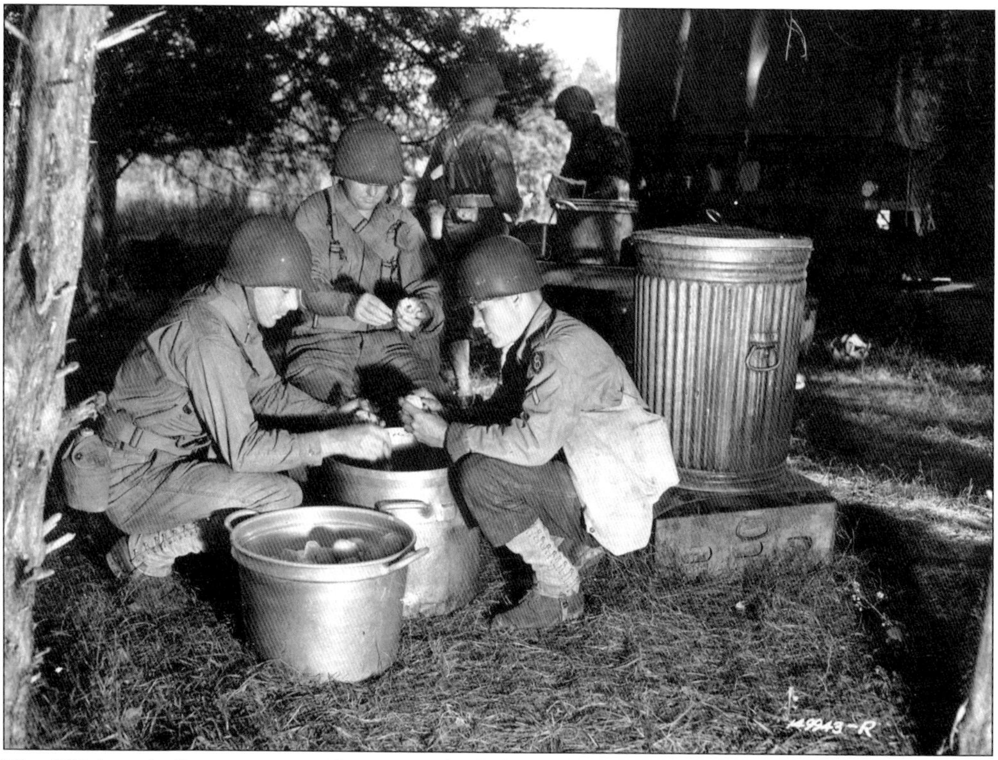

The US Army's Quartermaster Corps supplied the ingredients for three daily meals per soldier, while the company-level mess kitchen handled preparation. Typical meals included fresh bread, meat or fish, and vegetables and fruit—fuel for long training days and operations in the field. In this image, Pfc. Samuel Jackson, Sgt. James Netherland, and Pfc. Floyd Williams (left to right) peel potatoes, a staple that appeared in countless menus. The Army needed a tremendous amount of labor to move thousands of pounds of food from supply lines to mess tents to plates, day after day. (Courtesy of NARA.)

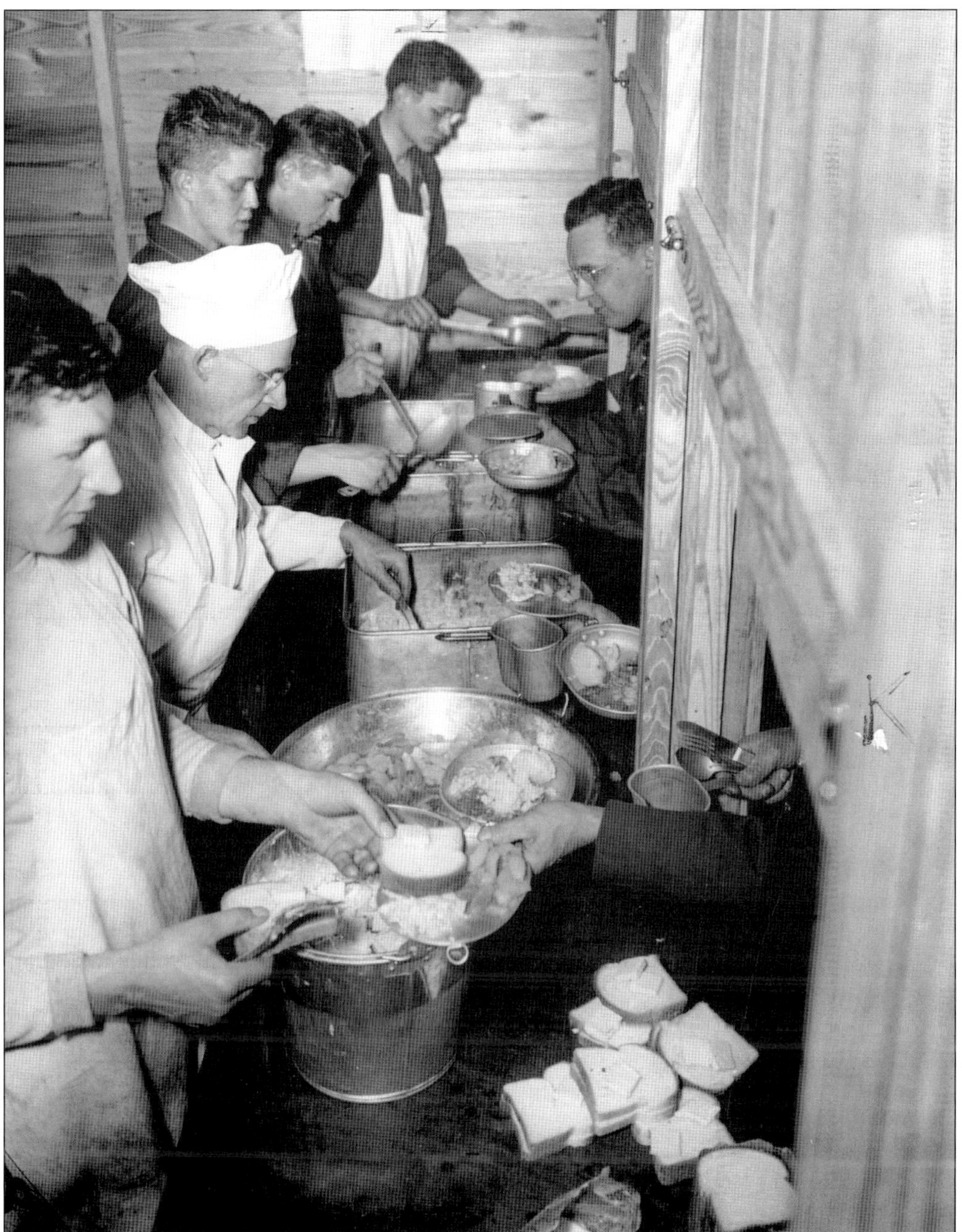

Across the United States, the Army operated intensive schools to train company cooks and bakers. Over a 21-day course, trainees studied food safety and storage, baking and cooking techniques, nutrition, and the basic theory behind large-scale meal preparation. Sound training mattered as a single batch of spoiled or improperly cooked food could sicken hundreds and disrupt an entire division. Fort Sheridan even loaned four chefs to bolster instruction at Camp Forrest. Day to day, meal quality depended on available foodstuffs and the skill of the mess team. Mess sergeants often judged the popularity of a menu by the amount of food in the trash cans. Pictured here, Headquarters Company cooks serve dinner as soldiers move through the chow line. (Courtesy of CFF.)

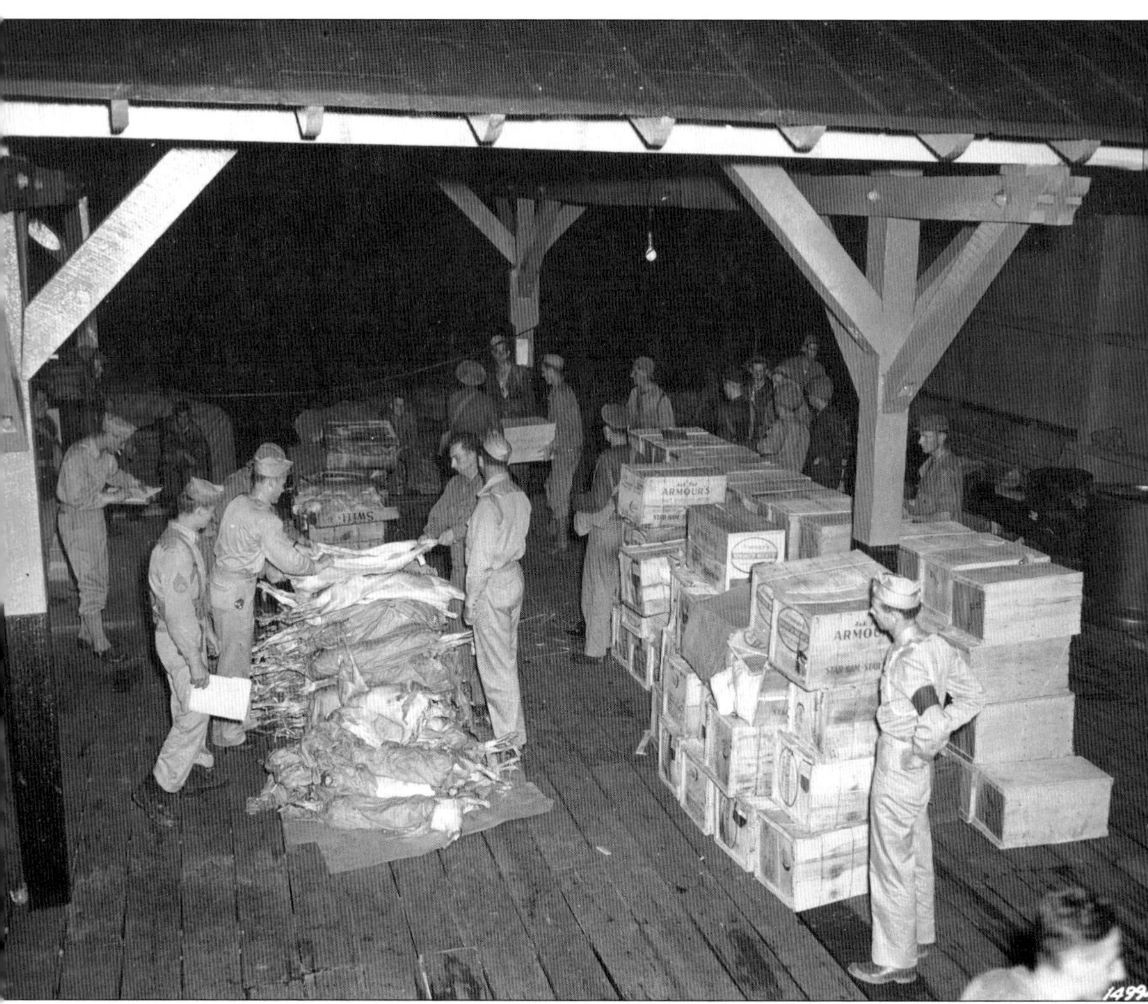

Company mess sergeants set menus weeks in advance, giving rail and truck deliveries time to arrive. Seasonal availability in nearby markets also determined the types of food served at meals. Here, soldiers unload provisions at a railhead in Tennessee to feed troops on maneuvers. Behind the chow line stood a vast logistical system from the Army and Quartermaster teams that procured, shipped, stored, and prepared food on a huge scale. Coordinating the feeding, movement, and care of hundreds of thousands of soldiers, vehicles, and equipment was daunting, yet the system usually ran smoothly thanks to planning and practice. (Courtesy of NARA.)

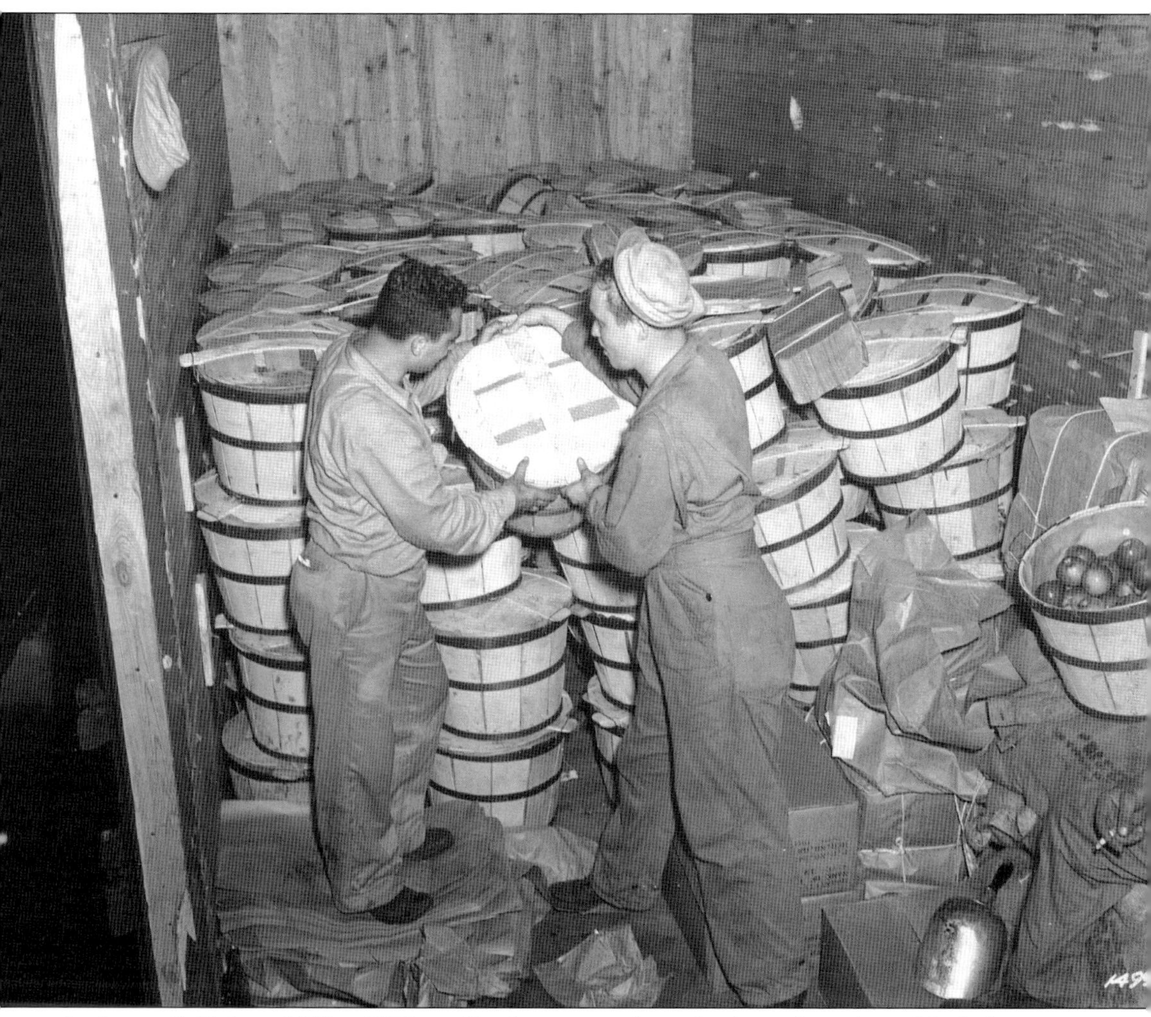

Lt. James C. Role and T.Sgt. Williams Reed supervise the unloading of supplies of fresh fruit in the fall of 1942 at a quartermaster field depot. (Courtesy of NARA.)

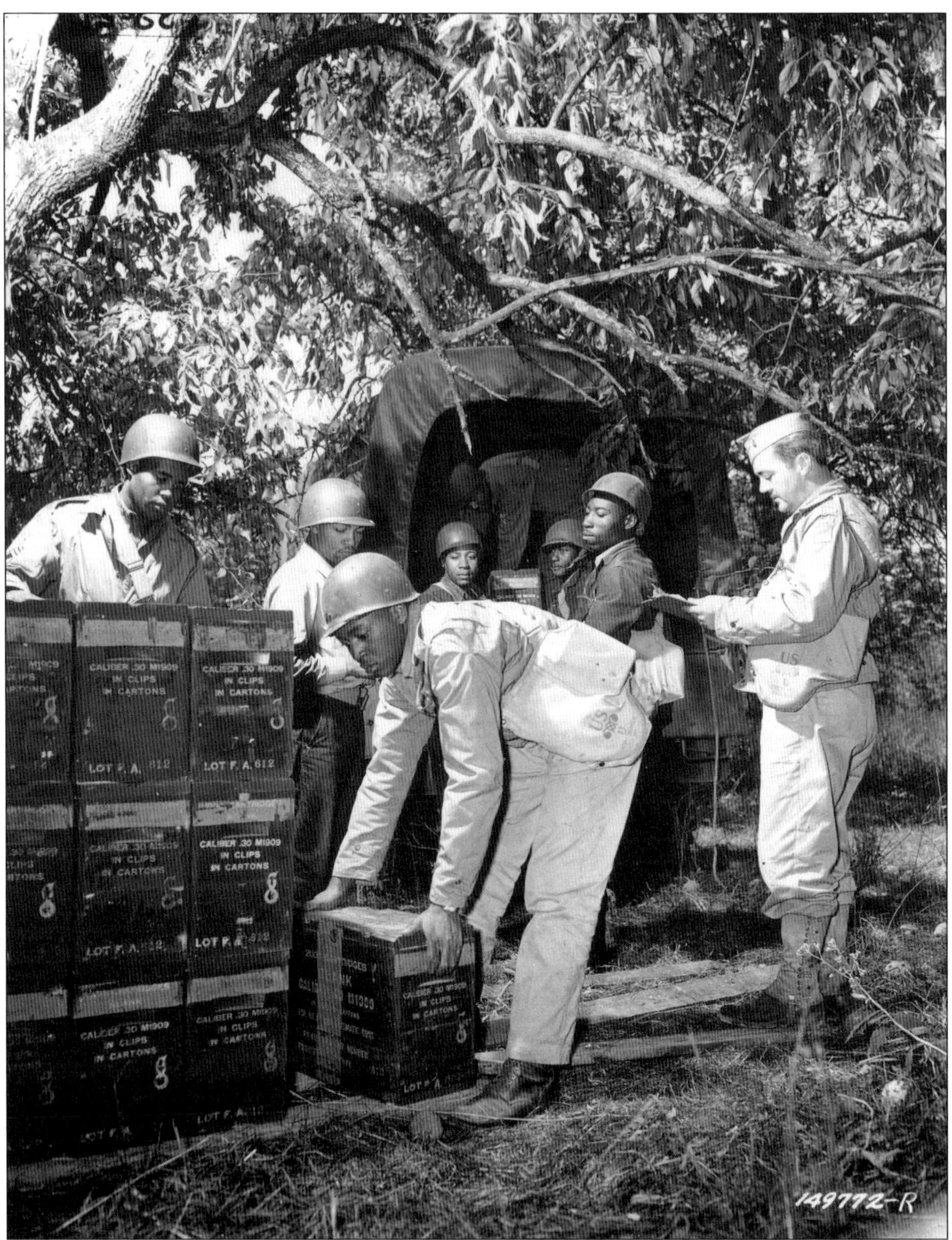

World War II mobile field kitchens typically fed 150 to 180 soldiers. Mess crews transported cooking equipment and foodstuffs in 2.5-ton cargo trucks equipped with trailers. Because perishables spoiled quickly, cooks relied on shelf-stable ingredients and issued C-rations when circumstances required. The sectional oven broke down into eight collapsible pieces, allowing crews to dismantle, move, and reassemble a kitchen in short order. The system prioritized hot meals as close to the front as possible while balancing speed, safety, and supply. (Courtesy of NARA.)

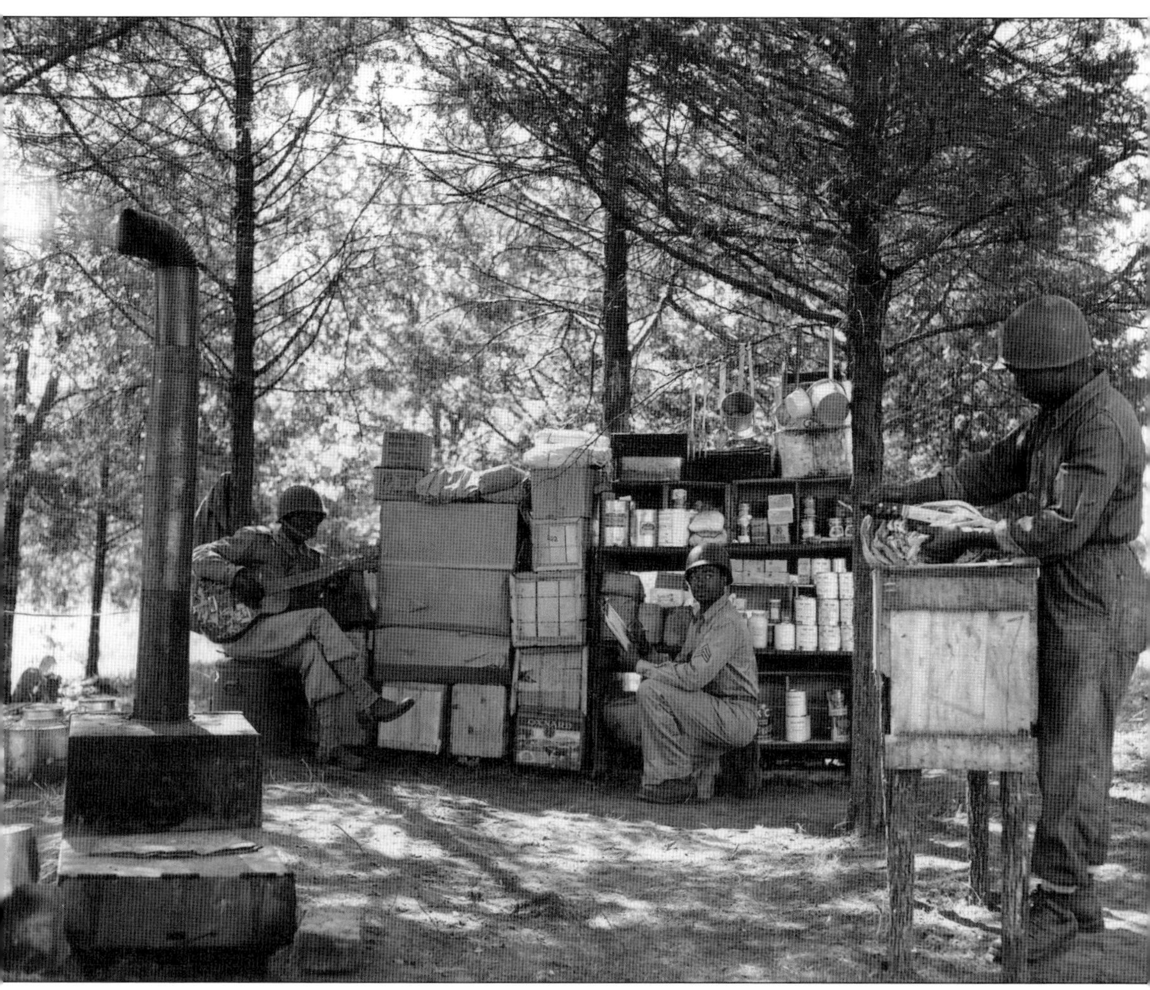

With millions of soldiers far from home, quartermasters and mess teams aimed to serve familiar foods whenever possible. For a large unit at Thanksgiving, that effort meant staggering quantities of foodstuffs: 3,284 turkeys, 6,900 cans of green peas and 6,900 cans of corn, 18,400 pounds of potatoes, 411 bushels of apples, 18,400 oranges, 1,840 cans of pineapple, 2,300 pounds of fresh cranberries, 2,760 heads of lettuce, and 9,200 pounds of tomatoes. (Courtesy of CFF.)

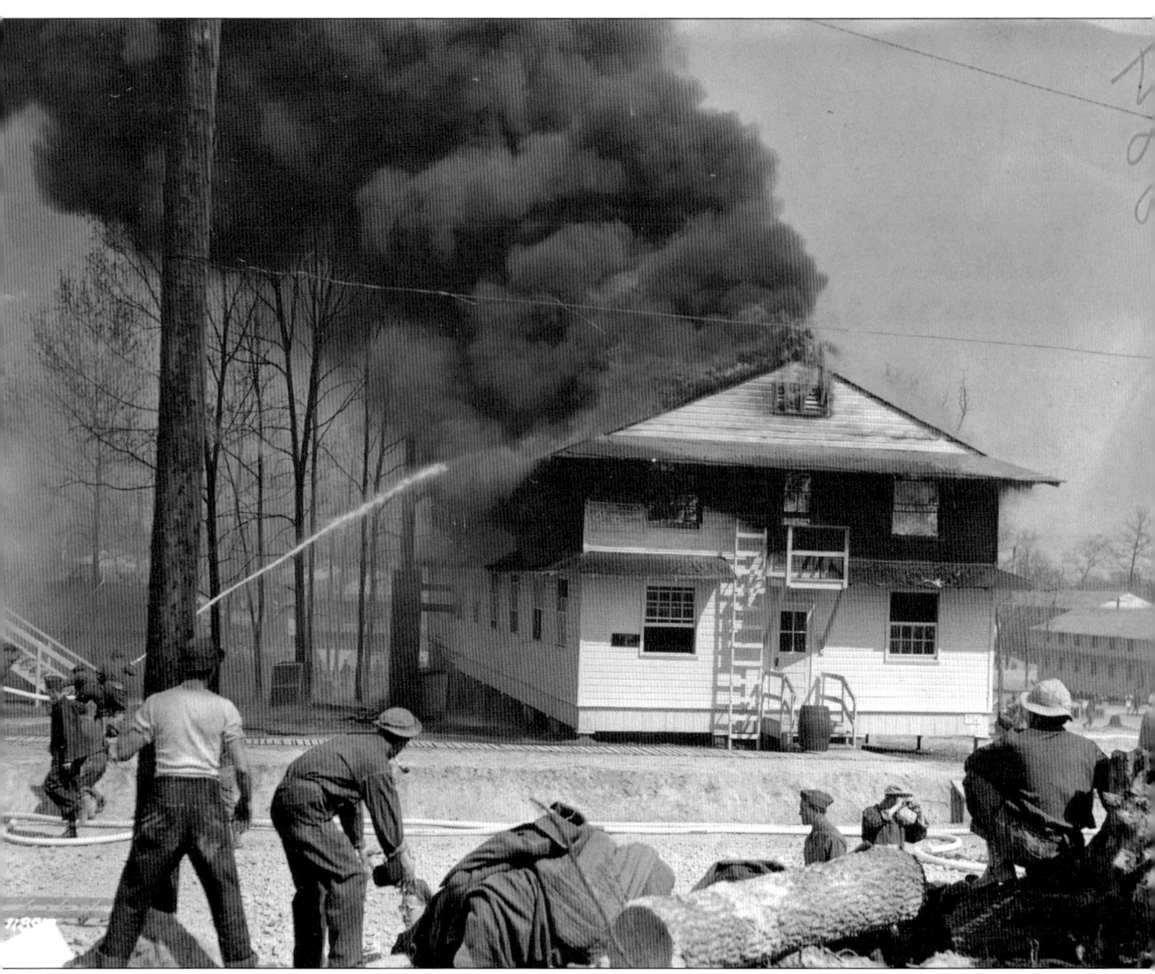

Camp Forrest's fire protection began with civilian crews. The 28 employees staffed the post's three stations and seven trucks until the 108th Ordnance Company, 33rd Division, arrived on March 21, 1941. At that point, Lt. Col. Merlin Bruce assumed responsibility from civilian fire chiefs William McKinney and Otto Von Almen as military personnel took over operating the cantonment. The photograph shows a barracks fire on April 7, 1941; the building burned quickly, but there were no injuries. Less than a year later, on January 2, 1942, Post Commander Waltz dispatched two fire trucks, an ambulance, and Army personnel off-post to help fight a blaze that threatened to destroy downtown Tullahoma. The episode illustrates how post resources supported both the installation and its surrounding community. (Courtesy of NARA.)

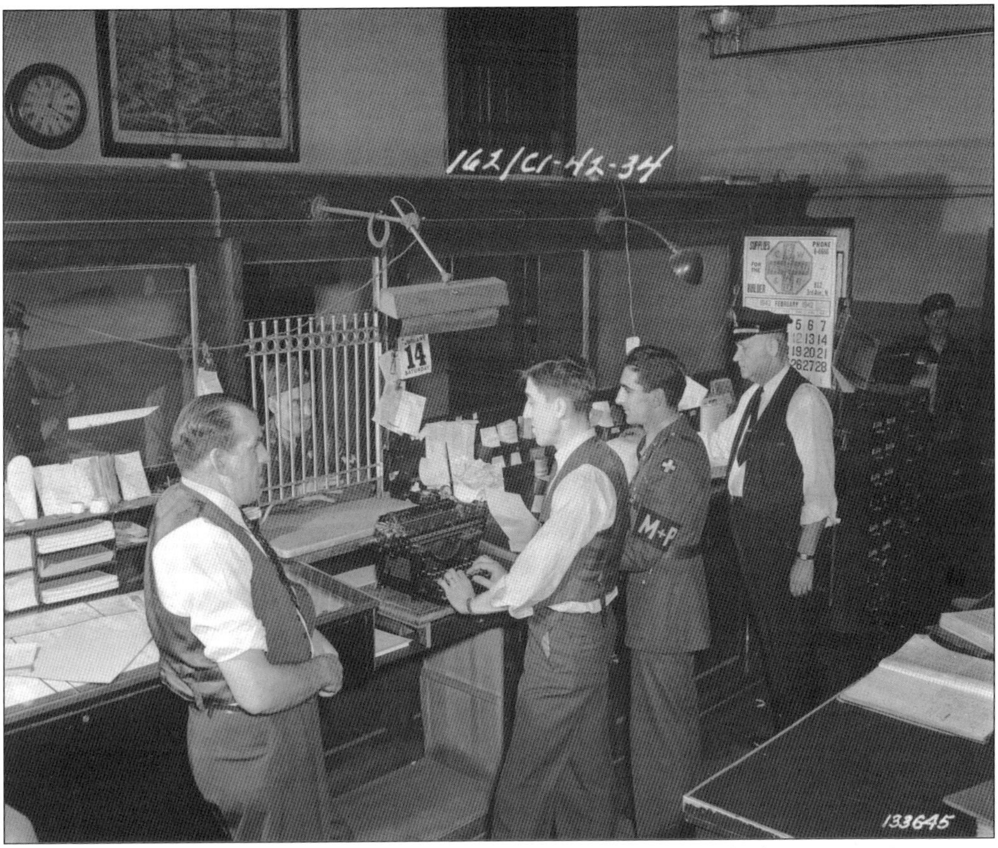

Camp Forrest's Military Police units maintained posts in Nashville and Chattanooga, Tennessee, and in Huntsville, Alabama, where they worked alongside local law enforcement when incidents involved off-duty soldiers. In this photograph, taken on Valentine's Day 1942, Pfc. Michel Imundo and MP Fred Wagner (at the window) of the 33rd MP Company meet with Nashville police officers Walter Gibbons, Thomas Beehan, and Lt. Frank Osborne (left to right) at police headquarters. Through liaison work, joint patrols, and case coordination, Camp Forrest MPs supported city departments while upholding the Army's good order and discipline. (Courtesy of NARA.)

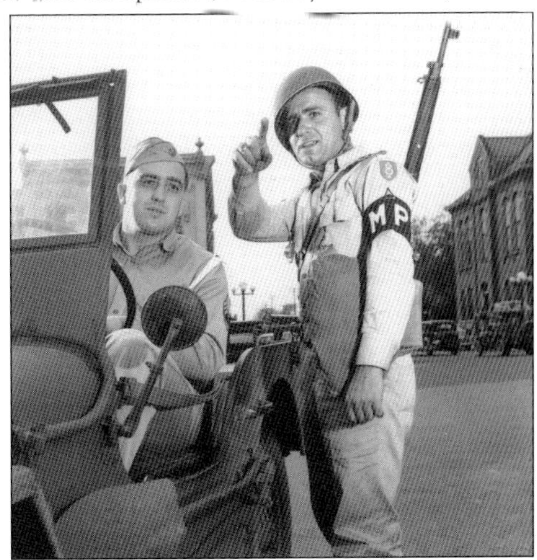

Maj. Ferris Foster was the head of the Camp Forrest Police Department. The post maintained 21 guardhouses for soldiers accused of minor offenses. Soldiers accused of felonies stayed in one of the two large post stockades until a court-martial convened. Armed guards staffed the stockades. The MPs were responsible for policing the 18,000-acre cantonment, patrolling the streets, directing traffic, guarding the camp's eight entrances, and assisting civilian police in nearby towns. In the photo, Staff Sergeant Radnovich receives directions from Military Police Corporal Gregorio. (Courtesy of NARA.)

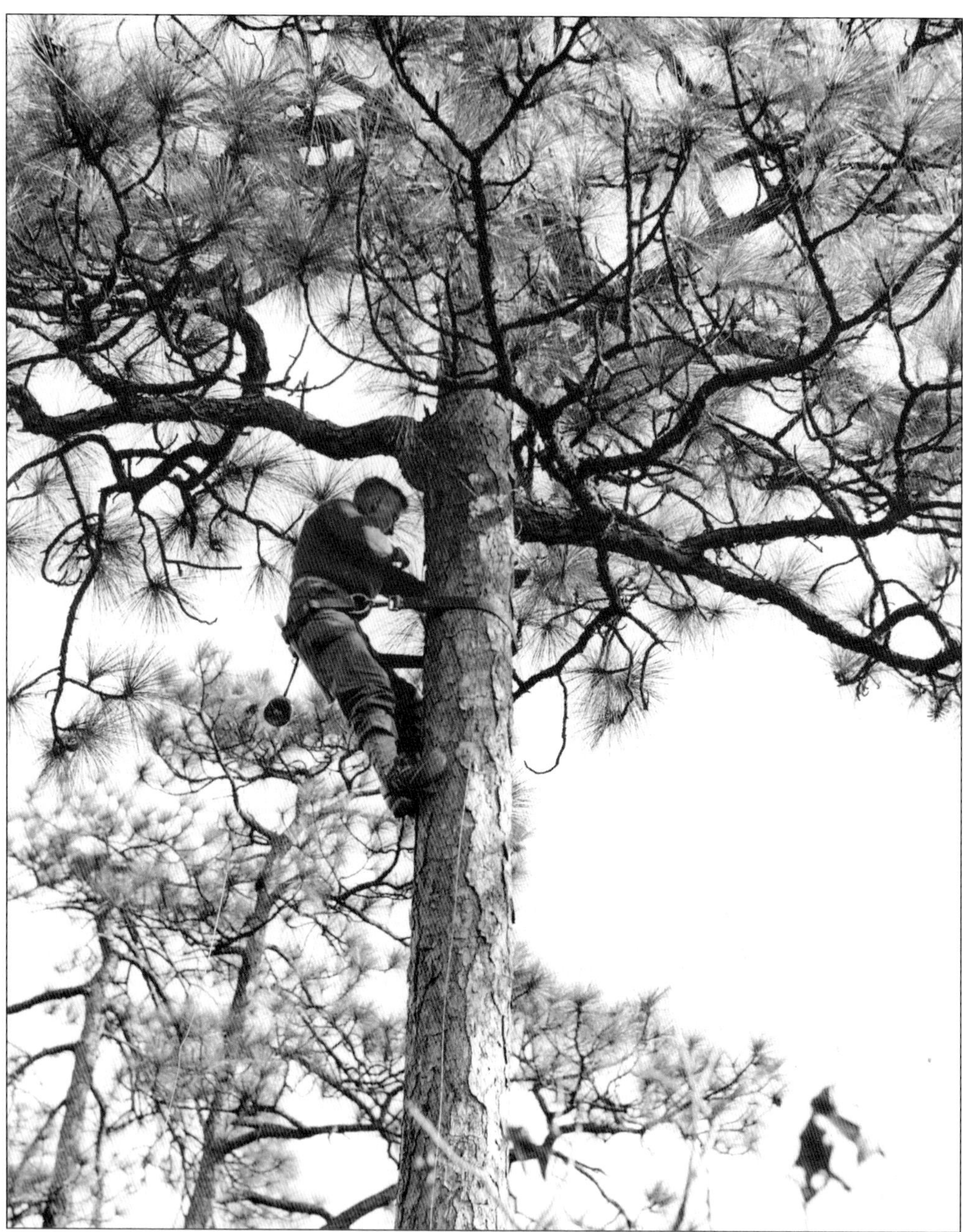

The US Army Signal Corps did far more than string wire. It managed battlefield communications, photography and motion-picture production, radar, homing-pigeon service, signal security and intelligence, and a system of training schools. In the field, line crews normally planted poles and unrolled hundreds of miles of wire to link forward units with headquarters by telephone and telegraph. When the ground made pole-setting impossible, soldiers improvised. Here, a 17th Airborne Division Signal Company soldier uses a pine tree as an expedient line support. During the large-scale maneuvers, Signal units worked with the opposing Red and Blue Armies to establish, protect, and repair communication networks, while photographic sections recorded operations on film and in still photographs for training, intelligence, and historical record. (Courtesy of CFF.)

T/5 Bart M. Williams attached wire to a cross frame set up on stony ground where it was impossible to use poles. (Courtesy of NARA.)

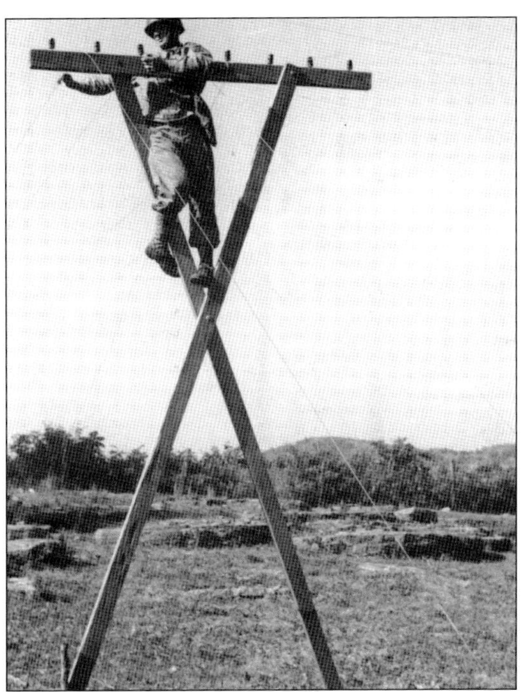

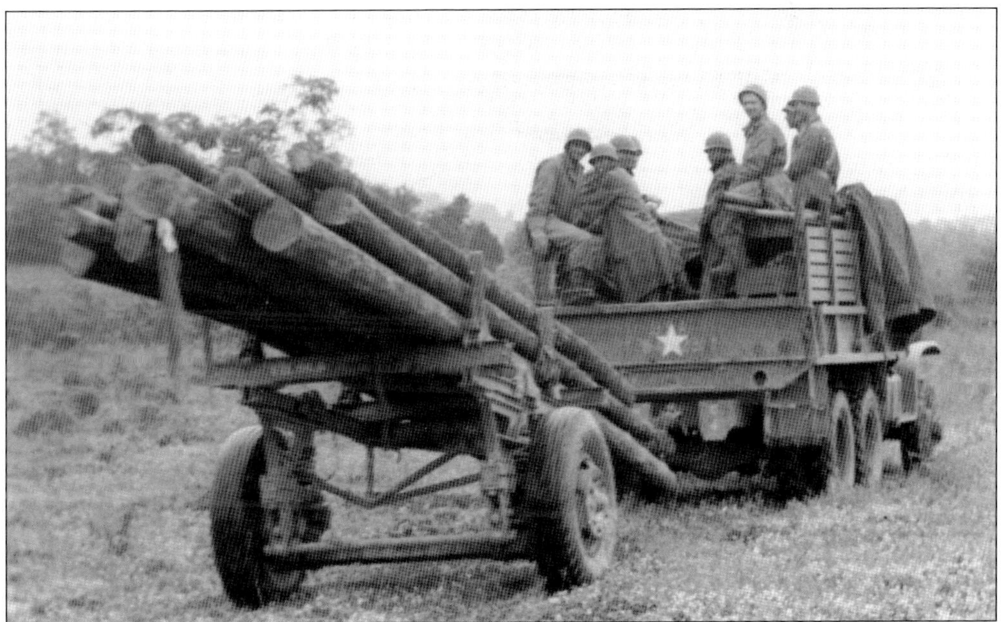

During World War II, the US Army Quartermaster Corps managed more than 70,000 different supply items, prepared about 24 million meals each day, and directed the recovery and burial of the fallen. In the field, Signal Corps line crews depended on that supply chain to connect units. Here, a trailer delivered utility poles to holes drilled by a portable auger; after setting each pole, soldiers strung wire to carry field telephone and telegraph traffic back to headquarters. The scene captures two sides of the same enterprise: the Quartermaster fed and equipped millions, and the Signal Corps networks moved information quickly to keep forces synchronized. (Courtesy of NARA.)

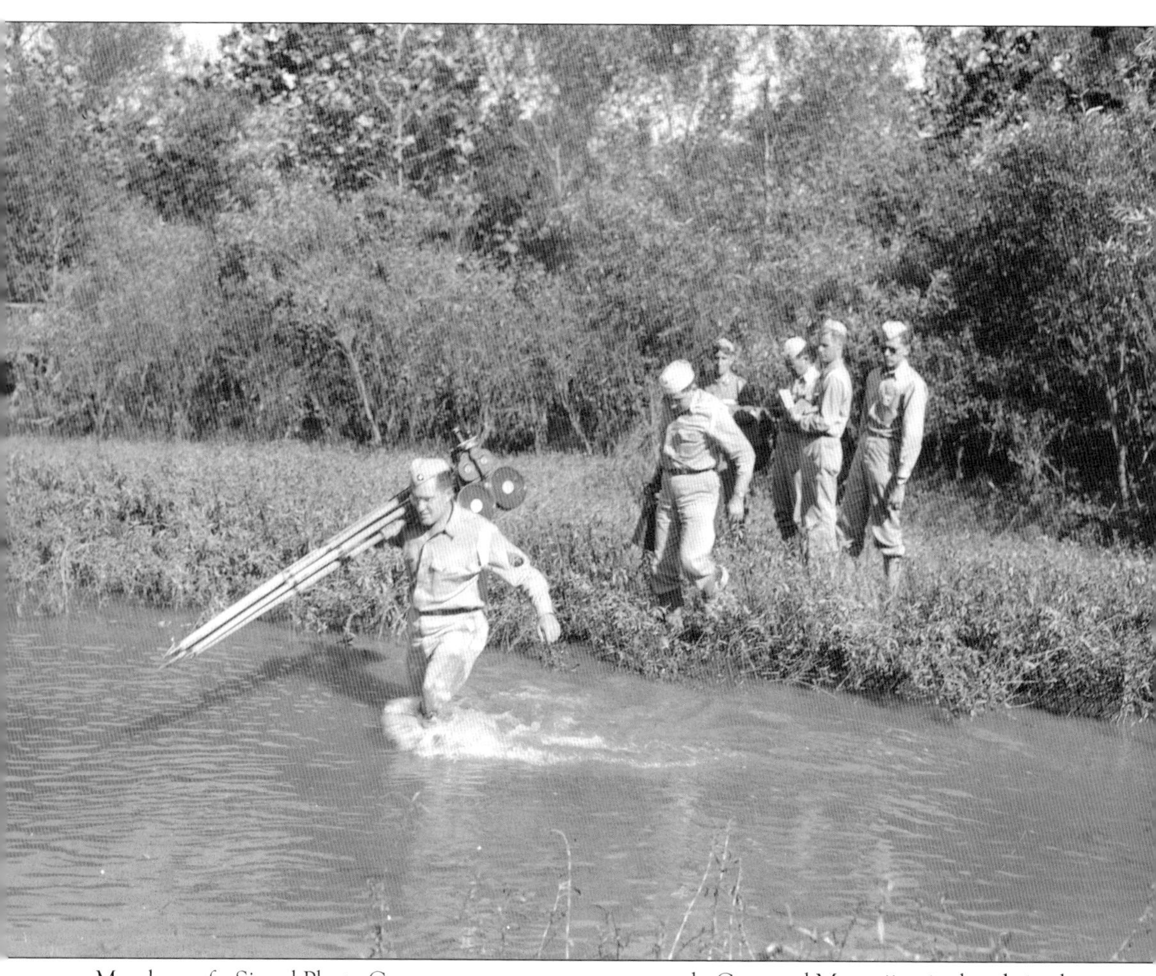

Members of a Signal Photo Company prepare to cross a creek. Corporal Manerjian is already in the water, while Pvt. Charles Klain, Pvt. J. Doyle, Private Martinson, and Pvt. A. Glosker follow close behind. (Courtesy of NARA.)

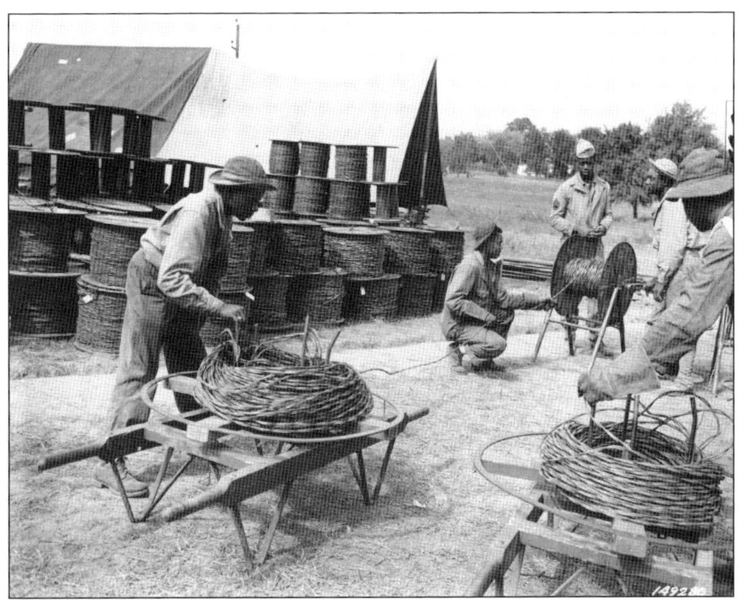

Staff Sergeant Jones and his crew service wire at the Signal Construction Company wire supply dump. (Courtesy of NARA.)

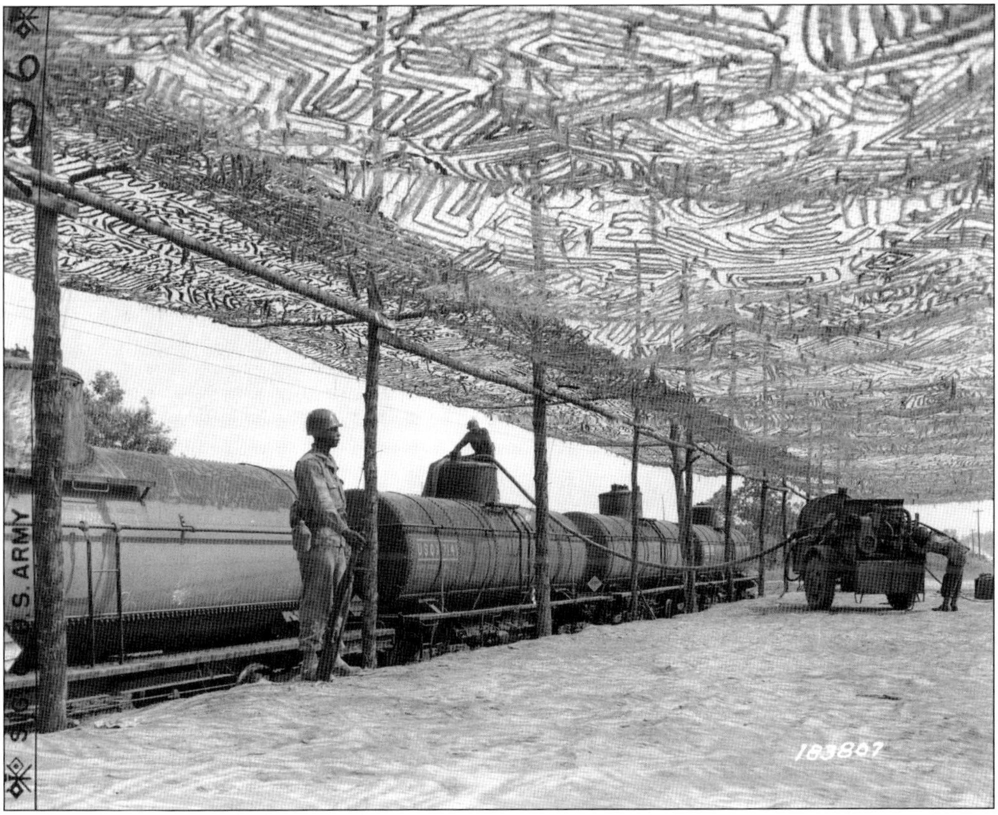

Gas tankers stopped at camouflaged refueling stations in maneuver areas, such as this one in Manchester, Tennessee. Units stopped at these stations to refuel vehicles and to obtain extra jerry cans. (Courtesy of NARA.)

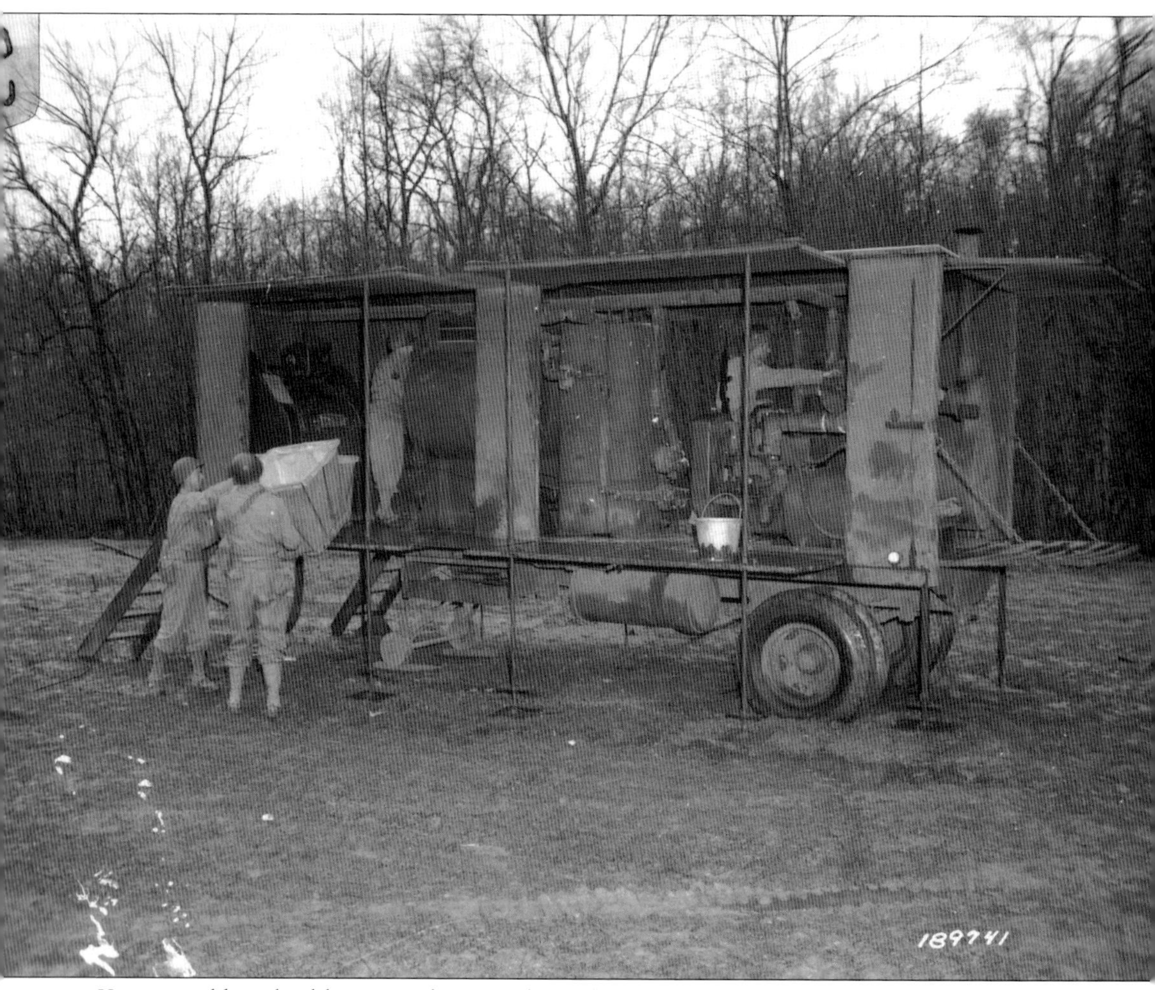

Keeping soldiers healthy meant keeping them clean. Lessons from earlier wars made clear that dirty uniforms and poor hygiene spread lice, infections, and disease. During World War II, the US Army treated cleanliness as a readiness issue. The Quartermaster Corps ran fixed-site laundries at US bases, while overseas the Army fielded mobile laundry units in Europe, the Pacific, the Mediterranean, and the China-Burma-India Theater. Truck-mounted plants washed and dried clothes within 40 minutes, but their size and visibility from the air meant they usually worked in rear areas. (Courtesy of NARA.)

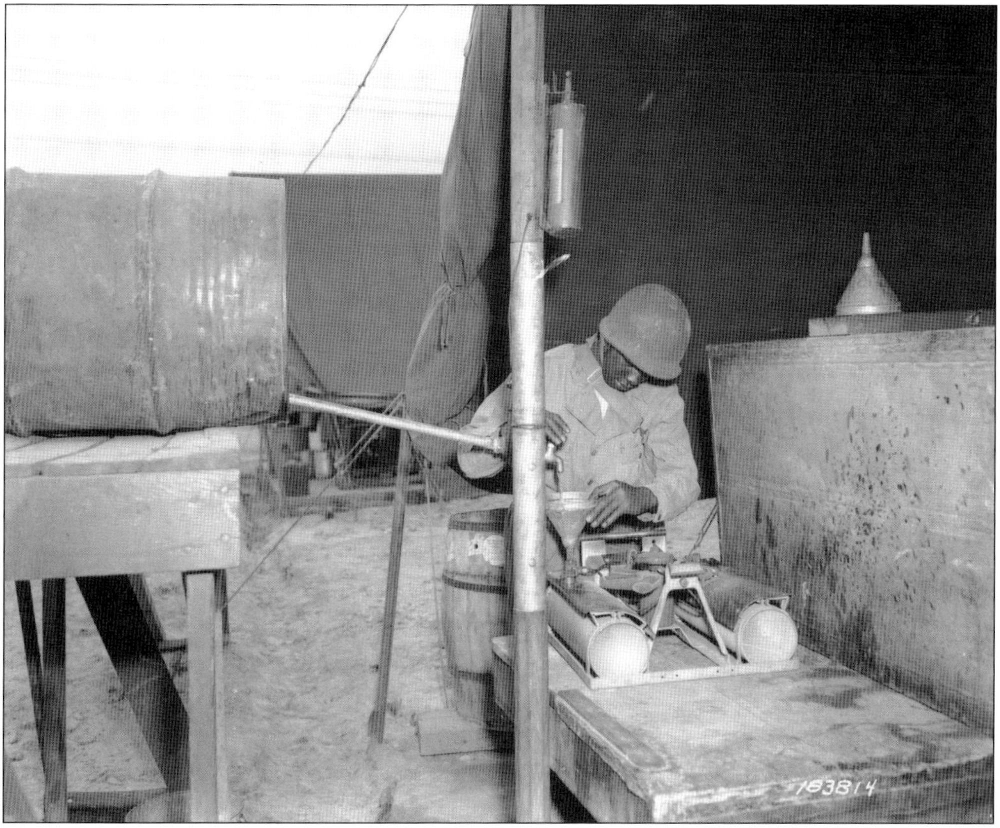

In May 1942, the federal government instituted gasoline rationing for civilians to guarantee the military had sufficient supplies. The petroleum industry underscored the need for ample fuel supplies for the military by pointing out that it required three tons of fuel to deliver a one-ton bomb and that the gasoline consumed to train a single pilot would last the average motorist 18 years. At Camp Forrest, 22 fueling stations kept operations moving. The photograph above illustrates fueling of the M-1937 burner used in field kitchens. (Courtesy of NARA.)

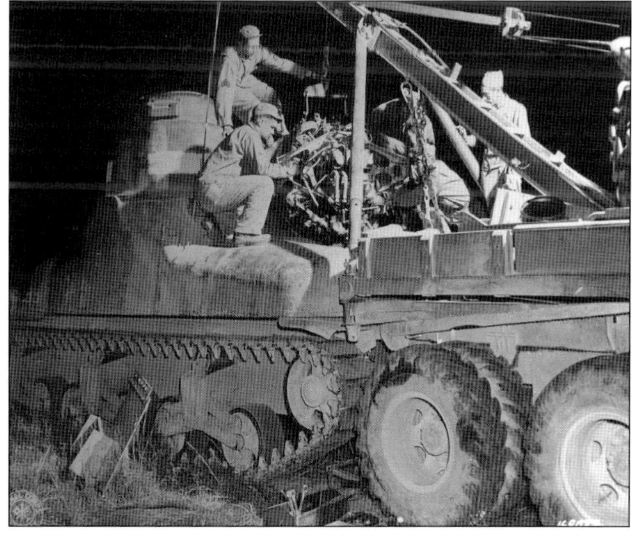

Here, soldiers use the crane boom on an Army wrecker to lift a tank's engine for repair. Military tow truck equipment included winches, cables, and boom cranes. Military personnel used these vehicles to either move or recover heavy equipment and vehicles, such as disabled tanks stuck in mud or sidelined by mechanical failure. Recovery crews worked alongside maintenance and supply units, turning battlefield breakdowns into quick returns to service. (Courtesy of NARA.)

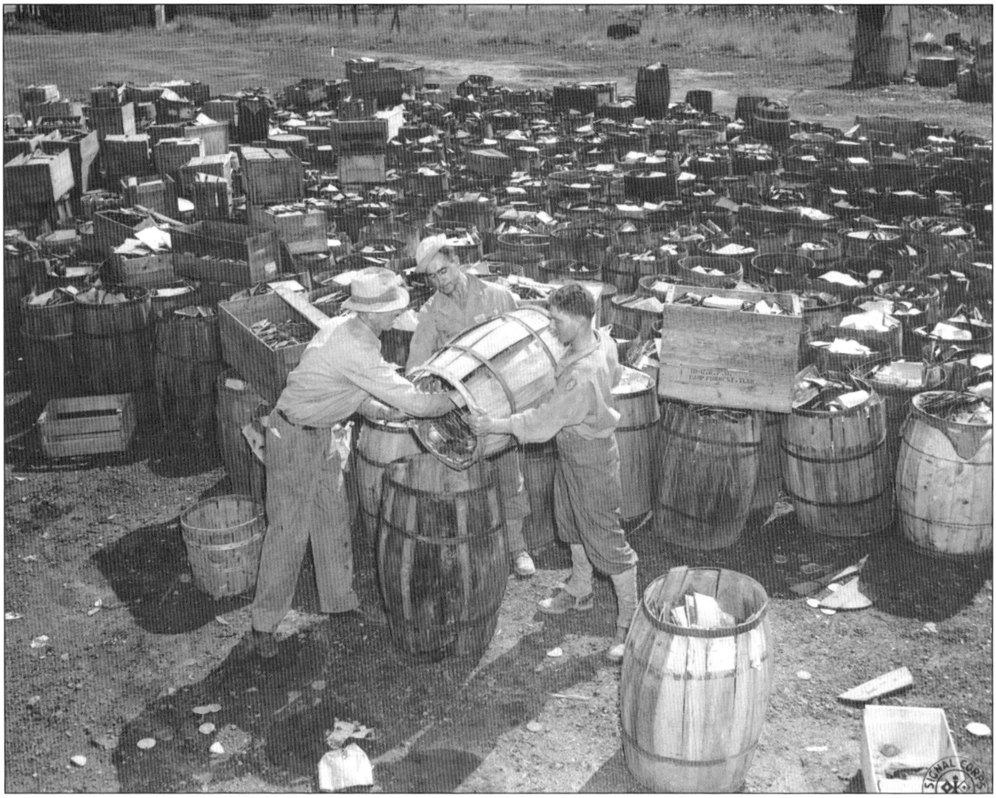

During World War II, posts like Camp Forrest ran salvage areas to reclaim metal for the war effort. In each photo, left to right, civilian employee J.E. Collier, Pvt. Eugene Zuzak, and Pvt. Leo Taylor stack recycled cans for processing. Salvage crews gathered metal from kitchens, shops, and barracks across the installation, sorted and compacted the material, and turned it over to civilian scrap drives for onward shipment and reuse. The steady routine of collecting, stacking, and dispatching scrap illustrates how conservation on the home front and in training camps supported wartime production. (Both, courtesy of CFF.)

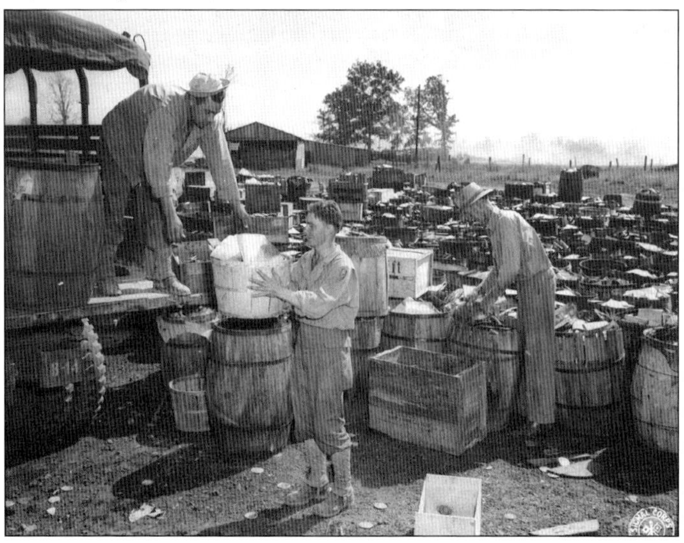

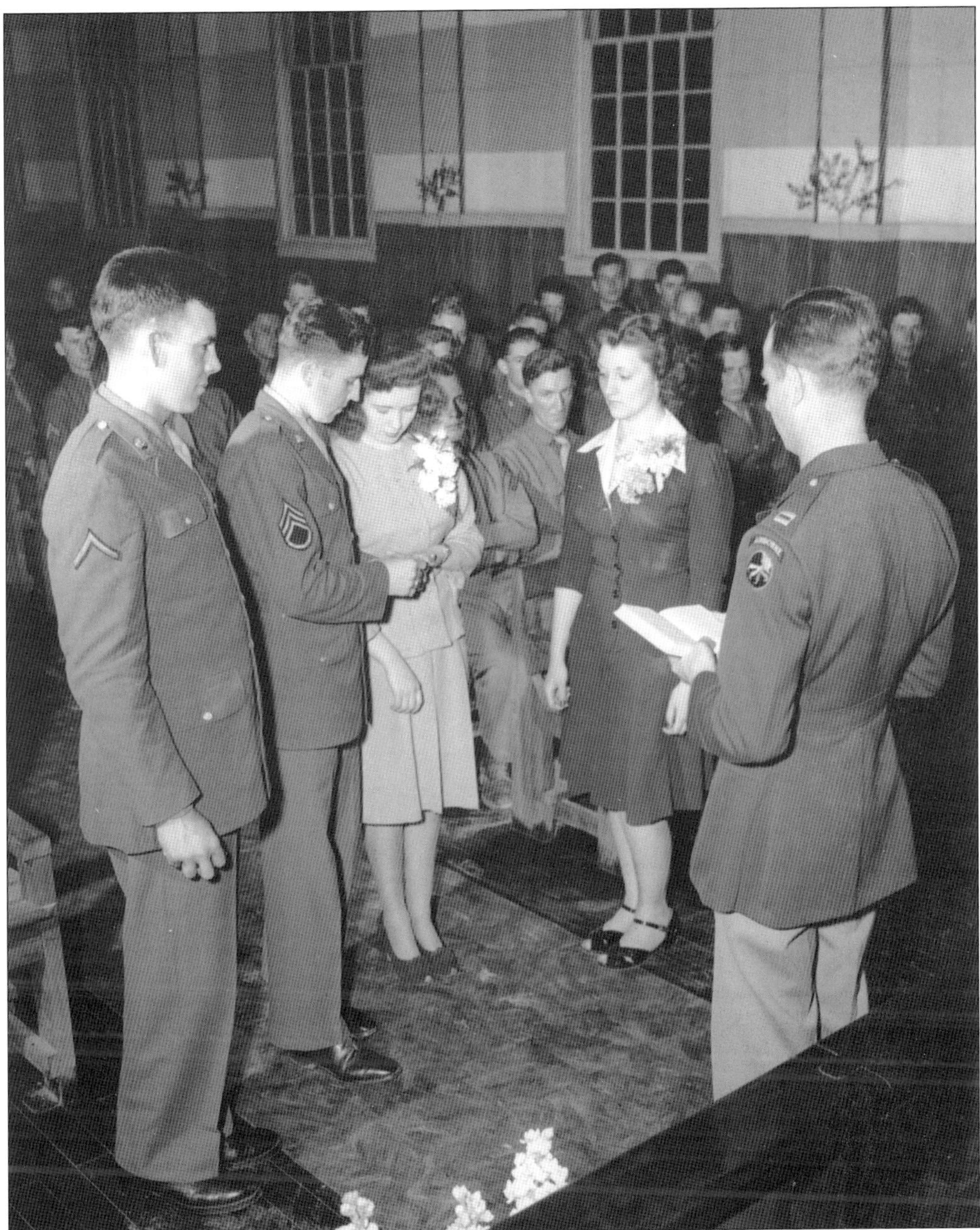

A couple stands before a chaplain at the altar inside Chapel 10 at Camp Forrest, exchanging wedding vows. The post chapels hosted more than 300 marriages during the camp's years of operation. (Courtesy of CFF.)

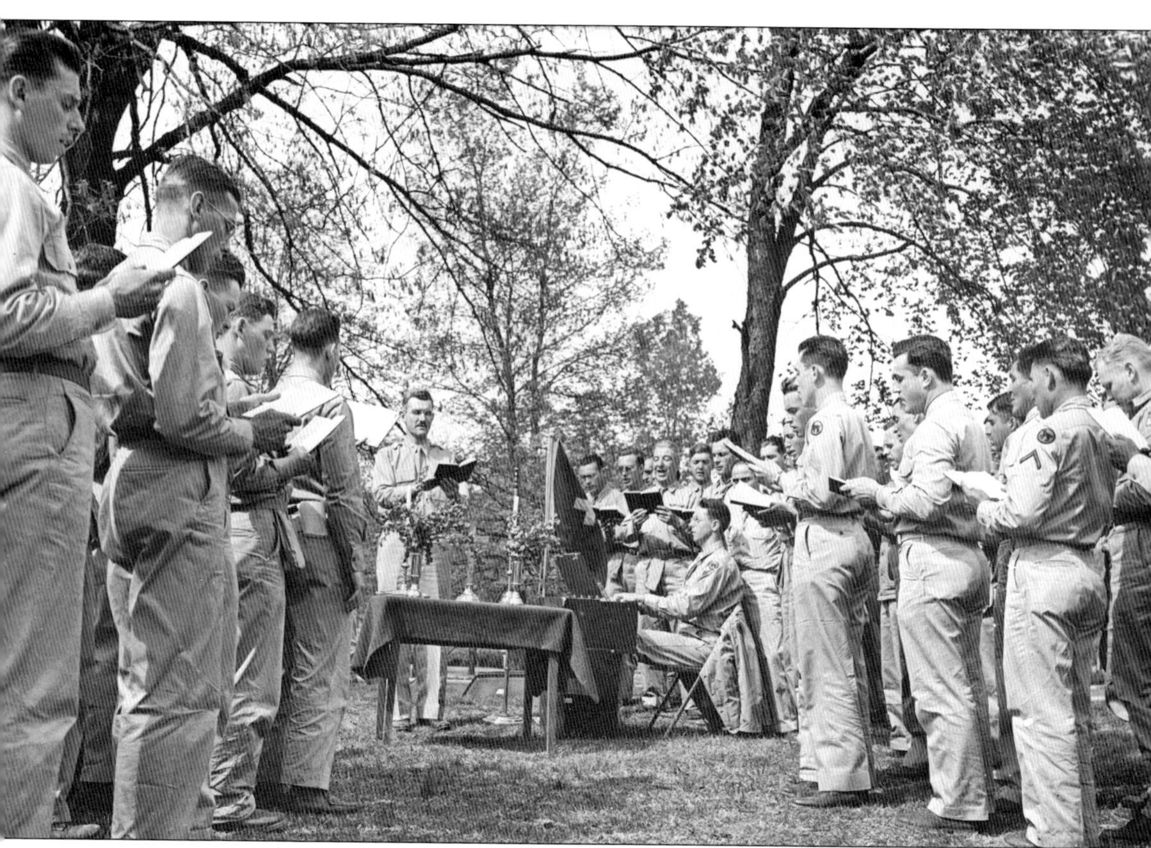

Army chaplains did not remain behind at base chapels; they accompanied units into training areas and into the field, where they led worship services, counseled soldiers, and offered spiritual support. Each chaplain carried a field kit tailored to their faith and included all items needed for services away from a chapel. Chaplain's assistants supported these efforts, sometimes providing music with portable pump organs. The chaplain carried prayer books, hymnals, chalices, and portable altars to bring a sense of continuity and community to men far from home. (Courtesy of MTSU.)

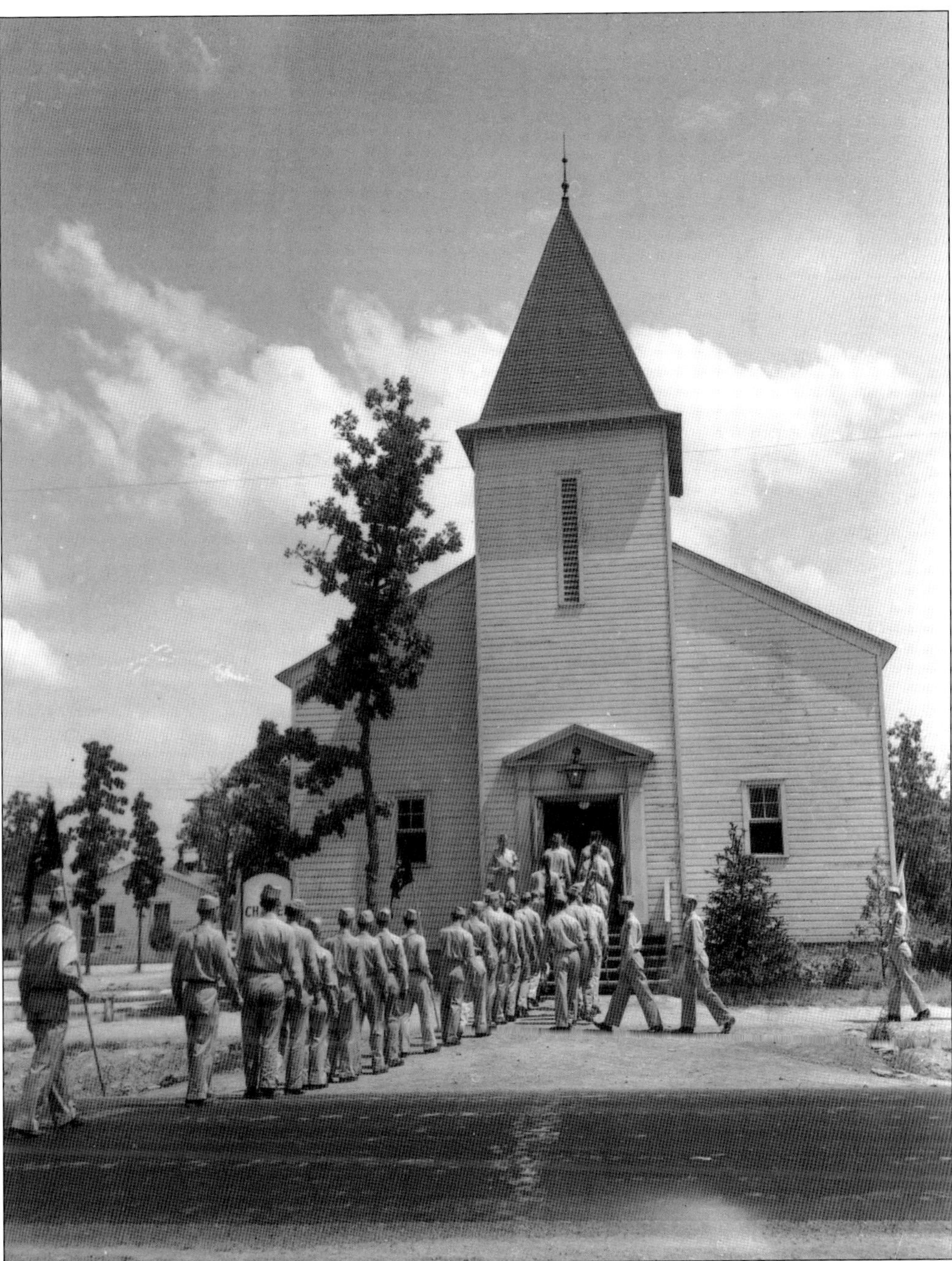

On November 22, 1941, Camp Forrest dedicated nine new chapels. These facilities hosted religious services, weddings, and community events for soldiers and their families. Chaplains from different faiths led worship throughout the week. Beyond services, chaplains offered counseling and comfort to soldiers. This photograph shows soldiers entering one of the chapels for a service shortly after their dedication, underscoring how spiritual life and routine worship integrated into Army training and camp life during World War II. (Courtesy of NARA.)

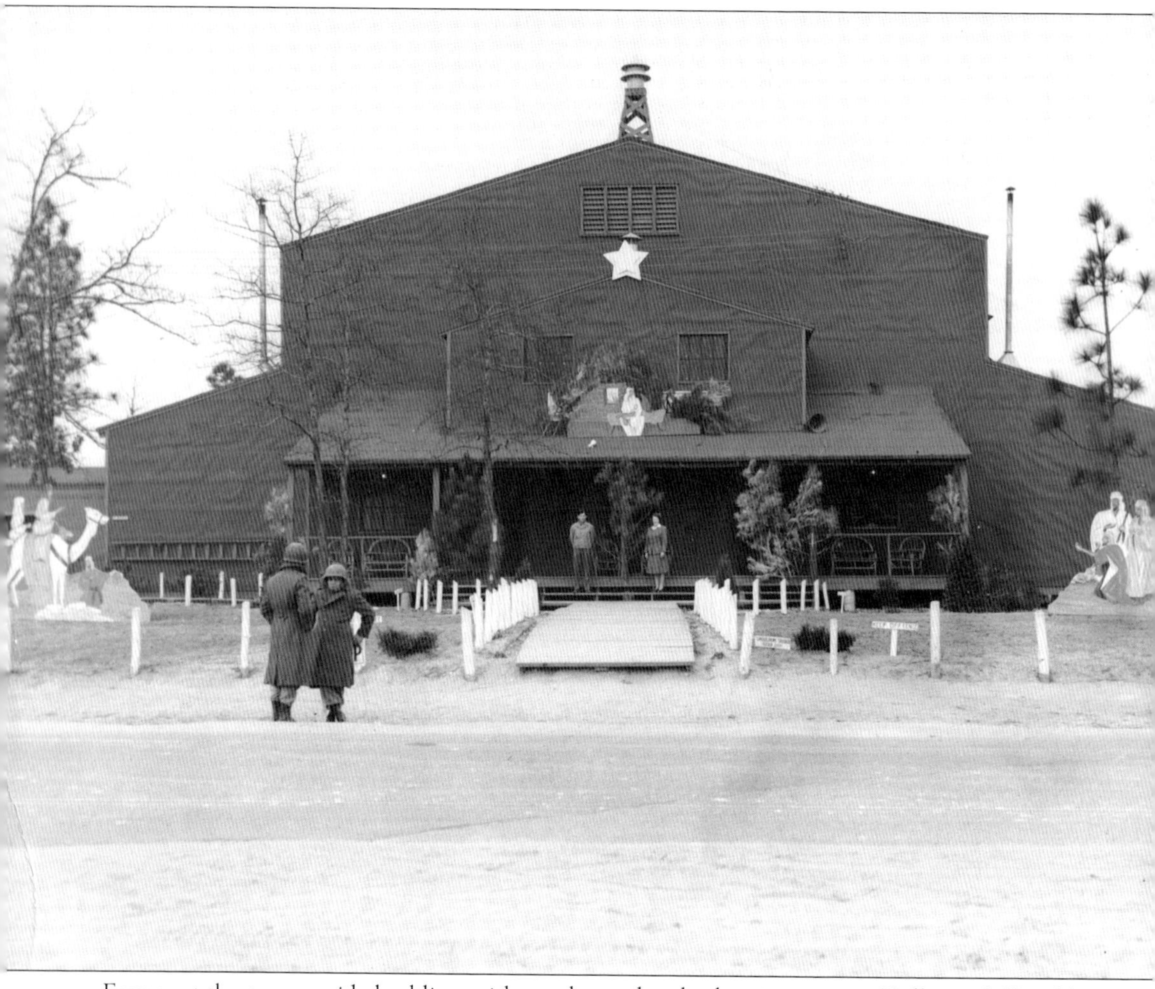

Four post theaters provided soldiers with a welcome break, showing current Hollywood films like *Blondie for Victory* (1942) and *Holiday Inn* (1942), along with Army training films and live stage productions. Each theater could seat 1,100 and ran several shows each evening to meet demand. Soldiers paid 20 cents for a Sunday matinee or bought ticket books for more affordable access. Base regulations stipulated that soldiers wear Full Class A uniforms, whether they attended the post theaters or one of the three theaters in Tullahoma. Theaters also reflected the seasons; at Christmastime, decorations, such as the ones shown in the photograph above, created a cheerful holiday atmosphere. These shared cultural experiences gave soldiers a sense of normalcy and connection to home during wartime service. (Courtesy of CFF.)

Posters outside the post theaters listed the day and time of each showing, ensuring soldiers knew when and where to line up. To spread the word more widely, the same posters hung across the installation: on unit bulletin boards, in Service Clubs, and at other high-traffic areas where troops gathered. The routine of checking the movie poster for the next show became part of daily life and a welcome distraction from training. (Both, courtesy of Jimmy Walker.)

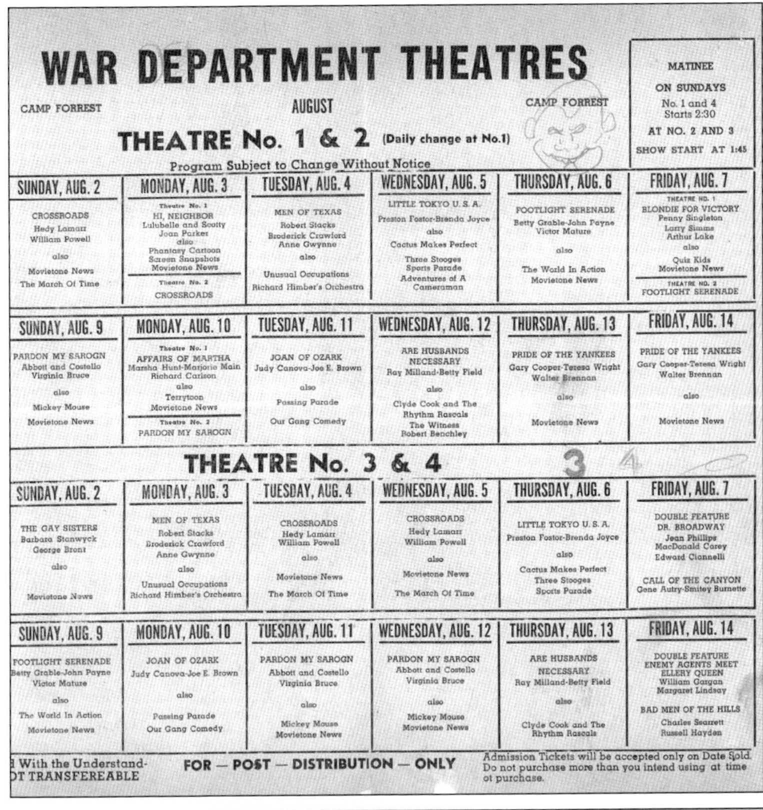

WAR DEPARTMENT THEATRES

CAMP FORREST — AUGUST — CAMP FORREST

MATINEE
ON SUNDAYS
No. 1 and 4
Starts 2:30
AT NO. 2 AND 3
SHOW START AT 1:45

THEATRE No. 1 & 2 (Daily change at No.1)

Program Subject to Change Without Notice

SUNDAY, AUG. 2	MONDAY, AUG. 3	TUESDAY, AUG. 4	WEDNESDAY, AUG. 5	THURSDAY, AUG. 6	FRIDAY, AUG. 7
CROSSROADS Hedy Lamarr William Powell also Movietone News The March Of Time	Theatre No. 1 HI, NEIGHBOR Lulubelle and Scotty Joan Parker also Phantasy Cartoon Screen Snapshots Movietone News Theatre No. 2 CROSSROADS	MEN OF TEXAS Robert Stacks Broderick Crawford Anne Gwynne also Unusual Occupations Richard Himber's Orchestra	LITTLE TOKYO U. S. A. Preston Foster-Brenda Joyce also Cactus Makes Perfect Three Stooges Sports Parade Adventures of A Cameraman	FOOTLIGHT SERENADE Betty Grable-John Payne Victor Mature also The World In Action Movietone News	THEATRE NO. 1 BLONDIE FOR VICTORY Penny Singleton Larry Simms Arthur Lake also Quiz Kids Movietone News THEATRE NO. 2 FOOTLIGHT SERENADE

SUNDAY, AUG. 9	MONDAY, AUG. 10	TUESDAY, AUG. 11	WEDNESDAY, AUG. 12	THURSDAY, AUG. 13	FRIDAY, AUG. 14
PARDON MY SAROGN Abbott and Costello Virginia Bruce also Mickey Mouse Movietone News	Theatre No. 1 AFFAIRS OF MARTHA Marsha Hunt-Marjorie Main Richard Carlson also Terrytoon Movietone News Theatre No. 2 PARDON MY SAROGN	JOAN OF OZARK Judy Canova-Joe E. Brown also Passing Parade Our Gang Comedy	ARE HUSBANDS NECESSARY Ray Milland-Betty Field also Clyde Cook and The Rhythm Rascals The Witness Robert Benchley	PRIDE OF THE YANKEES Gary Cooper-Teresa Wright Walter Brennan also Movietone News	PRIDE OF THE YANKEES Gary Cooper-Teresa Wright Walter Brennan also Movietone News

THEATRE No. 3 & 4

SUNDAY, AUG. 2	MONDAY, AUG. 3	TUESDAY, AUG. 4	WEDNESDAY, AUG. 5	THURSDAY, AUG. 6	FRIDAY, AUG. 7
THE GAY SISTERS Barbara Stanwyck George Brent also Movietone News	MEN OF TEXAS Robert Stacks Broderick Crawford Anne Gwynne also Unusual Occupations Richard Himber's Orchestra	CROSSROADS Hedy Lamarr William Powell also Movietone News The March Of Time	CROSSROADS Hedy Lamarr William Powell also Movietone News The March Of Time	LITTLE TOKYO U. S. A. Preston Foster-Brenda Joyce also Cactus Makes Perfect Three Stooges Sports Parade	DOUBLE FEATURE DR. BROADWAY Jean Phillips MacDonald Carey Edward Ciannelli CALL OF THE CANYON Gene Autry-Smiley Burnette

SUNDAY, AUG. 9	MONDAY, AUG. 10	TUESDAY, AUG. 11	WEDNESDAY, AUG. 12	THURSDAY, AUG. 13	FRIDAY, AUG. 14
FOOTLIGHT SERENADE Betty Grable-John Payne Victor Mature also The World In Action Movietone News	JOAN OF OZARK Judy Canova-Joe E. Brown also Passing Parade Our Gang Comedy	PARDON MY SAROGN Abbott and Costello Virginia Bruce also Mickey Mouse Movietone News	PARDON MY SAROGN Abbott and Costello Virginia Bruce also Mickey Mouse Movietone News	ARE HUSBANDS NECESSARY Ray Milland-Betty Field also Clyde Cook and The Rhythm Rascals	DOUBLE FEATURE ENEMY AGENTS MEET ELLERY QUEEN William Gargan Margaret Lindsay BAD MEN OF THE HILLS Charles Starrett Russell Hayden

d With the Understand-
DT TRANSFEREABLE

FOR — POST — DISTRIBUTION — ONLY

Admission Tickets will be accepted only on Date Sold. Do not purchase more than you intend using at time of purchase.

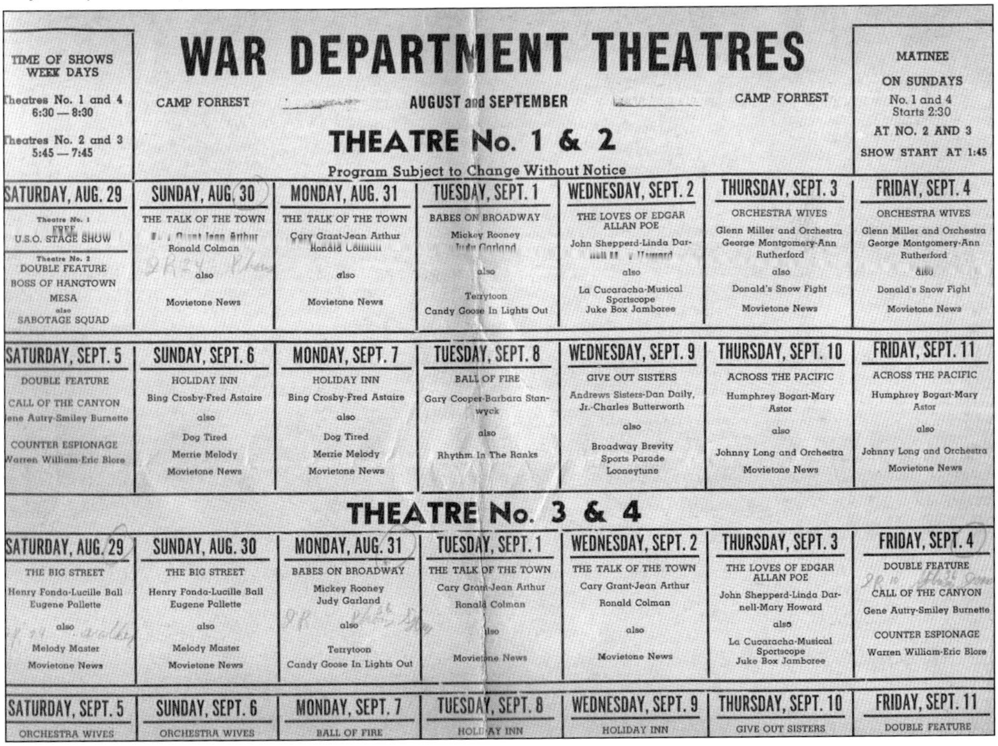

WAR DEPARTMENT THEATRES

TIME OF SHOWS WEEK DAYS
Theatres No. 1 and 4
6:30 — 8:30
Theatres No. 2 and 3
5:45 — 7:45

CAMP FORREST — AUGUST and SEPTEMBER — CAMP FORREST

MATINEE
ON SUNDAYS
No. 1 and 4
Starts 2:30
AT NO. 2 AND 3
SHOW START AT 1:45

THEATRE No. 1 & 2

Program Subject to Change Without Notice

SATURDAY, AUG. 29	SUNDAY, AUG. 30	MONDAY, AUG. 31	TUESDAY, SEPT. 1	WEDNESDAY, SEPT. 2	THURSDAY, SEPT. 3	FRIDAY, SEPT. 4
Theatre No. 1 FREE U.S.O. STAGE SHOW Theatre No. 2 DOUBLE FEATURE BOSS OF HANGTOWN MESA also SABOTAGE SQUAD	THE TALK OF THE TOWN [illegible] Ronald Colman also Movietone News	THE TALK OF THE TOWN Cary Grant-Jean Arthur Ronald Colman also Movietone News	BABES ON BROADWAY Mickey Rooney Judy Garland also Terrytoon Candy Goose In Lights Out	THE LOVES OF EDGAR ALLAN POE John Shepperd-Linda Dar- [illegible] also La Cucaracha-Musical Sportscope Juke Box Jamboree	ORCHESTRA WIVES Glenn Miller and Orchestra George Montgomery-Ann Rutherford also Donald's Snow Fight Movietone News	ORCHESTRA WIVES Glenn Miller and Orchestra George Montgomery-Ann Rutherford also Donald's Snow Fight Movietone News

SATURDAY, SEPT. 5	SUNDAY, SEPT. 6	MONDAY, SEPT. 7	TUESDAY, SEPT. 8	WEDNESDAY, SEPT. 9	THURSDAY, SEPT. 10	FRIDAY, SEPT. 11
DOUBLE FEATURE CALL OF THE CANYON Gene Autry-Smiley Burnette COUNTER ESPIONAGE Warren William-Eric Blore	HOLIDAY INN Bing Crosby-Fred Astaire also Dog Tired Merrie Melody Movietone News	HOLIDAY INN Bing Crosby-Fred Astaire also Dog Tired Merrie Melody Movietone News	BALL OF FIRE Gary Cooper-Barbara Stan-wyck also Rhythm In The Ranks	GIVE OUT SISTERS Andrews Sisters-Dan Daily, Jr.-Charles Butterworth also Broadway Brevity Sports Parade Looneytune	ACROSS THE PACIFIC Humphrey Bogart-Mary Astor also Johnny Long and Orchestra Movietone News	ACROSS THE PACIFIC Humphrey Bogart-Mary Astor also Johnny Long and Orchestra Movietone News

THEATRE No. 3 & 4

SATURDAY, AUG. 29	SUNDAY, AUG. 30	MONDAY, AUG. 31	TUESDAY, SEPT. 1	WEDNESDAY, SEPT. 2	THURSDAY, SEPT. 3	FRIDAY, SEPT. 4
THE BIG STREET Henry Fonda-Lucille Ball Eugene Pallette also Melody Master Movietone News	THE BIG STREET Henry Fonda-Lucille Ball Eugene Pallette also Melody Master Movietone News	BABES ON BROADWAY Mickey Rooney Judy Garland also Terrytoon Candy Goose In Lights Out	THE TALK OF THE TOWN Cary Grant-Jean Arthur Ronald Colman also Movietone News	THE TALK OF THE TOWN Cary Grant-Jean Arthur Ronald Colman also Movietone News	THE LOVES OF EDGAR ALLAN POE John Shepperd-Linda Dar-nell-Mary Howard also La Cucaracha-Musical Sportscope Juke Box Jamboree	DOUBLE FEATURE CALL OF THE CANYON Gene Autry-Smiley Burnette COUNTER ESPIONAGE Warren William-Eric Blore

SATURDAY, SEPT. 5	SUNDAY, SEPT. 6	MONDAY, SEPT. 7	TUESDAY, SEPT. 8	WEDNESDAY, SEPT. 9	THURSDAY, SEPT. 10	FRIDAY, SEPT. 11
ORCHESTRA WIVES	ORCHESTRA WIVES	BALL OF FIRE	HOLIDAY INN	HOLIDAY INN	GIVE OUT SISTERS	DOUBLE FEATURE

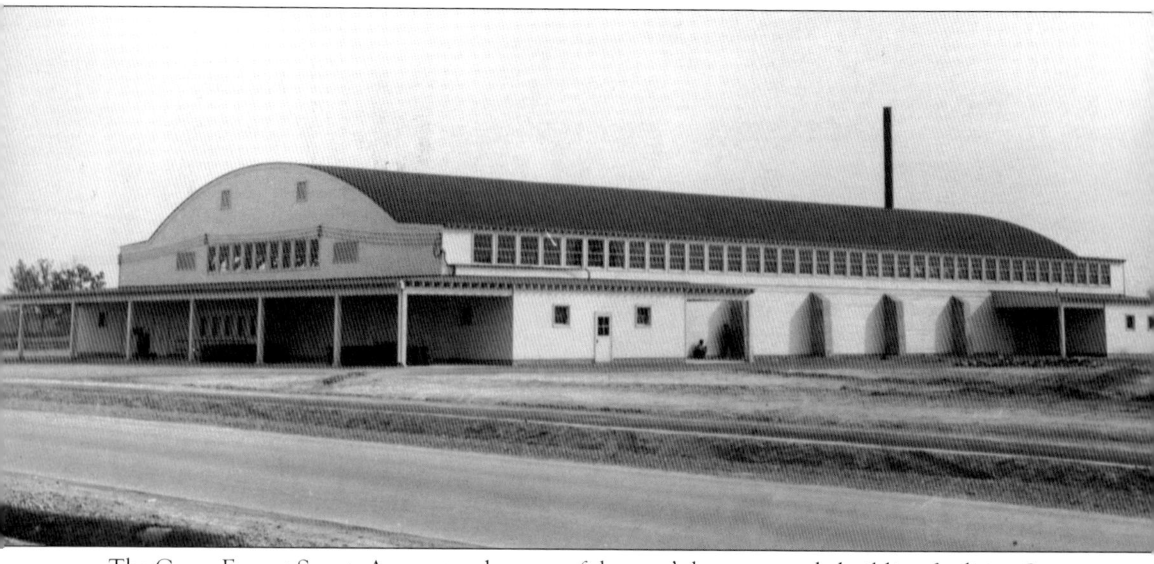

The Camp Forrest Sports Arena stood as one of the post's largest morale-building facilities. Seating more than 8,000, the arena hosted chapel services, concerts, stage productions, and athletic events that broke up the rigors of training. Soldiers competed in a wide variety of sports that included baseball, football, basketball, boxing, fencing, volleyball, soccer, and golf. Teams organized at both regimental and post levels. By early 1942, the camp supported 12 regimental basketball teams, playing against one another and against teams from across the Southeast. This integration into regional competition connected soldiers with surrounding communities, bringing visibility to the Army's presence while providing entertainment for civilians. The arena also welcomed professional events such as the Southern Golden Gloves Tournament, an exhibition by the Boston Celtics, and a tour by the Red Heads women's basketball team. Together, these activities built morale, created camaraderie, and gave soldiers a touch of normal life during wartime. (Courtesy of NARA.)

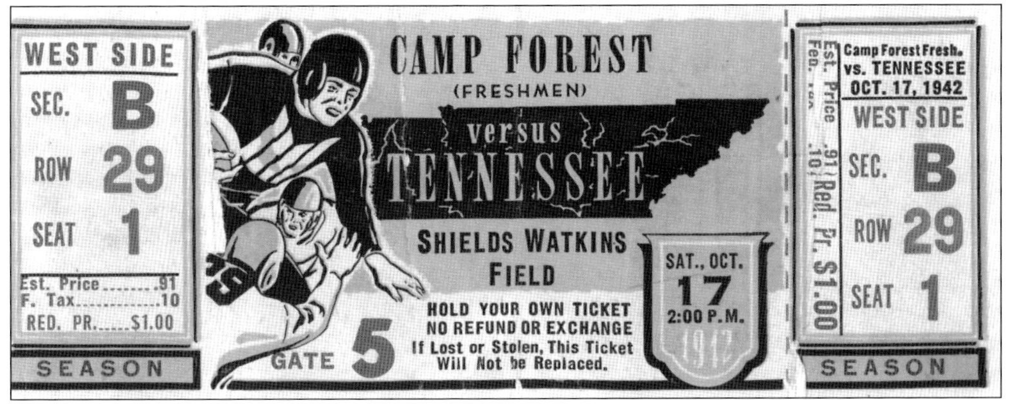

Military teams frequently competed with college squads during World War II, providing both spirited contests and entertainment for soldiers and civilians alike. On October 17, 1942, the Camp Forrest Freshman Eleven traveled to Knoxville to play the University of Tennessee freshmen at Shields Watkins Field. The game ended decisively, with the Vols running up eight touchdowns to claim a 51-0 victory. The *Knoxville Journal* reported the contest with the memorable headline, "Tennessee Freshmen Manhandle Camp Forrest Soldiers, 51-0." Artifacts such as this ticket stub highlight the role of athletics in wartime, connecting service members with local communities and demonstrating how sports helped sustain morale far from home. (Both, courtesy of Jimmy Walker.)

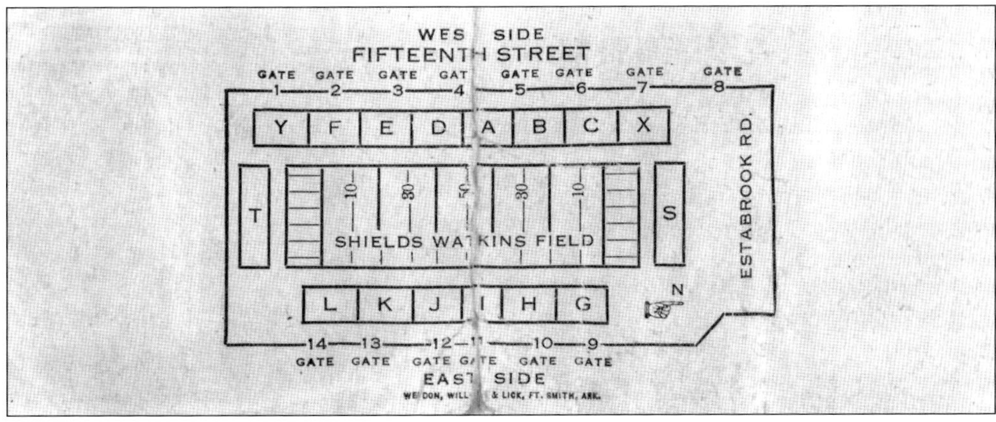

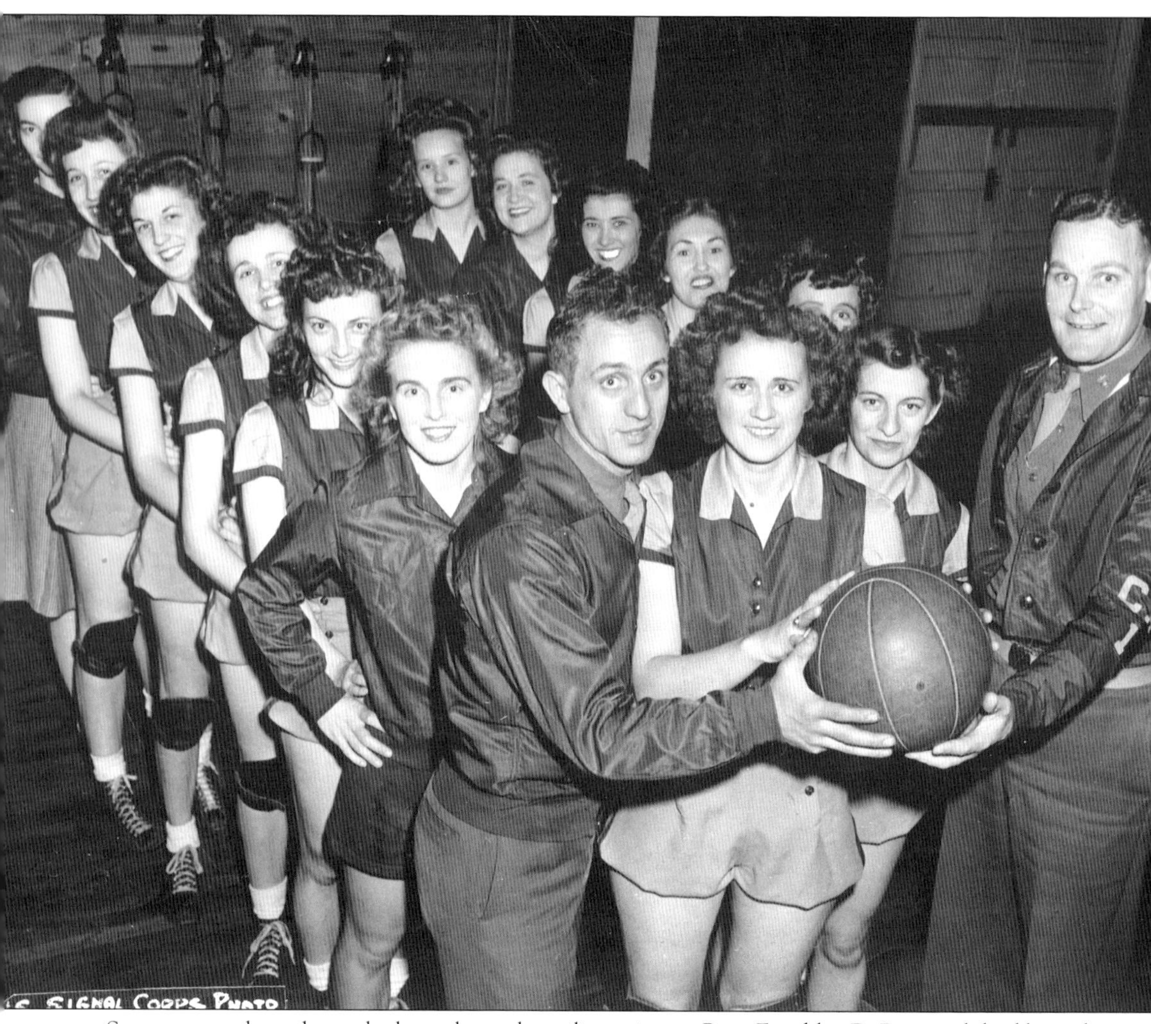

Sports strengthened morale throughout the military, just as Pres. Franklin D. Roosevelt had hoped. One of Camp Forrest's most popular athletic attractions was the Camp Forrest Lassies, a civilian women's basketball team organized under the post-quartermaster laundry officer, Capt. Gaylord F. Schad. Sgt. Melvin Fromm, the camp's recreational director, coached the team, and Coffee County native Carmine Todd captained it. Todd, who first played at Noah Elementary School, drew praise in local newspapers for her leadership on the court. Her sister, Callie, also joined the roster. The Lassies won most of their contests and were considered the best independent women's basketball team in Middle Tennessee. Their games brought soldiers and townspeople together, providing spirited competition, wholesome entertainment, and a sense of community during the wartime years. (Courtesy of Andrew V. Turner.)

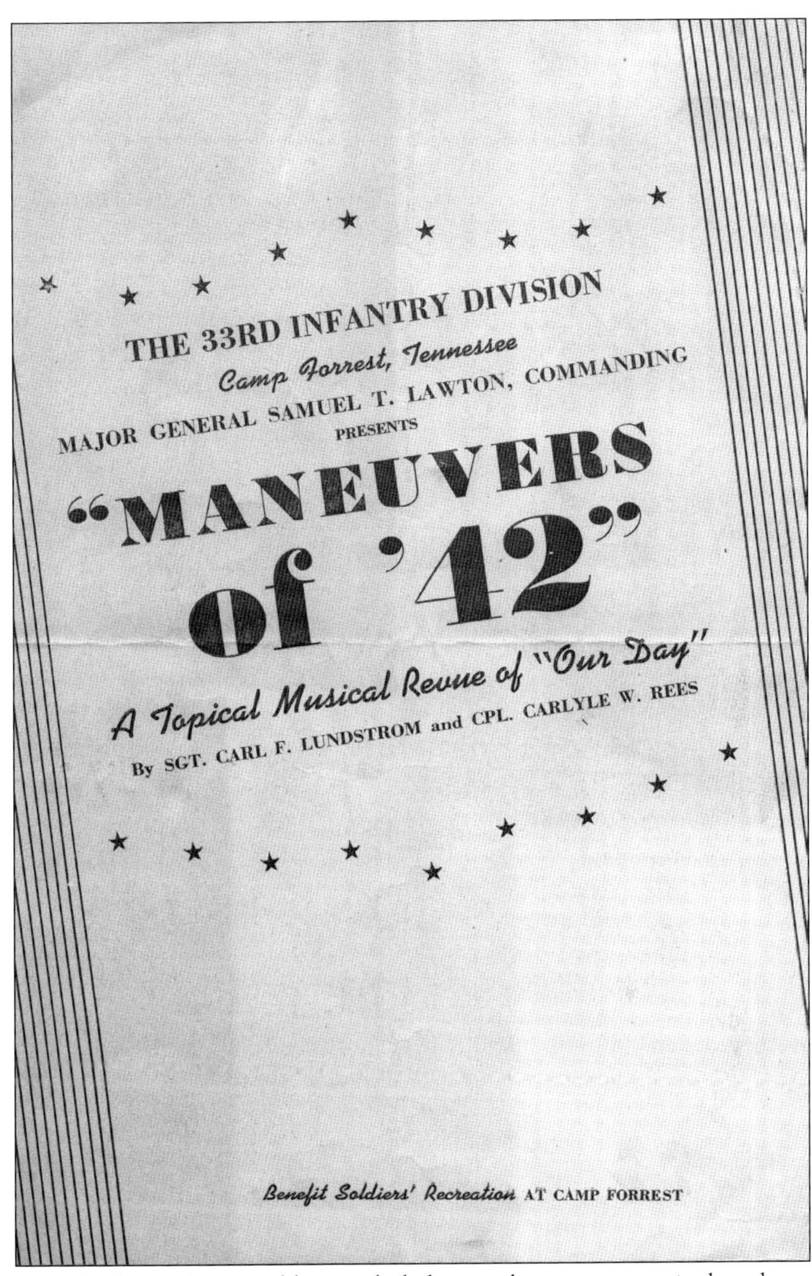

Entertainment for Camp Forrest soldiers included not only sports or movies but also servicemen who created their own theatrical productions. Members of the 33rd Infantry Division staged "Maneuvers of '42," a topical musical revue with songs and humor drawn from Army life. Sgt. Carl Lindstrom composed the score, while Cpl. Carlyle Rees wrote the lyrics. Their show gained notice beyond the post when they submitted it to WGM's Great American Operetta contest, a national competition highlighting new works. Though it did not win top honors, "Maneuvers of '42," reflected the talent, energy, and creativity of soldiers who found ways to blend discipline with self-expression. Productions like this helped sustain morale and reinforced a sense of community during the demanding training cycle at Camp Forrest. Pictured is a playbill from "Maneuvers of '42." (Courtesy of CFF.)

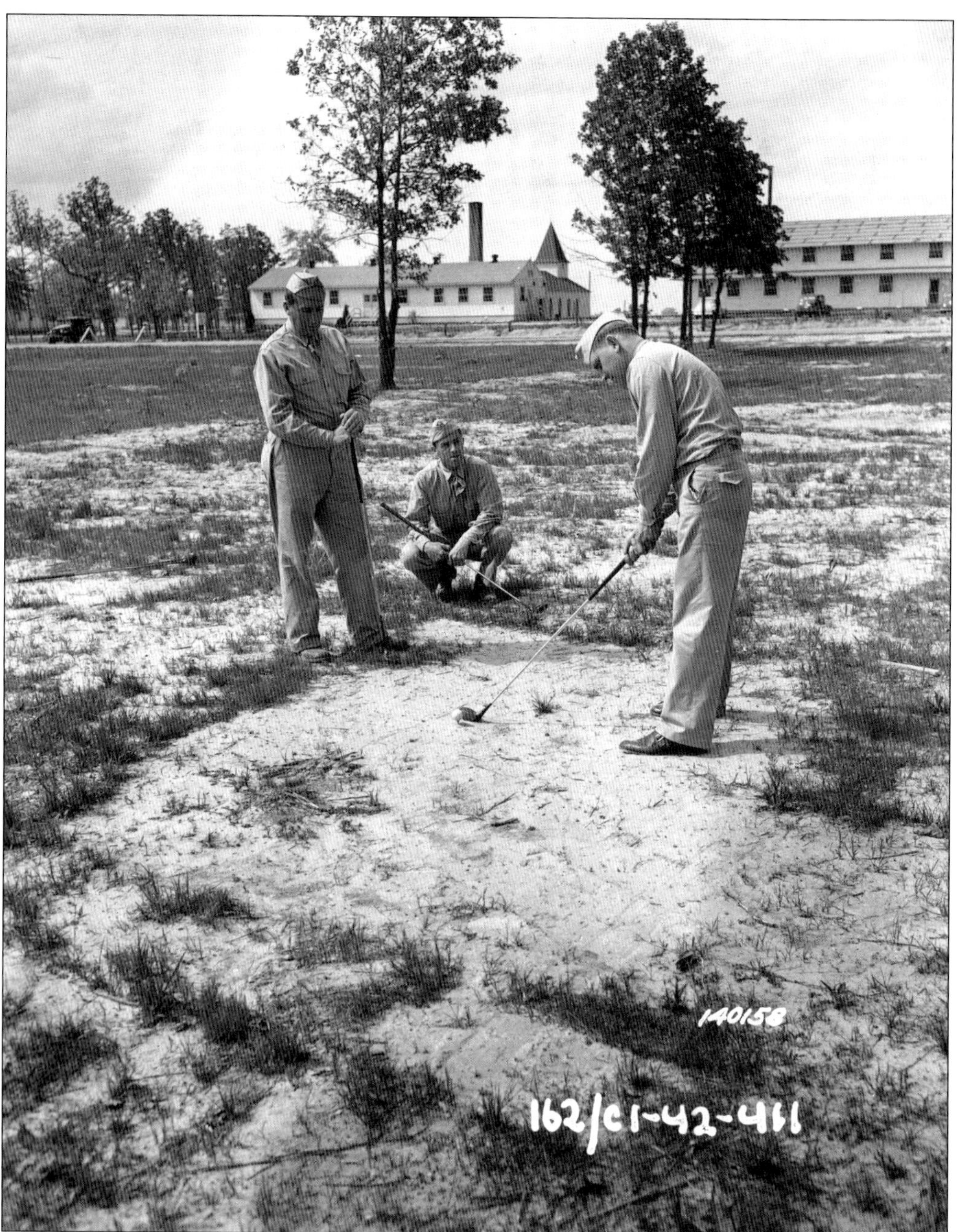

The opening of Camp Forrest's nine-hole golf course gave soldiers another outlet for recreation. *The Chattanooga Times* as well as Chattanooga area golfers donated clubs and balls. Novices eager to learn or improve their game benefited from the guidance of former pros who volunteered their time. Golf joined a wide range of sports at the post, from baseball and basketball to fencing and boxing, reinforcing Pres. Franklin D. Roosevelt's view that athletics were essential to morale. In this photograph, Sgt. Frank J. Alie lines up a drive from the tee while Pvt. Bill Walsh and Pvt. Harry J. Brown look on. (Courtesy of NARA.)

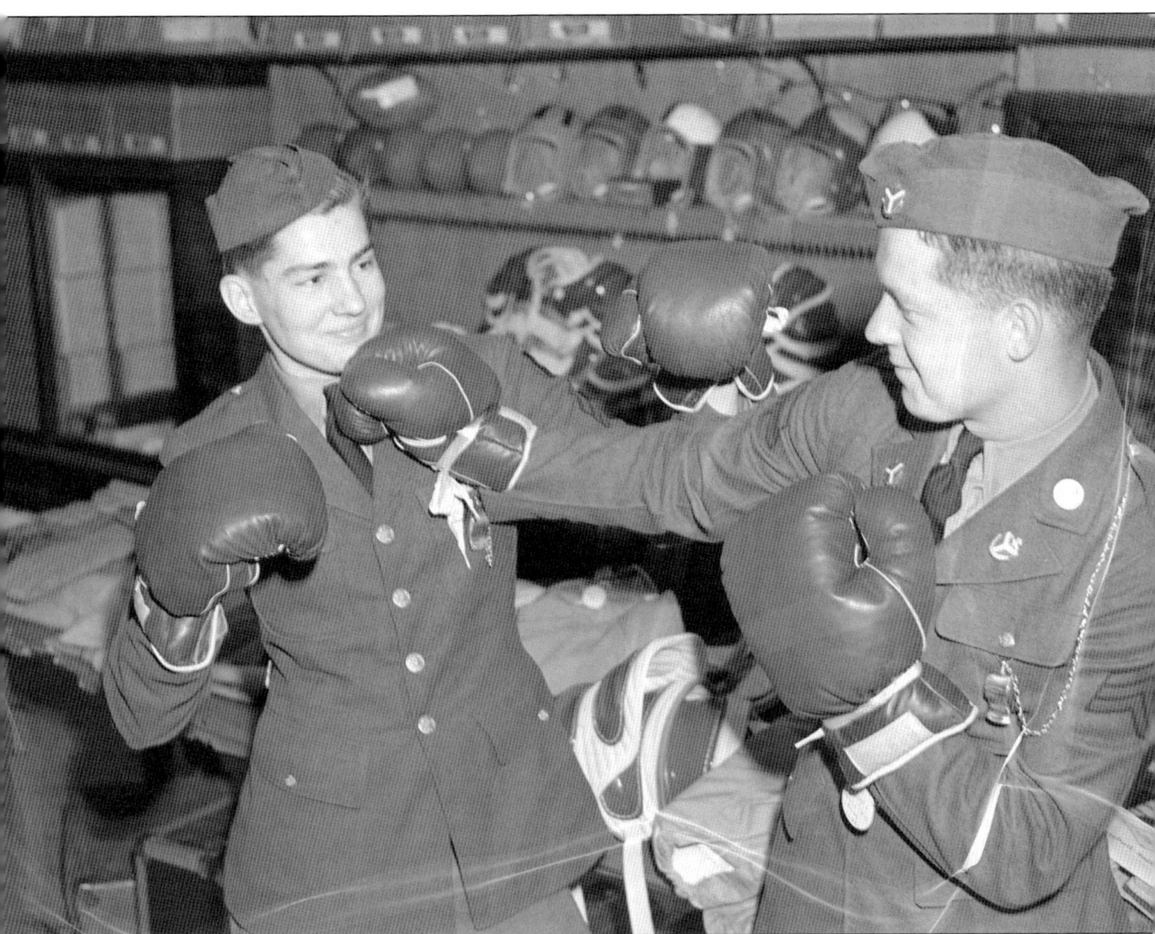

Civic support extended beyond the gates of Camp Forrest. In Chicago, citizens and organizations such as the Young Men's Club raised money to purchase sports equipment for soldiers of the 33rd Infantry Division to take to Tennessee. Athletics were essential for morale, conditioning, and camaraderie, whether on the gun range or in off-duty hours. Before the men departed, two soldiers staged a lighthearted boxing match inside a local sporting goods store, giving a preview of the spirited competition their new equipment encouraged. Scenes like this highlight the close bond between civilian communities and the soldiers they equipped, entertained, and supported during the early months of World War II. (Courtesy of Illinois Digital Archives.)

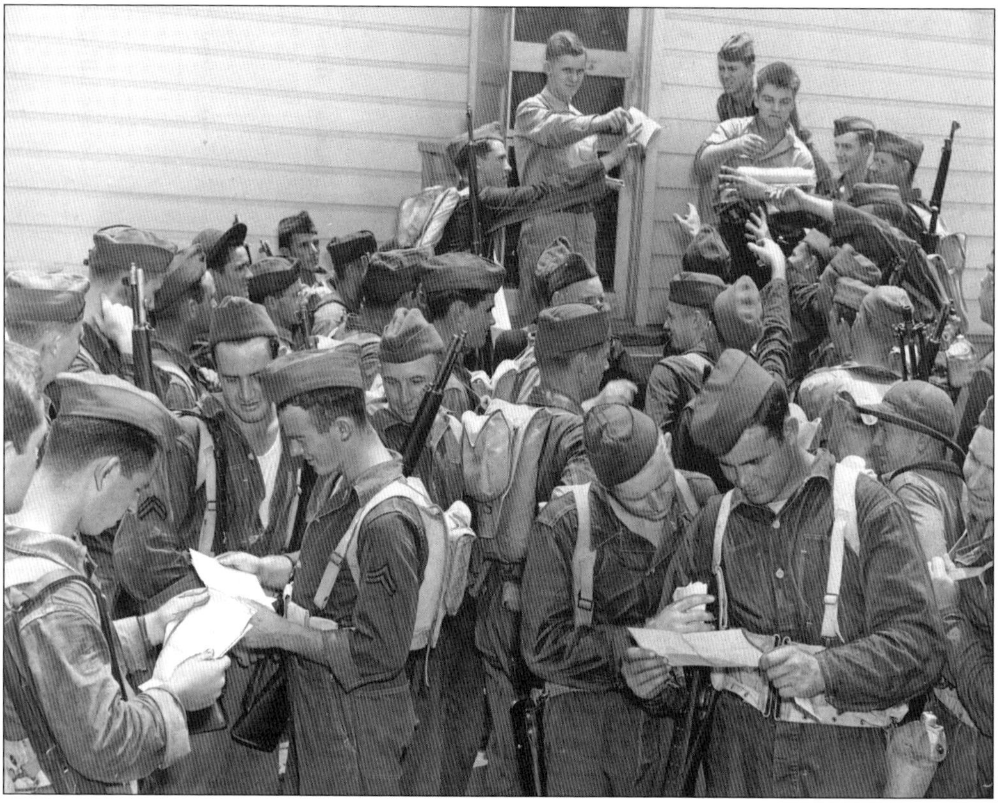

Mail was one of the most important morale boosters at Camp Forrest. Soldiers gathered eagerly at company mail calls, where letters from home brought comfort or sometimes disappointment. In the scene above, Company I of the 138th Infantry received mail as Pfc. Raymond Clemens shared the difficult news with Pvt. Charles Taylor: his sweetheart back home in Missouri was dating someone else. Behind the scenes, the camp post office, at Forrest Boulevard and Main Road, operated 12 hours daily to handle the enormous volume of mail and packages. Even in bivouac areas, mail stations kept detailed records of registered letters, as seen below with Pfc. Armad LaRose (front) and Pfc. Edward Stabile, who ensured safe delivery even in the field. (Above, courtesy of CFF; below, courtesy of NARA.)

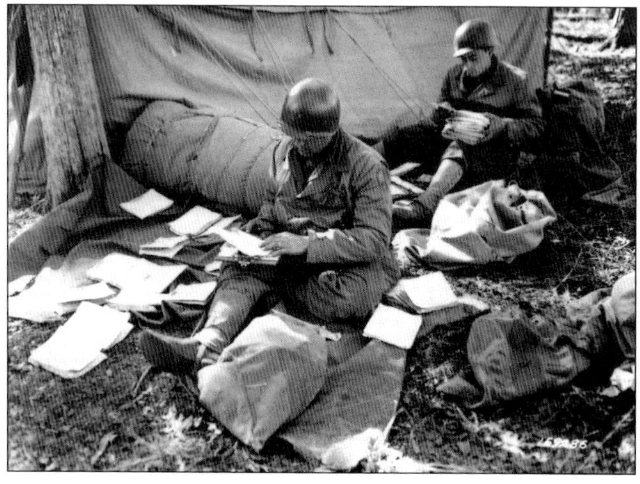

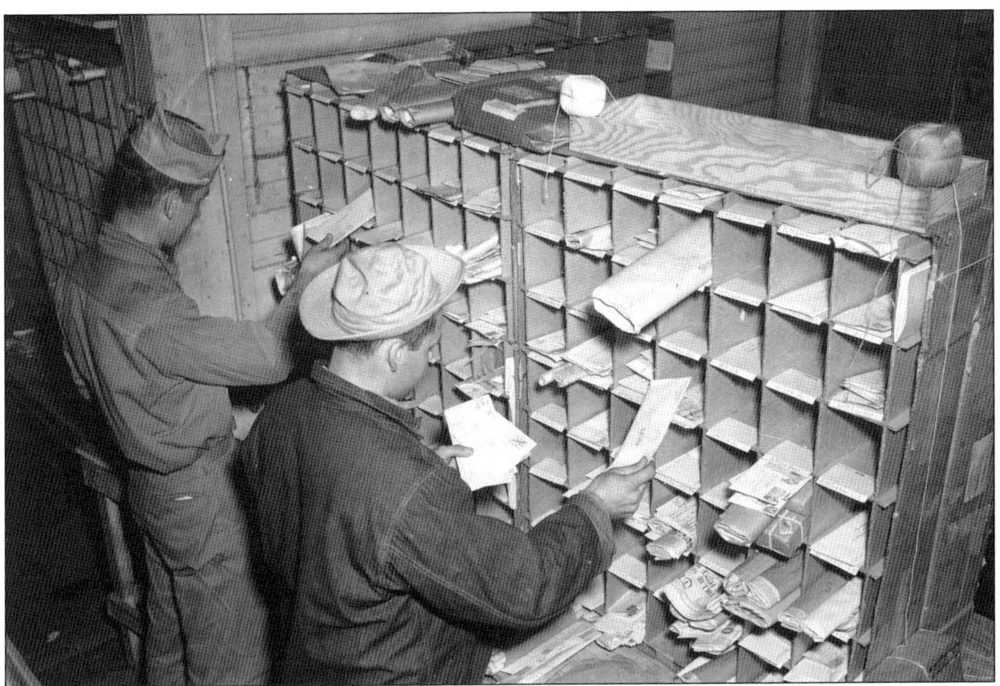

The Camp Forrest Post Office was a lifeline between soldiers and the outside world. Private First-Class Shea and Sergeant Barnowski sorted mail by unit, a task made more efficient using Army Post Office (APO) numbers. Each division typically had a specific APO number for the duration of the war, streamlining delivery across vast troop movements. Mail mattered deeply to morale; soldiers longed for letters from family, friends, or anyone willing to write. As units departed, men sometimes tossed slips of paper with their names and addresses to bystanders along the roadside, hoping for correspondence. Many of these spontaneous pen pal exchanges blossomed into long-lasting friendships, underscoring the power of letters to sustain connections during wartime. (Courtesy of NARA.)

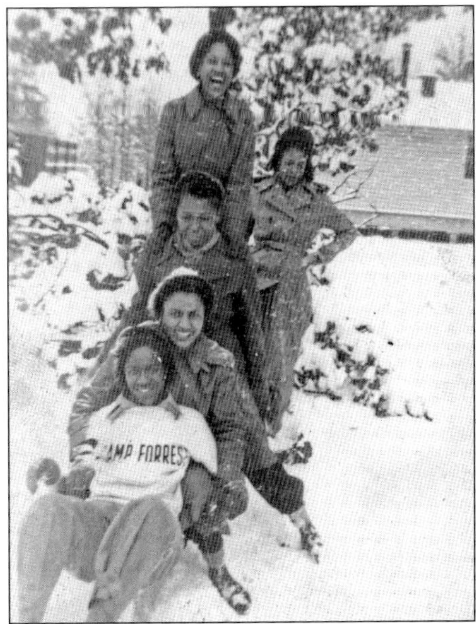

Many African American women were already serving in medical detachments in the Armed Services when the 6888th Central Postal Directory Battalion was activated. The 6888th Central Postal Directory Battalion was the only Black battalion of the Women's Army Corps and stationed at Camp Forrest. Mail delivery and distribution overseas were not as efficient as home front postal services. A backlog of letters and packages sent to the European Theater Operations (ETO) began to fill aircraft hangars. The 6888th stayed true to their motto "No mail, low morale" and disseminated the backlog of mail in England and France in record time. (Courtesy of Hoover Institution, Stanford University.)

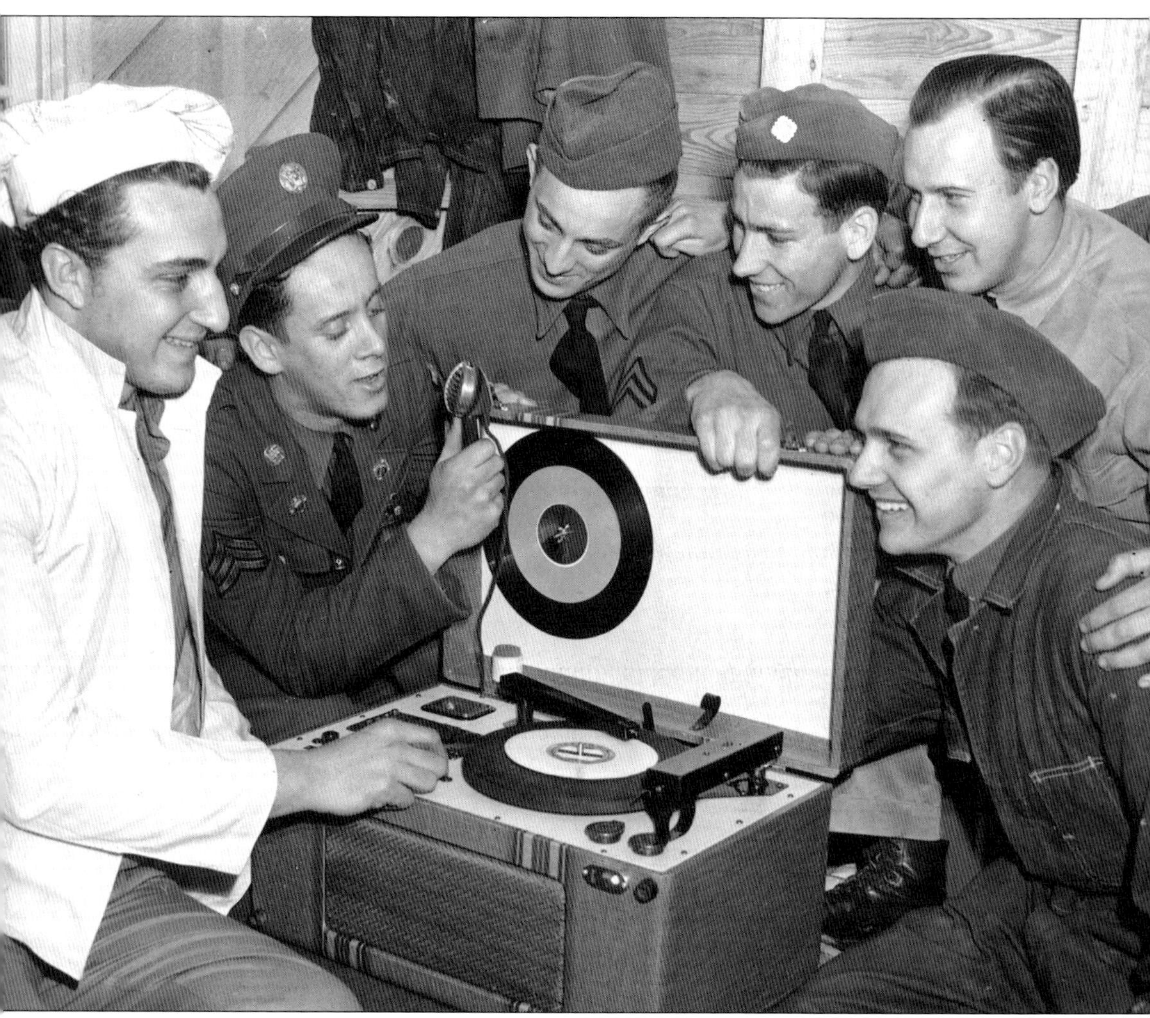

Letters were not the only way soldiers stayed connected with home. Many stores and USO clubs installed recording booths that allowed service members to make brief phonograph records of their voices. These "voice mail" messages, mailed in protective sleeves, gave families the rare chance to hear their loved one's voice while they were away. At Camp Forrest, soldiers of the 33rd Infantry Division gathered around the record-making machine to share stories of Army life. In this image, the group includes First Cook Louis S. Lawrence of the 108th Ordnance Company, Sgt. Carl Randolph, Sgt. Melvin Fromm, Cpl. William Fox, Edward Anderson, and Sgt. John Kirnbauer (left to right). Recordings like these brought comfort, familiarity, and a powerful sense of presence across long wartime distances. (Courtesy of CFF.)

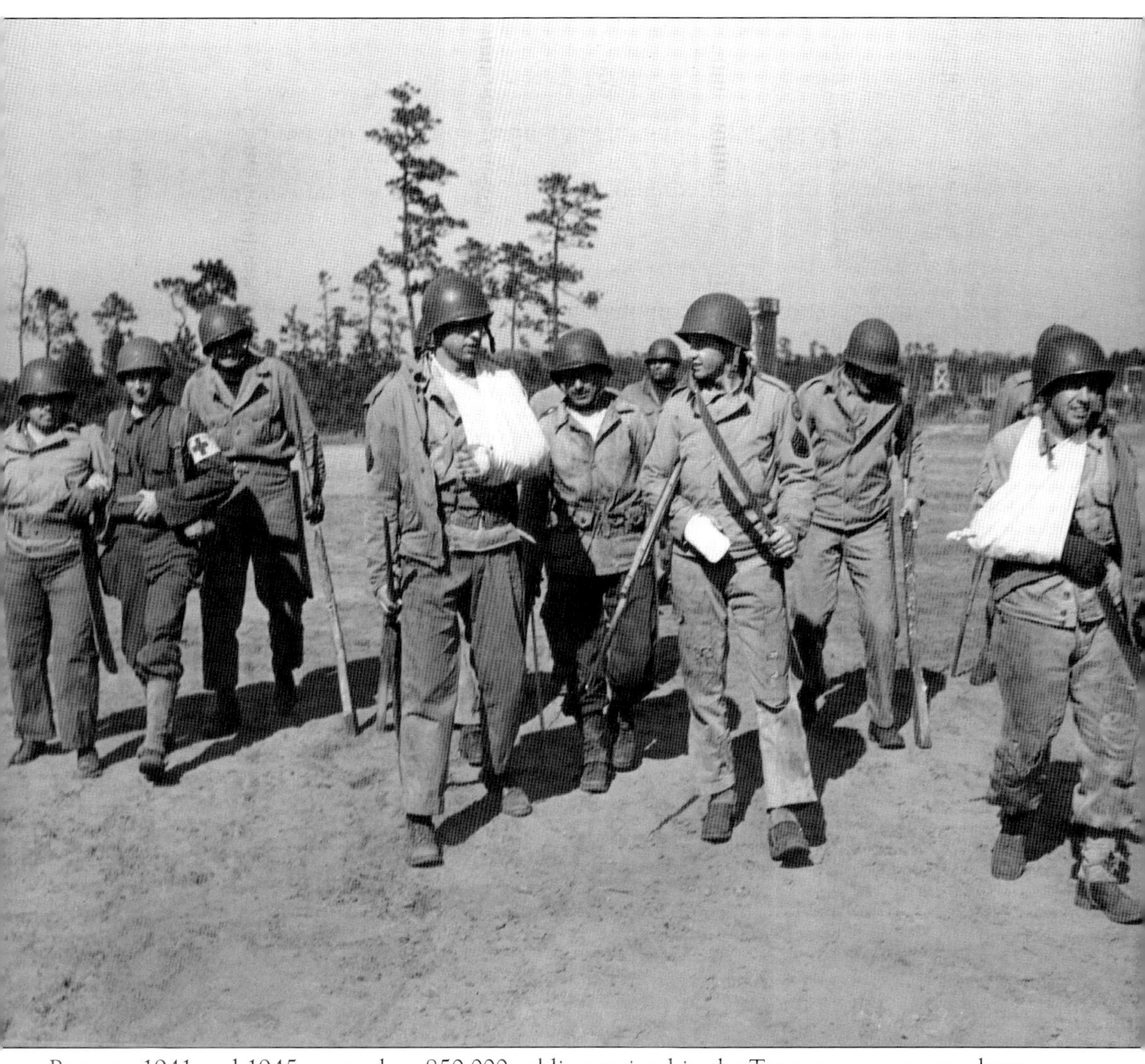

Between 1941 and 1945, more than 850,000 soldiers trained in the Tennessee maneuvers, large-scale war games designed to test both men and machines before they entered combat. These exercises often brought more troops into rural Middle Tennessee than the total civilian population, yet fewer than two percent of participants required hospitalization. Camp Forrest's station hospital played a vital role in sustaining the fighting force throughout its five years of operation. In that time, it recorded 83,715 admissions, 582 births, and 177 deaths, and issued 8,000 certificates of disability and discharge. These statistics reveal the immense scope of the Army's medical care during wartime, balancing readiness for combat with the treatment of injuries, illnesses, and the day-to-day needs of soldiers. (Courtesy of CFF.)

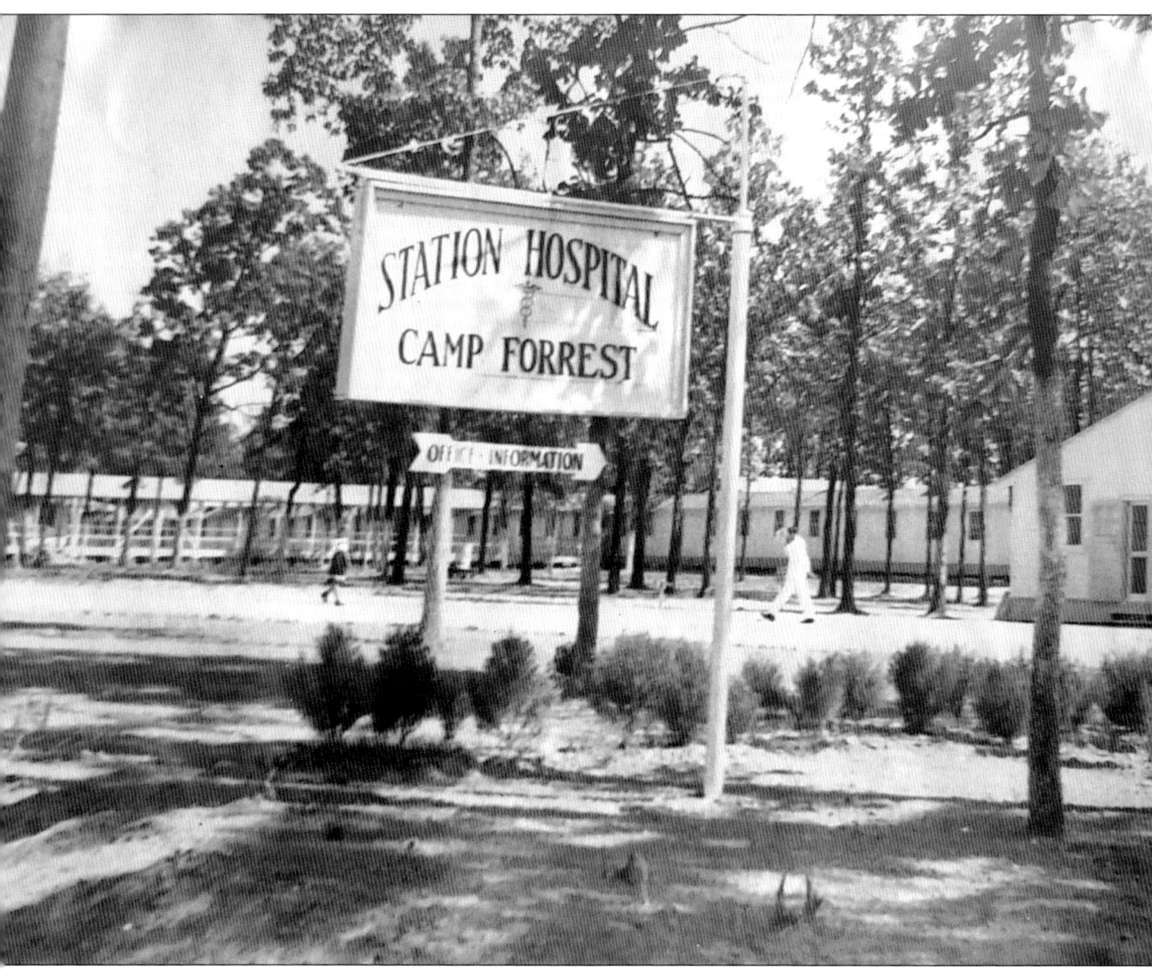

Camp Forrest's station hospital was a fully equipped medical complex designed to provide immediate and long-term care for soldiers. At its peak, the facility comprised 68 buildings, including an administration building, six nurses' quarters, two officers' quarters, an officers' mess, nine barracks, two non-emergency care clinics, four dental clinics, a physiotherapy building, 32 convalescence wards, a modern operating room, five storehouses, a morgue, and a central heating plant. Its two-thousand-bed hospital ranked among the most advanced in the region. As the camp's population grew, the hospital expanded several times to meet the demands of soldiers in training and patients requiring extended recovery. The scale and sophistication of the complex reflected the Army's commitment to medical readiness and the importance of health care as part of overall military effectiveness during World War II. (Courtesy of Dr. Paul Wylie family.)

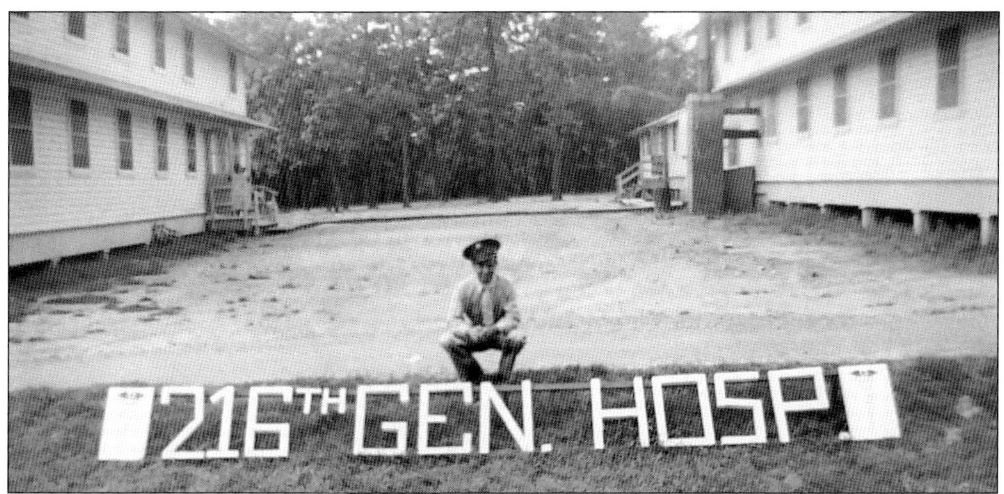

The Camp Forrest medical complex provided comprehensive care for thousands of soldiers and dependents. Facilities included surgical suites, dental and vision clinics, emergency and non-emergency wards, laboratories, and extensive recovery areas. A permanent staff of both military personnel and civilian employees kept the hospital operating at full capacity. Within the complex, the 300th General Hospital and the 216th General Hospital carried out their duties, while divisional medical detachments managed clinics for routine care. Beyond medical services, camp headquarters promoted beautification projects throughout each division's block. Landscaping with flowers, shrubs, and stonework not only improved an area's appearance but also reduced mud after rain and controlled dust from passing vehicles. These projects enhanced both morale and daily living conditions, reflecting the Army's concern for the health and well-being of its soldiers. (Courtesy of CFF.)

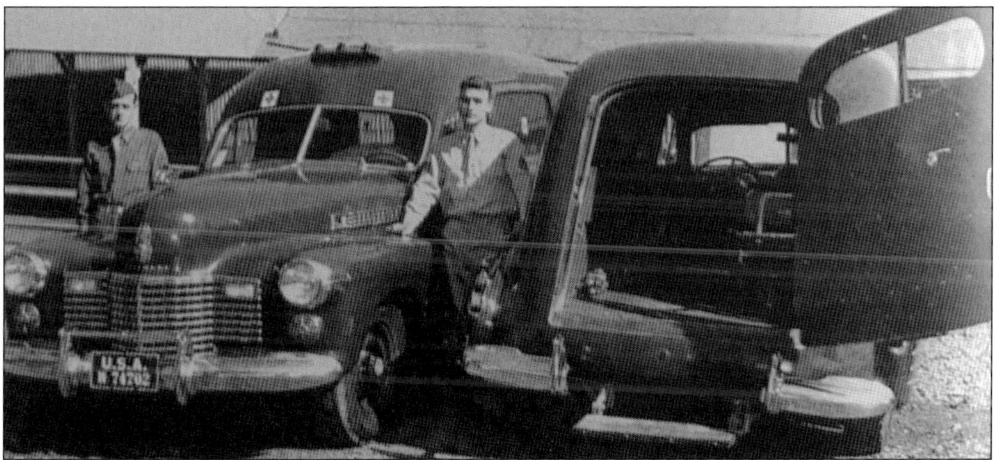

Training at Camp Forrest pushed soldiers to their limits, and injuries were a frequent consequence. Some exercises, such as the rough-and-tumble game of pushball, were notorious for breaking bones and knocking out teeth. Medical support began at the divisional level: soldiers reported first to their unit's medical clinic for treatment of routine ailments. Soldiers with serious cases were given a referral by their unit's medical staff for treatment at the station hospital. Soldiers requiring urgent attention went directly to the hospital. For emergencies inside the camp itself, the station hospital kept ambulances on call, ensuring injured personnel reached the hospital quickly for treatment. This system of clinics, referrals, and hospital care reflected the Army's emphasis on readiness and the importance of maintaining health even amid the hazards of training. (Courtesy of CFF.)

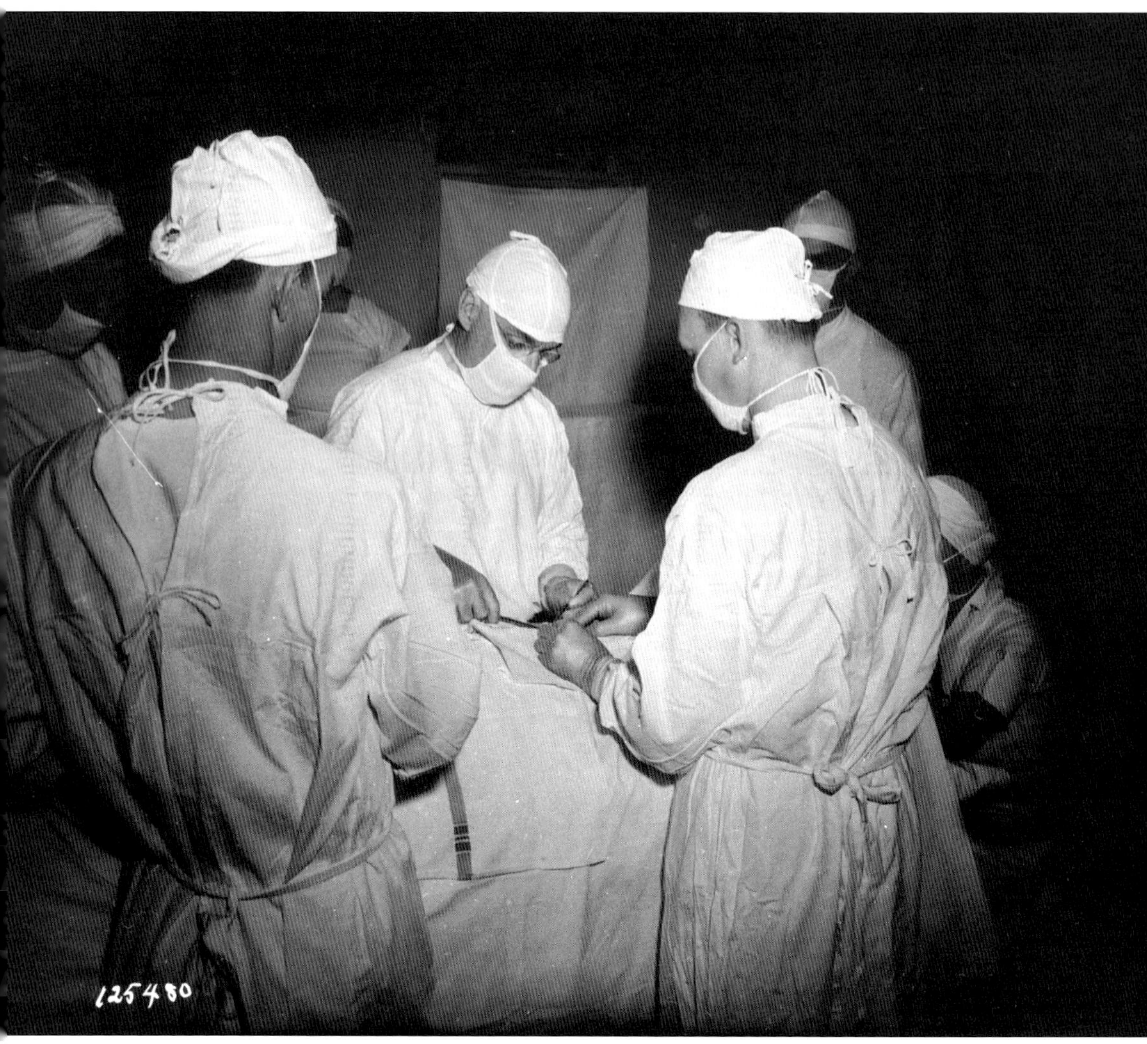

Camp Forrest's Station Hospital was among the largest and most advanced medical facilities of its kind during World War II. In this image, doctors bandage a patient's incision inside one of its operating rooms. Many of the nation's leading physicians and surgeons received orders to serve here, bringing specialized skills to a camp that trained hundreds of thousands of soldiers. The 40-acre complex featured covered walkways connecting its 68 buildings, allowing staff and patients to move between wards and treatment areas protected from rain and harsh weather. Within its first year, the hospital expanded rapidly, with exponential growth in its permanent staff of doctors, nurses, and civilian employees. (Courtesy of NARA.)

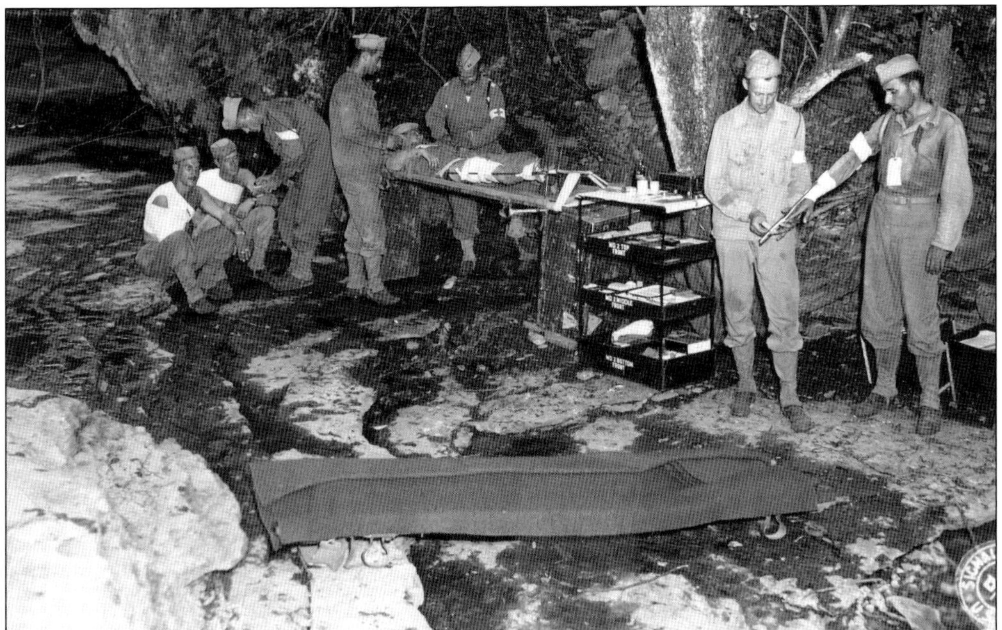

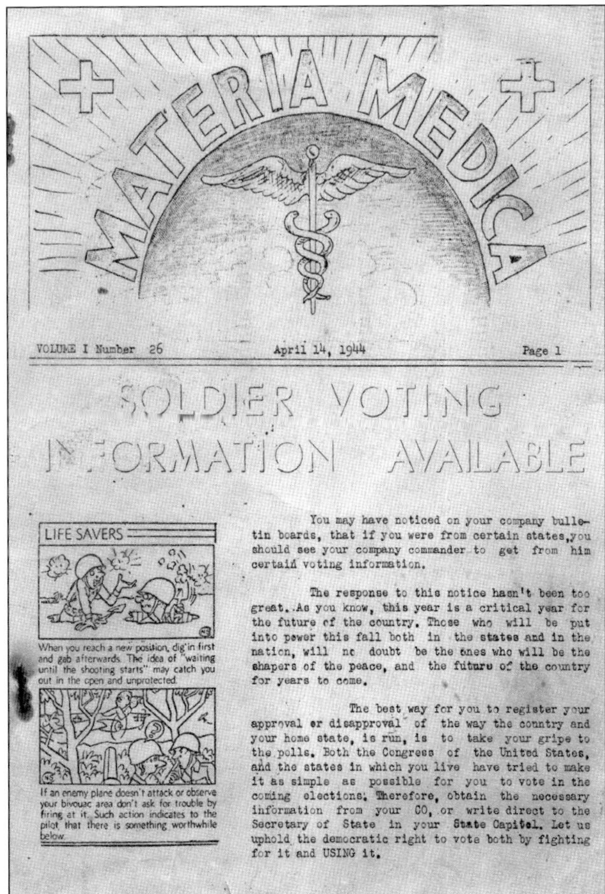

MATERIA MEDICA

VOLUME I Number 26 April 14, 1944 Page 1

SOLDIER VOTING INFORMATION AVAILABLE

LIFE SAVERS

When you reach a new position, dig in first and gab afterwards. The idea of "waiting until the shooting starts" may catch you out in the open and unprotected.

If an enemy plane doesn't attack or observe your bivouac area don't ask for trouble by firing at it. Such action indicates to the pilot that there is something worthwhile below.

You may have noticed on your company bulletin boards, that if you were from certain states, you should see your company commander to get from him certain voting information.

The response to this notice hasn't been too great. As you know, this year is a critical year for the future of the country. Those who will be put into power this fall both in the states and in the nation, will no doubt be the ones who will be the shapers of the peace, and the future of the country for years to come.

The best way for you to register your approval or disapproval of the way the country and your home state, is run, is to take your gripe to the polls. Both the Congress of the United States, and the states in which you live have tried to make it as simple as possible for you to vote in the coming elections. Therefore, obtain the necessary information from your CO, or write direct to the Secretary of State in your State Capitol. Let us uphold the democratic right to vote both by fighting for it and USING it.

Medical personnel at Camp Forrest prepared for deployment by completing basic military training and refining their specialties within the post hospital complex. Field hospital practice was also part of large-scale maneuvers, ensuring medical staff could work effectively in combat conditions. Overseas, both Axis and Allied powers agreed not to bomb hospitals marked with large red crosses, yet the enemy still attacked them during the war. The distinctive markings on buildings and tents were meant to signal protected facilities visible from the air. Alongside medical training, units also published newsletters to build community and morale. One example was *Materia Medica*, the weekly paper of the 331st Medical Group Special Service, first issued April 14, 1944. It carried news of the group's personnel as well as updates on nearby units such as the 468th, 467th, 469th, and 86th Battalion Headquarters. (Above, courtesy of MTSU; below, courtesy of CFF.)

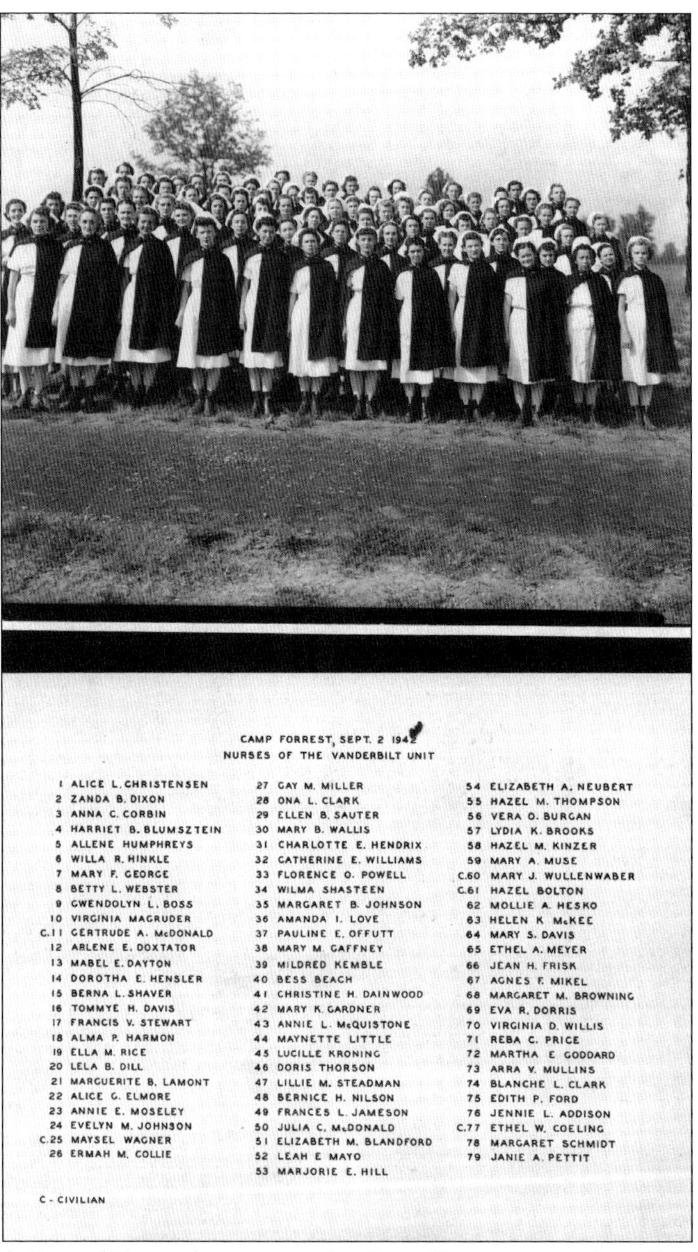

CAMP FORREST, SEPT. 2 1942
NURSES OF THE VANDERBILT UNIT

1 ALICE L. CHRISTENSEN
2 ZANDA B. DIXON
3 ANNA C. CORBIN
4 HARRIET B. BLUMSZTEIN
5 ALLENE HUMPHREYS
6 WILLA R. HINKLE
7 MARY F. GEORGE
8 BETTY L. WEBSTER
9 GWENDOLYN L. BOSS
10 VIRGINIA MAGRUDER
C.11 GERTRUDE A. McDONALD
12 ARLENE E. DOXTATOR
13 MABEL E. DAYTON
14 DOROTHA E. HENSLER
15 BERNA L. SHAVER
16 TOMMYE H. DAVIS
17 FRANCIS V. STEWART
18 ALMA P. HARMON
19 ELLA M. RICE
20 LELA B. DILL
21 MARGUERITE B. LAMONT
22 ALICE G. ELMORE
23 ANNIE E. MOSELEY
24 EVELYN M. JOHNSON
C.25 MAYSEL WAGNER
26 ERMAH M. COLLIE
27 GAY M. MILLER
28 ONA L. CLARK
29 ELLEN B. SAUTER
30 MARY B. WALLIS
31 CHARLOTTE E. HENDRIX
32 CATHERINE E. WILLIAMS
33 FLORENCE O. POWELL
34 WILMA SHASTEEN
35 MARGARET B. JOHNSON
36 AMANDA I. LOVE
37 PAULINE E. OFFUTT
38 MARY M. GAFFNEY
39 MILDRED KEMBLE
40 BESS BEACH
41 CHRISTINE H. DAINWOOD
42 MARY K. GARDNER
43 ANNIE L. McQUISTONE
44 MAYNETTE LITTLE
45 LUCILLE KRONING
46 DORIS THORSON
47 LILLIE M. STEADMAN
48 BERNICE H. NILSON
49 FRANCES L. JAMESON
50 JULIA C. McDONALD
51 ELIZABETH M. BLANDFORD
52 LEAH E MAYO
53 MARJORIE E. HILL
54 ELIZABETH A. NEUBERT
55 HAZEL M. THOMPSON
56 VERA O. BURGAN
57 LYDIA K. BROOKS
58 HAZEL M. KINZER
59 MARY A. MUSE
C.60 MARY J. WULLENWABER
C.61 HAZEL BOLTON
62 MOLLIE A. HESKO
63 HELEN K McKEE
64 MARY S. DAVIS
65 ETHEL A. MEYER
66 JEAN H. FRISK
67 AGNES F. MIKEL
68 MARGARET M. BROWNING
69 EVA R. DORRIS
70 VIRGINIA D. WILLIS
71 REBA C. PRICE
72 MARTHA E GODDARD
73 ARRA V. MULLINS
74 BLANCHE L. CLARK
75 EDITH P. FORD
76 JENNIE L. ADDISON
C.77 ETHEL W. COELING
78 MARGARET SCHMIDT
79 JANIE A. PETTIT

C - CIVILIAN

When the 300th General Hospital was activated at Camp Forrest, many of its officers came directly from Vanderbilt University Medical School or were current staff members at Nashville hospitals. According to Capt. James Benton Neal, a former Nashville dentist, physicians closed their private practices to answer the Army's call for medical professionals. The hospital's nurses, known as "The Fighting 300th," were the first female soldiers to serve at Camp Forrest. Their dedication and visibility made an impression: during Pres. Franklin D. Roosevelt's 1943 inspection tour, they were the only group on post to receive a salute from the commander in chief. Their service underscored both the sacrifice of medical personnel who left civilian careers behind and the critical role of women in sustaining military readiness during World War II. (Courtesy of Vanderbilt Medical Library.)

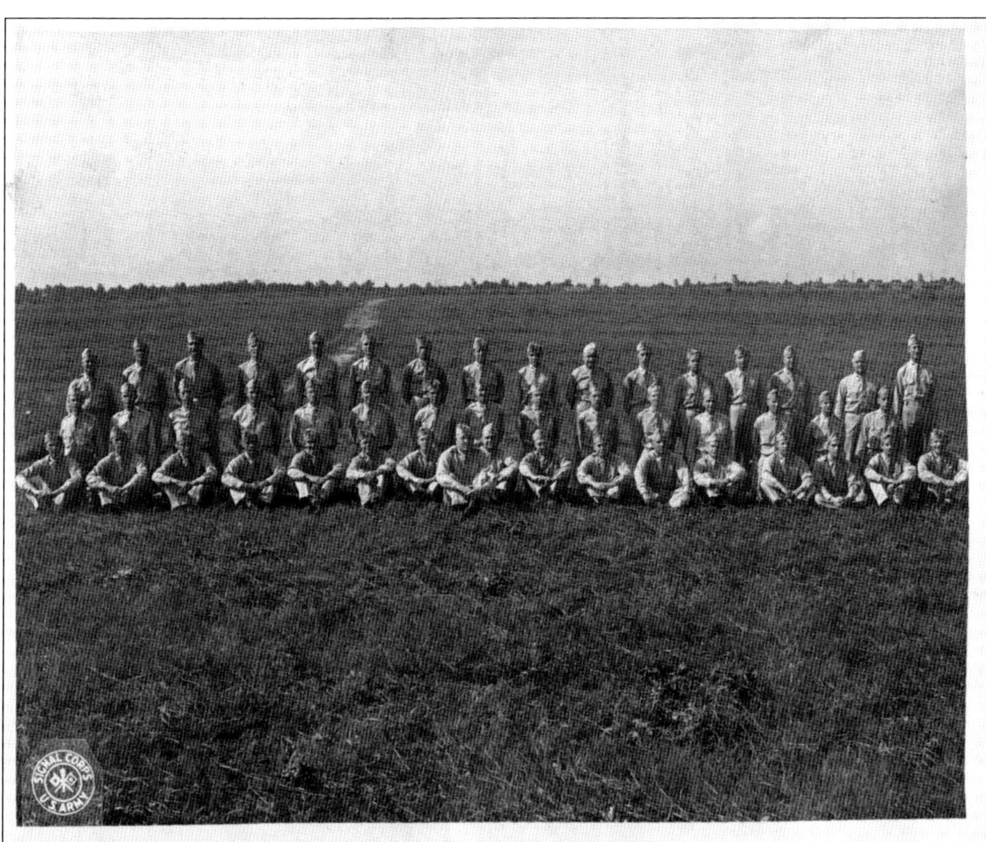

The War Department ordered the 300th General Hospital to report to Camp Forrest on July 15, 1942. For the next 13 months, the unit trained intensively in the post's medical complex, preparing doctors, nurses, and enlisted personnel for overseas service. The hospital staff learned to manage both large-scale facilities and mobile field units, practicing surgery, recovery, and emergency care under simulated combat conditions. In August 1943, after more than a year of preparation, the 300th General Hospital deployed to Italy, where it supported Allied campaigns and treated thousands of wounded soldiers. Their journey from Tennessee to the Mediterranean illustrated how Camp Forrest served as a critical training ground for personnel destined for all of the battlefronts. (Courtesy of Vanderbilt Medical Library.)

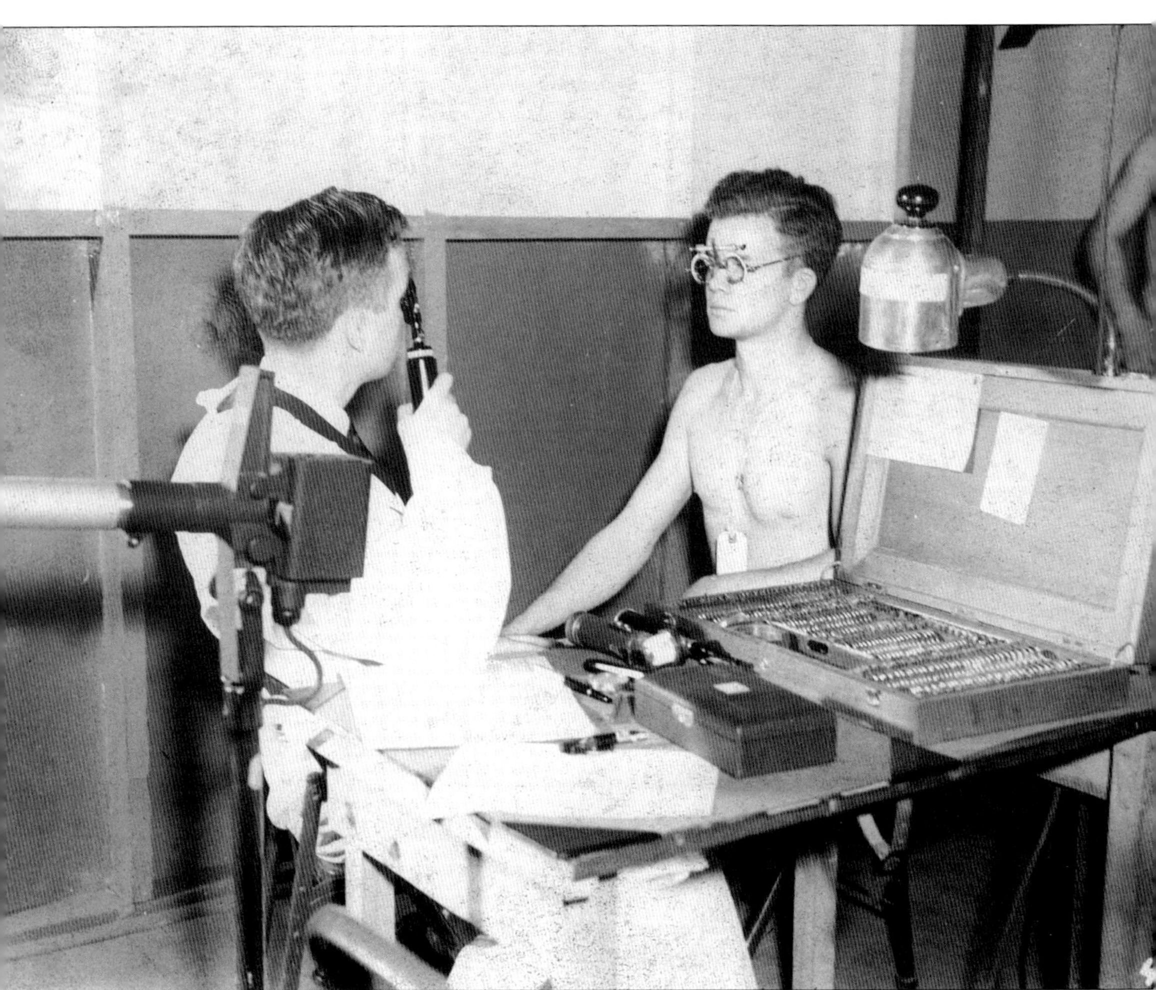

Medical examinations were a key part of the World War II induction process. Recruits underwent thorough physical evaluations to ensure they met the Army's standards for service. In the image above, an optometrist conducts an eye exam, checking vision against minimum requirements. As the war intensified and the need for manpower grew, the military lowered some qualification criteria to expand the pool of eligible soldiers. Individuals who did not meet the minimum physical, mental, or moral standards were classified 4F, a term widely recognized by both the military and civilians as unfit for service. The 4F designation carried weight far beyond the induction center, often shaping how individuals experienced the war years at home. (Courtesy of CFF.)

Dental care became an essential part of military readiness during World War II. The Army Dental Corps expanded rapidly, with more than 18,000 practitioners providing comprehensive oral care to America's soldiers. At Camp Forrest, Capt. Stanley F. Steele reported to the Tennessee State Dental Association in May 1942 that military personnel had received 2,500 tooth repairs in just 10 months. His presentation also addressed the effects of various drugs used during oral surgery, reflecting the evolving science of wartime dentistry. In the images shown here, Lieutenant Slavin and his assistant, Corporal Schock, conduct a dental examination on Sergeant Benjamin using the well-equipped field dental set of the 68th Medical Regiment. Such portable equipment ensured dentists were able to provide oral healthcare not only at large installations like Camp Forrest but also in the field, close to the front lines. (Both, courtesy of NARA.)

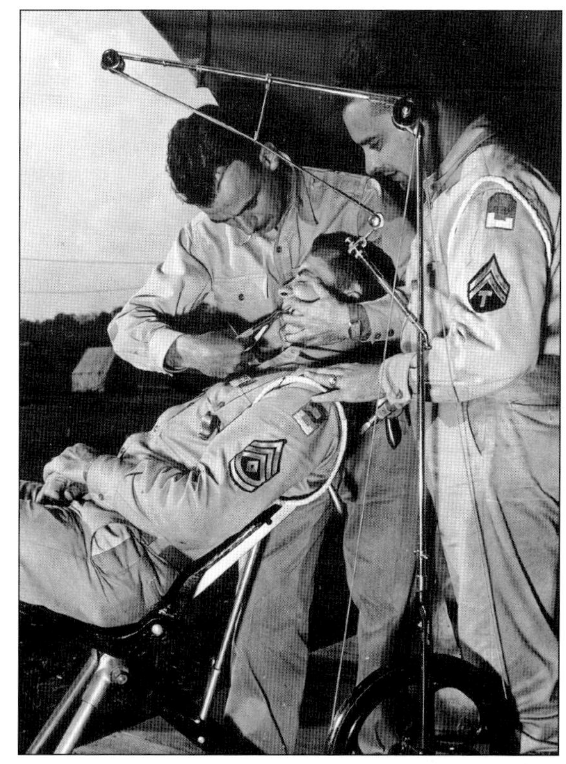

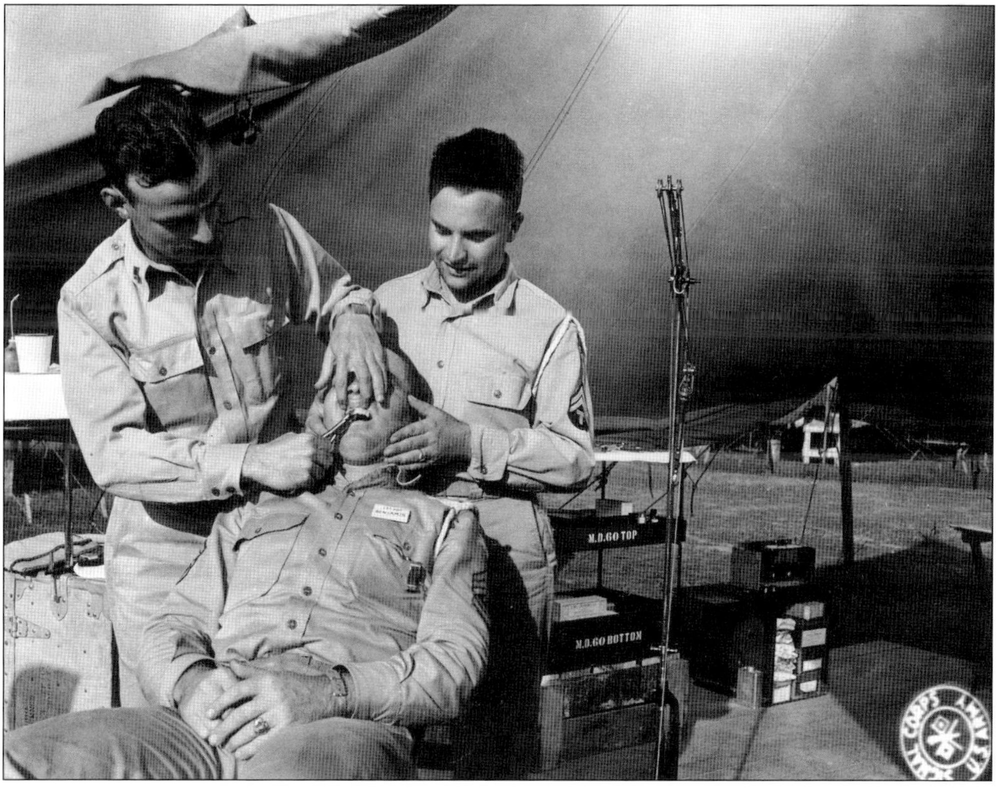

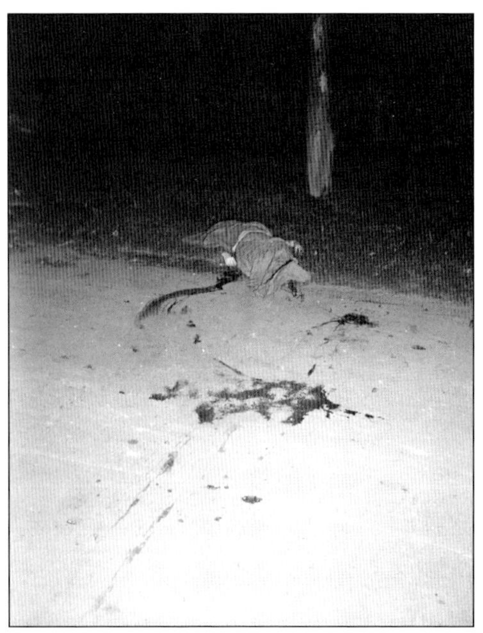

Not all wartime fatalities occurred on the battlefield. At Camp Forrest, more than 175 soldiers died during training or in accidents. Causes included drownings, firearms and knife incidents, explosions, burns, and vehicle crashes. Civilian populations near the camp and maneuver areas also suffered losses, with a significant percentage of deaths in this period linked to accidents involving military vehicles on local roads. In the photograph, the soldier shown died of injuries sustained in a vehicle accident. Such tragedies underscored the inherent risks of training and the impact of a large military presence on surrounding communities, even far from combat zones. (Courtesy of CFF.)

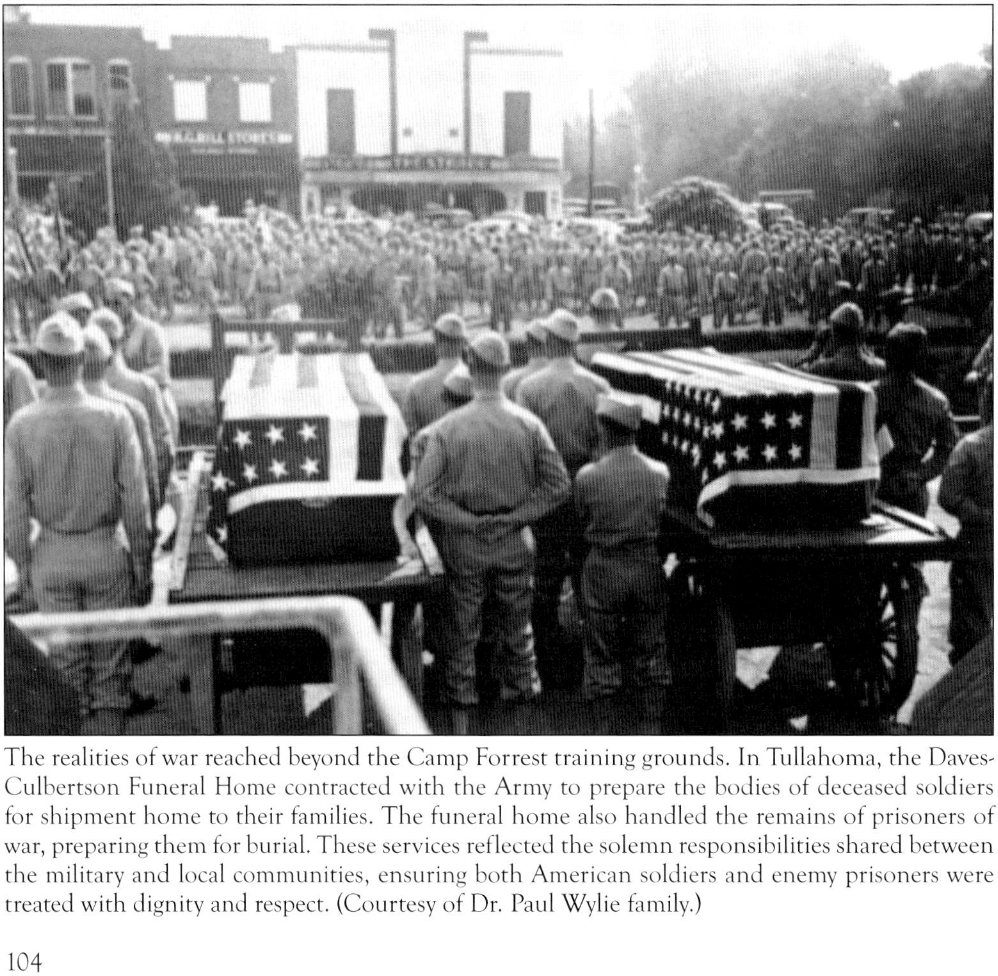

The realities of war reached beyond the Camp Forrest training grounds. In Tullahoma, the Daves-Culbertson Funeral Home contracted with the Army to prepare the bodies of deceased soldiers for shipment home to their families. The funeral home also handled the remains of prisoners of war, preparing them for burial. These services reflected the solemn responsibilities shared between the military and local communities, ensuring both American soldiers and enemy prisoners were treated with dignity and respect. (Courtesy of Dr. Paul Wylie family.)

Four

Home Front Support for Victory

Civilian and Industrial Services

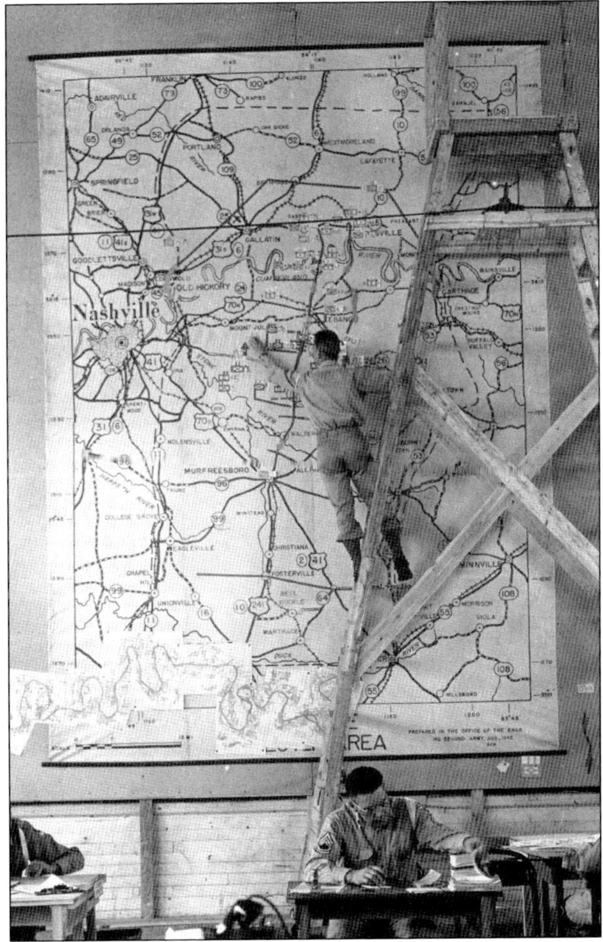

For many soldiers, Camp Forrest was their first experience away from home. The small towns of Middle Tennessee softened that separation, with residents often bending the rules to lend a hand to soldiers in training. Official regulations discouraged civilians from helping during maneuvers, but in practice these rules were frequently ignored. Acts of hospitality, such as sharing food, offering directions, or simply extending kindness, made the soldiers' adjustment less painful. While the Tennessee Maneuvers were serious war games that tested strategy and endurance, they unfolded in a landscape shaped by Southern generosity. In this photograph, soldiers track the movements of opposing forces on a giant map of the battle area, blending the rigors of training with the human connections that defined life in wartime Tennessee. (Courtesy of NARA.)

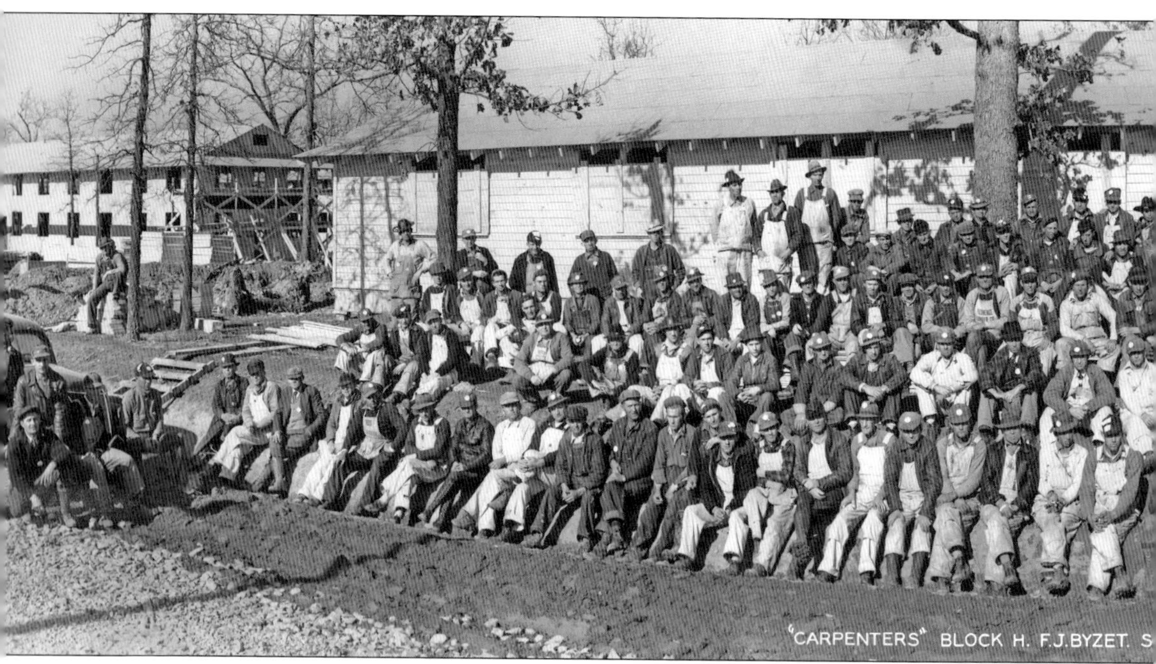

In 1940, the Quartermaster Corps oversaw a massive program to build 50 new Army cantonments across the United States. After reviewing the dossier of Nashville's Creighton Company, the Construction Advisory Board invited owners Don and Wilber Creighton Sr. to Washington, DC, where they confirmed a partnership with Hardaway Contracting Company of Columbus, Georgia. Together, the firms signed the nation's second wartime construction contract, valued at $8,379,510 ($193.4 million in 2025), to build a major installation in Middle Tennessee. The agreement, dated

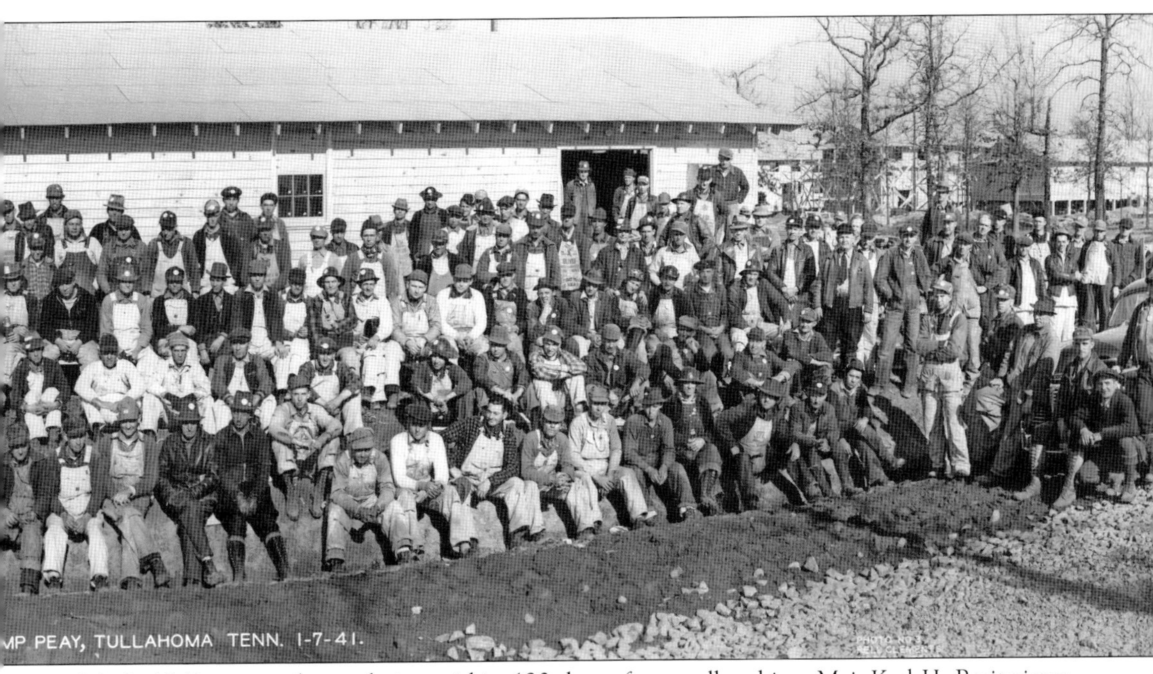

July 2, 1940, required completion within 120 days of groundbreaking. Maj. Karl H. Breitwieser of the Army's Construction Quartermaster received the order to begin construction on October 10, 1940. At the height of the project, more than 20,300 local and union workers labored day and night to meet the deadline. Federal authorities ordered workers not to discuss camp matters with outsiders. Pictured is one of the Camp Forrest construction crews. (Courtesy of CFF.)

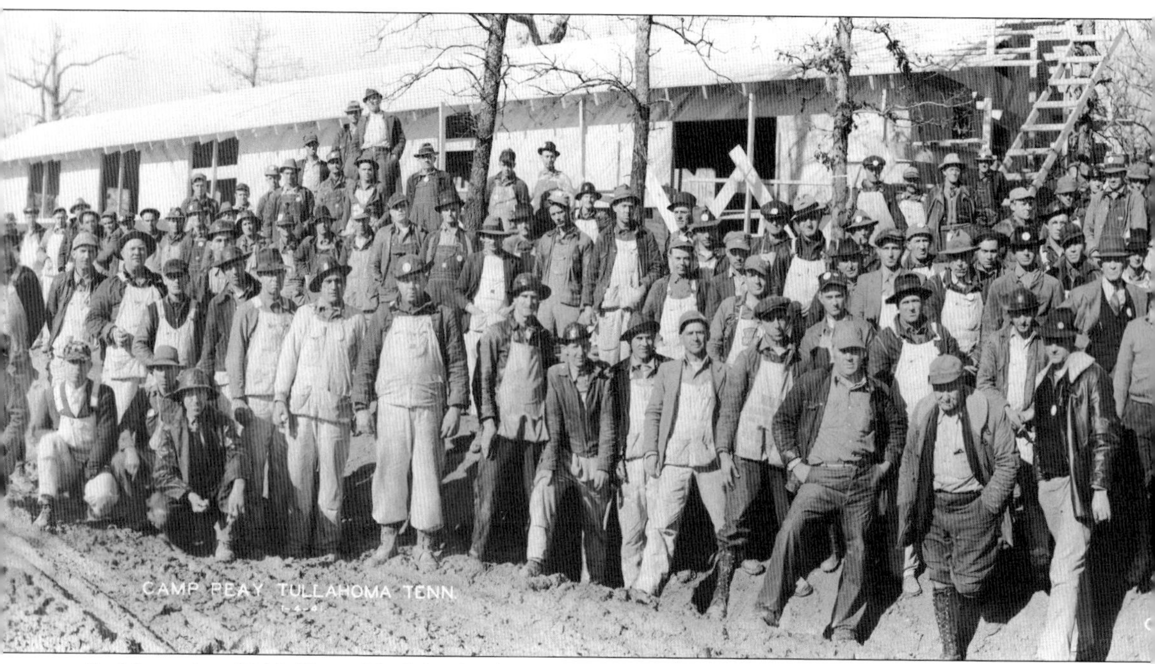

By November 1940, Troop E of the Sixth Cavalry had arrived from Fort Oglethorpe, Georgia, to assume administrative and policing duties for the 15,000-acre construction project at Camp Forrest. At the same time, the Quartermaster General and the Army Corps of Engineers introduced new guidelines for military housing. The new standardized blueprints and simplified designs allowed work crews to operate in an assembly-line fashion: one crew set the concrete forms, the next poured the foundation, and a third began erecting the exterior walls. Once finished, each team

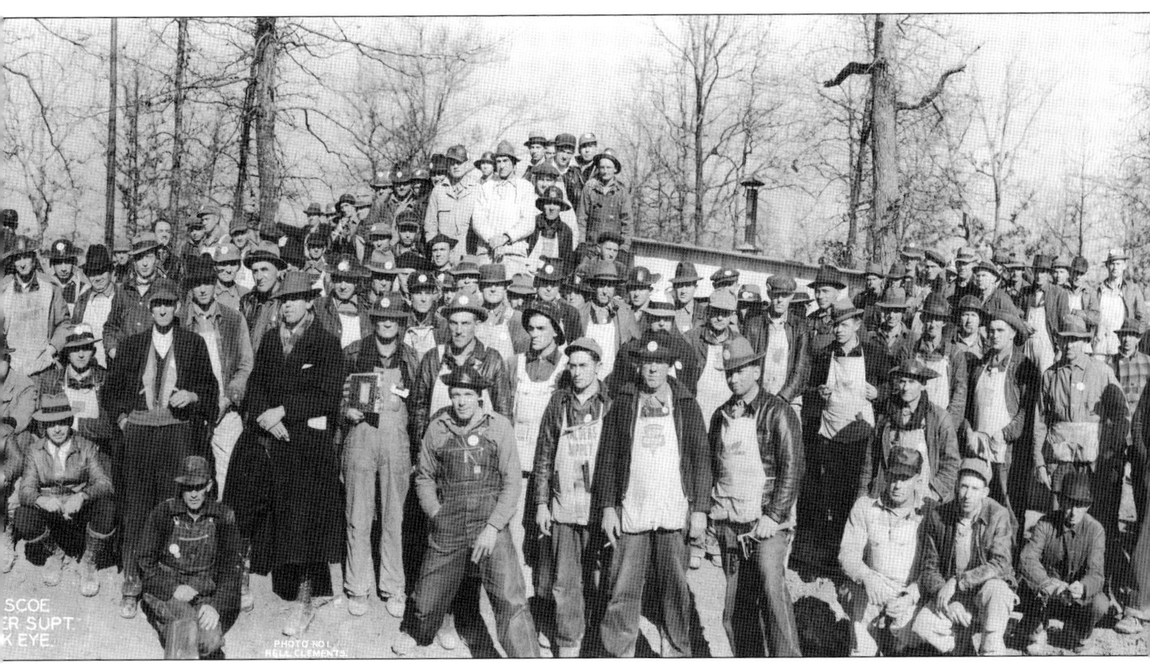

moved to the next site, repeating the process. This streamlined system increased efficiency, lowered costs, and improved safety, enabling thousands of buildings to rise within months. In December 1941, overall construction responsibility formally shifted from the Quartermaster Corps to the US Army Corps of Engineers. Pictured here is a second construction crew working at Camp Forrest. (Courtesy of Tommy Bradley.)

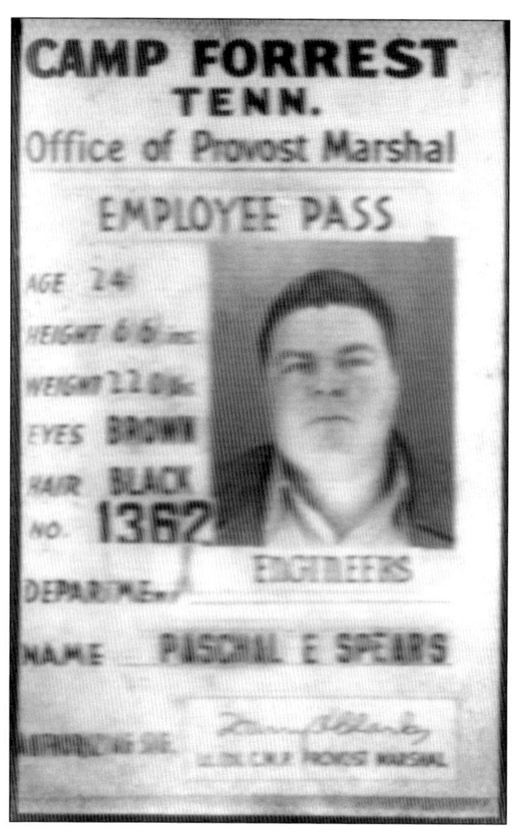

The unemployment rate in America began to decline in 1939. However, it was still at 17 percent when the federal government announced the major construction project on the outskirts of Tullahoma. Thousands of men secured construction jobs, but there were many more who traveled to Tullahoma hoping to find work. Crowds of over 2,500 unemployed men lingered in Tullahoma until officials announced no additional construction jobs were forthcoming. The workforce grew to more than 20,000 individuals, causing employee identification badges to evolve from simple brass tags to numbered push pins, then to photo IDs with identifying details, as shown here in the badge issued to Paschal E. Spears. Base regulations mandated workers always have their badge on them. (Left, courtesy of CFF; below, courtesy of Brady-Hughes-Beasley Archives at Magness Library.)

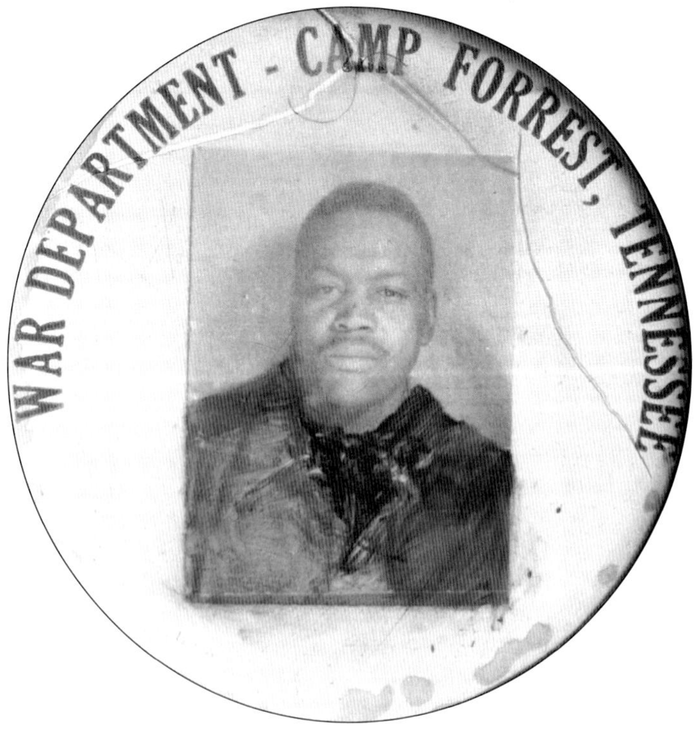

VISITOR

-- TO --

Camp Forrest, Tennessee

The officers and men stationed at Camp Forrest welcome you to the reservation. On the reverse side of this card you will find a map of the camp and information concerning the location of troop units.

Gates number 1, 2 and 3 are the authorized entrances to the camp areas. On roads 4 and 5 you will find the headquarters of the various units in training at this camp. Permission must be obtained at these headquarters to visit within unit area.

Please observe traffic signs. Intoxicating liquor is forbidden on the reservation.

Display This Card On Windshield

Visitors to Camp Forrest obtained permits that authorized their presence on the installation. The permit came with a card that was displayed on the front windshield of the visitor's vehicle, such as the images shown here. A map printed on the reverse side guided newcomers through the vast military post. Transportation within the camp included buses and taxis, but neither was free. Soldiers and visitors paid 5 cents to ride a bus within the installation or 10 cents for a trip into Tullahoma. Taxis charged 50 cents for a single passenger or 25 cents each when two or more shared the ride. These systems helped regulate access to the post while also keeping people and goods moving smoothly across the busy wartime installation. (Both, courtesy of Jimmy Walker.)

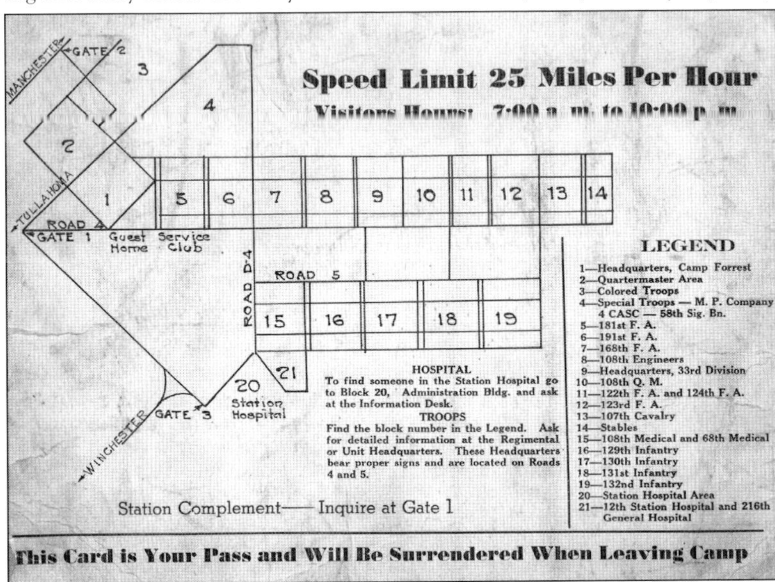

App. not req.

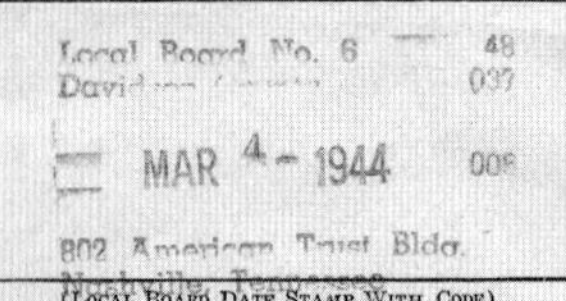

(Local Board Date Stamp With Code)

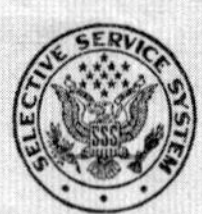

SELECTIVE SERVICE SYSTEM

Order to Report
Preinduction Physical Examination

March 4, 1944
(Date of mailing)

The President of the United States,

To Harry - Jordan 1206
(First name) (Middle name) (Last name) (Order No.)

Greeting:

You are hereby directed to report for preinduction physical examination at

802 American Trust Bldg.,
(Place of reporting)

at 7;30 AM m., on the 8th of March, 1944
(Hour of reporting) (Day) (Month)

Bus leaves at 8AM for Camp Forrest

Chas Nelson
(Member or clerk of Local Board)

Chas Nelson

IMPORTANT NOTICE TO REGISTRANT

Registrant who believes he has a disqualifying defect.—If you believe that you have some defect which will disqualify you for service you may, on or before the .... day of ...., 194..., appear in person at the office of the Local Board, or, if you are unable by reason of such defect to personally appear, you may submit an affidavit from a reputable physician or an official statement by an authorized representative of a Federal or State agency to the effect that such physician has personal professional knowledge or such authorized representative has official knowledge of your defect, the character thereof, and that you are unable to personally appear due to the character of the defect. The Local Board may send you to the Local Board examining physician, and, if it does so, it shall be your duty to appear at the time and place designated by the Local Board and to submit to such examination as the examining physician shall direct. If the Local Board determines that your defect does disqualify you for service you will receive a Notice of Classification (Form 57) advising you that you have been placed in Class IV–F. Unless prior to the date fixed for your preinduction physical examination, you receive such a Notice of Classification (Form 57) advising you that you have been placed in Class IV–F, you must report for your preinduction physical examination as directed.

Every registrant.—When you report for preinduction physical examination you will be forwarded to an induction station where you will be given a complete physical examination to determine whether you are physically fit for service. If you sign a Request for Immediate Induction (Form 219), and you are found qualified for service, you will be inducted immediately following the completion of your preinduction physical examination. Otherwise, upon completion of your preinduction physical examination, you will be returned to this Local Board. You will be furnished transportation and meals and lodgings when necessary. Following your preinduction physical examination you will receive a certificate issued by the commanding officer of the induction station showing your physical fitness for service or lack thereof.

If you fail to report for preinduction physical examination as directed, you will be delinquent and will be immediately ordered to report for induction into the armed forces. You will also be subject to fine and imprisonment under the provisions of section 11 of the Selective Training and Service Act of 1940, as amended.

If you are so far from your own Local Board that reporting in compliance with this order will be a hardship and you desire to report to the Local Board in the area in which you are now located, take this order and go immediately to that Local Board and make written request for transfer for preinduction physical examination.

DSS Form 215

16—37979-1 U. S. GOVERNMENT PRINTING OFFICE

At Camp Forrest's induction station, recruits began their transformation from civilians to soldiers. Each man underwent physical and mental examinations, received immunizations, and was issued uniforms and basic equipment. Reception center staff also classified recruits according to aptitude and skill sets, helping determine future assignments. Between November 1941 and January 1944, more than 250,000 soldiers from various branches of the armed forces received their physicals at Camp Forrest. The induction letter, such as the example shown here, provided instructions on when and where to report for examination to see if an individual met the Army's standards. In late September 1944, the induction center closed, prompting Tullahoma civic leaders to petition the War Department to establish a separation center at the post for returning soldiers. (Courtesy of CFF.)

Rail and bus service kept Camp Forrest connected to the wider world. Soldiers boarded NC & St. L. trains at the Tullahoma depot, either bound for new assignments or enjoying leave time away from camp. To accommodate the heavy passenger traffic, railroad engineers often added four to eight extra cars to scheduled trains. Around the clock, two bus companies, Greyhound and Consolidated Bus Line, provided continuous service between the camp and neighboring towns. Reliable transportation was essential for managing the constant flow of soldiers in and out of Middle Tennessee during the war years. (Courtesy of Dr. Paul Wylie family.)

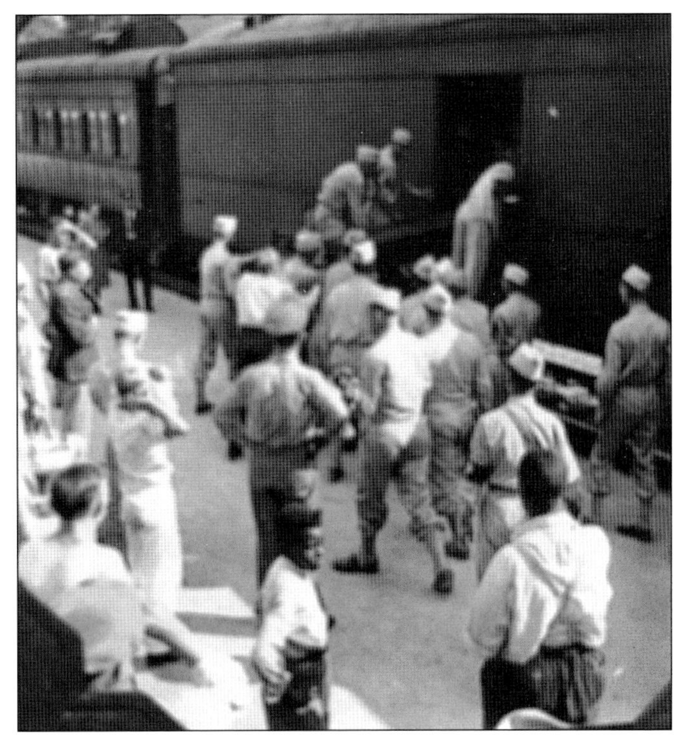

944

OCT 27 1942

Oct 21st 1942
(Date)

Secretary of State of: Washington

Being on active duty in the armed forces of the United States and desiring to vote in the coming election, I hereby apply for an official war ballot.

My home address is Rt. 5 ~~Arlington~~, in the city,
(Number and street)

town, or village of Arlington, in the county of Snohomish, in the State of Washington, and my voting district or precinct to the best of my knowledge is [illegible]

I desire that the ballot be sent to me at the following address Co. B. 319th Inf. A.P.O. #80 Camp Forrest Tenn

Pvt Hans L A. Westman
(Signed)

Signature certified by:

Lt Glen S Lund
(To be signed by any commissioned officer)

W. D., A. G. O. Form No. 560
September 17, 1942

GPO 16—30238-1

Even in wartime, elections continued at the federal, state, and local levels. Soldiers stationed at Camp Forrest could request absentee ballots from their home election boards, though the acceptance of completed ballots remained at the discretion of state and local authorities. Information about candidates reached the soldiers through newspapers, letters from home, and conversations with friends and family. Despite the distance, the Army sought to maintain democratic participation, reminding troops that civic duty at the ballot box was as important as duty on the training grounds. (Courtesy of CFF.)

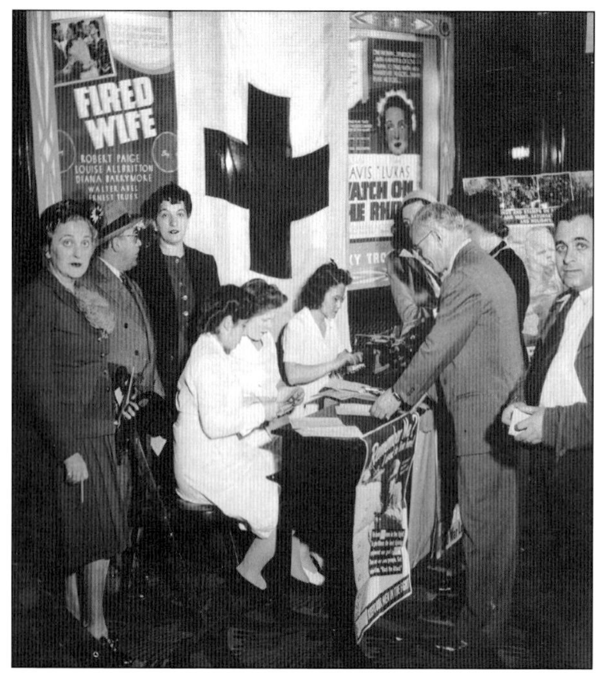

The American Red Cross played a vital role in supporting soldiers stationed at Camp Forrest. On January 3, 1942, construction began on a new Red Cross building along Forrest Boulevard, located next to its Guest House. The completed facility included a reception room, four offices, and living quarters for the field director, Leland Zink. Red Cross staff provided guidance to soldiers dealing with family or business problems and assisted with war relief campaigns. They also helped secure supplies for both stateside and overseas service members. The organization's presence at Camp Forrest offered practical aid as well as reassurance, reminding soldiers that connections to home and community were never far away. (Courtesy of CFF.)

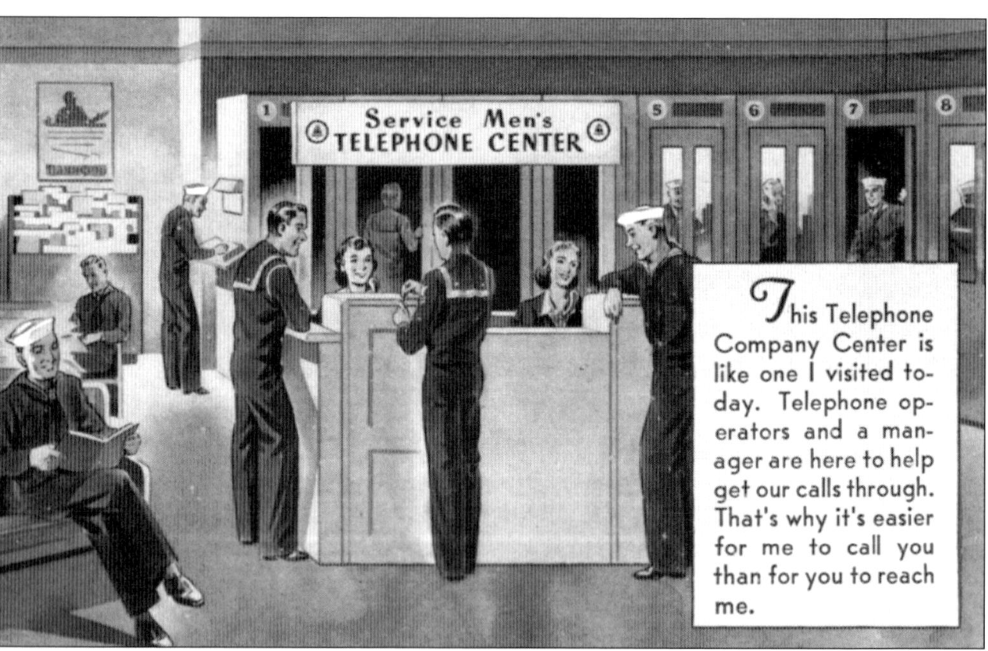

Communication with home was one of the most valued services at Camp Forrest. A public telephone center operated on 8th Street between Forrest Boulevard and Avenue F, staffed with operator-attendants to assist callers. Long-distance calls required operator connection, and soldiers paid the charges once the call ended. To meet demand, the government installed special long-distance lines so that military personnel could connect with family and friends beyond the immediate area. The telephone center became a vital link between camp life and loved ones at home, offering soldiers a chance to share news, reassurance, and a sense of connection during their time in training. (Courtesy of CFF.)

Community and national organizations worked to provide wholesome recreation for soldiers stationed at Camp Forrest. Trucks from across the country continually delivered items such as pianos, musical instruments, sports equipment, and cigarettes to ensure soldiers had opportunities for relaxation beyond their training schedules. In the spring of 1941, for example, the 33rd Division received a piano shipped from Bloomington, Illinois. (Courtesy of Illinois Digital Archives.)

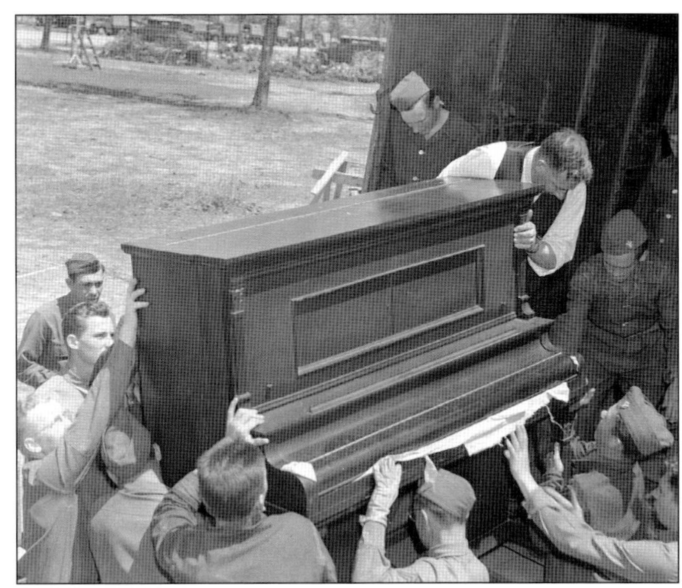

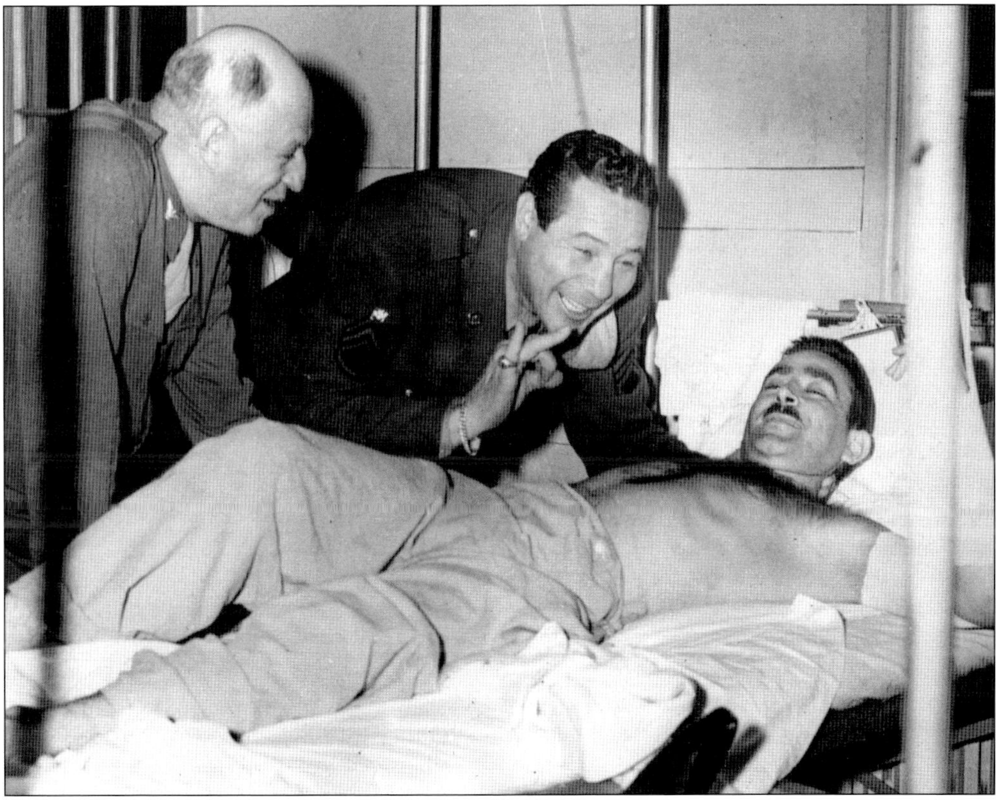

Movie, radio, and sports celebrities frequently visited Camp Forrest to support recruitment, promote war bond sales, and lift soldiers' spirits. Among them was former World Heavyweight Boxing champion S.Sgt. Max Baer. During his stay, Baer was a referee for several boxing matches at William Northern Army Airfield and toured the Camp Forrest station hospital. In his trademark good humor, he encouraged Cpl. Samuel Denmark to "Keep your chin up, kid," as Col. Thomas Ferenbaugh, the hospital's commanding officer, looked on. (Courtesy of CFF.)

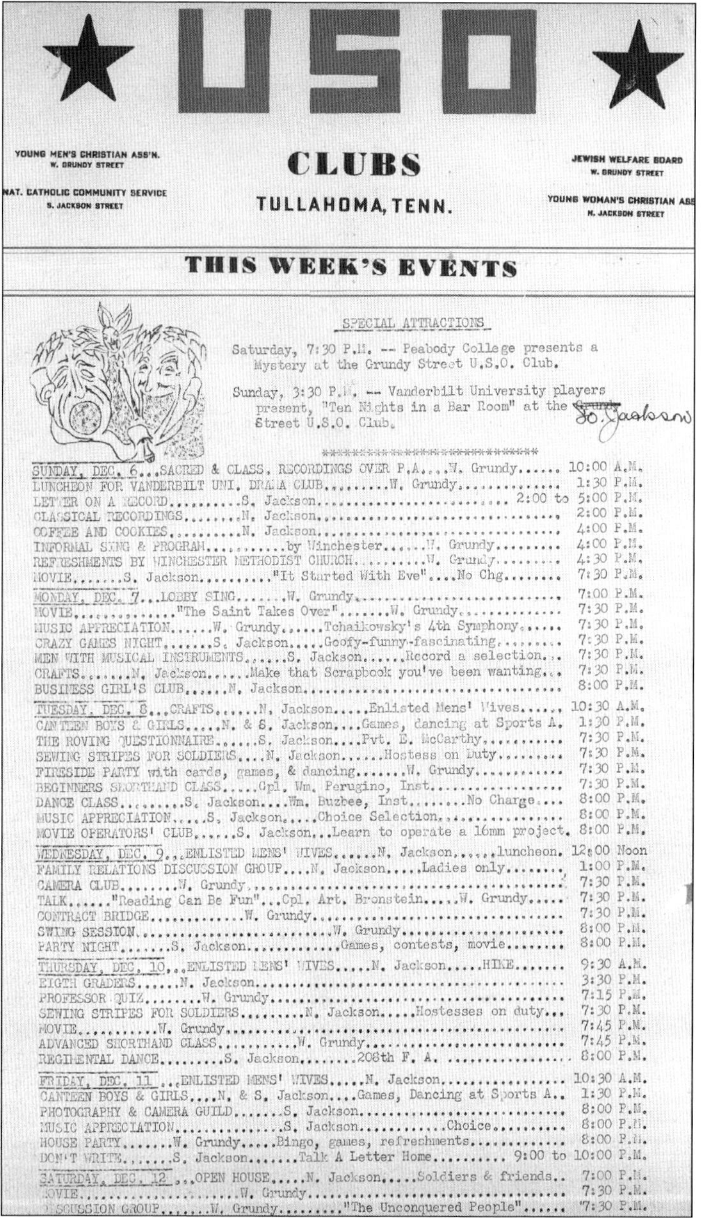

★ USO ★

YOUNG MEN'S CHRISTIAN ASS'N.
W. GRUNDY STREET

NAT. CATHOLIC COMMUNITY SERVICE
S. JACKSON STREET

CLUBS

TULLAHOMA, TENN.

JEWISH WELFARE BOARD
W. GRUNDY STREET

YOUNG WOMAN'S CHRISTIAN ASS
N. JACKSON STREET

THIS WEEK'S EVENTS

SPECIAL ATTRACTIONS

Saturday, 7:30 P.M. -- Peabody College presents a Mystery at the Grundy Street U.S.O. Club.

Sunday, 3:30 P.M. -- Vanderbilt University players present, "Ten Nights in a Bar Room" at the ~~Grundy~~ So. Jackson Street U.S.O. Club.

****

SUNDAY, DEC. 6...SACRED & CLASS. RECORDINGS OVER P.A....W. Grundy...... 10:00 A.M.
LUNCHEON FOR VANDERBILT UNI. DRAMA CLUB.........W. Grundy.............. 1:30 P.M.
LETTER ON A RECORD..........S. Jackson.......................... 2:00 to 5:00 P.M.
CLASSICAL RECORDINGS........N. Jackson.................................. 2:00 P.M.
COFFEE AND COOKIES..........N. Jackson.................................. 4:00 P.M.
INFORMAL SING & PROGRAM............by Winchester......W. Grundy......... 4:00 P.M.
REFRESHMENTS BY WINCHESTER METHODIST CHURCH..........W. Grundy......... 4:30 P.M.
MOVIE.......S. Jackson.........."It Started With Eve"....No Chg......... 7:30 P.M.

MONDAY, DEC. 7...LOBBY SING.......W. Grundy.............................. 7:00 P.M.
MOVIE................"The Saint Takes Over".......W. Grundy.............. 7:30 P.M.
MUSIC APPRECIATION......W. Grundy......Tchaikowsky's 4th Symphony...... 7:30 P.M.
CRAZY GAMES NIGHT.......S. Jackson.....Goofy-funny-fascinating.......... 7:30 P.M.
MEN WITH MUSICAL INSTRUMENTS......S. Jackson......Record a selection... 7:30 P.M.
CRAFTS........N. Jackson......Make that Scrapbook you've been wanting... 7:30 P.M.
BUSINESS GIRL'S CLUB......N. Jackson................................... 8:00 P.M.

TUESDAY, DEC. 8...CRAFTS......N. Jackson.....Enlisted Mens' Wives...... 10:30 A.M.
CANTEEN BOYS & GIRLS.....N. & S. Jackson....Games, dancing at Sports A. 1:30 P.M.
THE ROVING QUESTIONNAIRE......S. Jackson....Pvt. E. McCarthy........... 7:30 P.M.
SEWING STRIPES FOR SOLDIERS....N. Jackson......Hostess on Duty.......... 7:30 P.M.
FIRESIDE PARTY with cards, games, & dancing.......W. Grundy............. 7:30 P.M.
BEGINNERS SHORTHAND CLASS.....Cpl. Wm. Perugino, Inst.................. 7:30 P.M.
DANCE CLASS.........S. Jackson....Wm. Buzbee, Inst........No Charge.... 8:00 P.M.
MUSIC APPRECIATION.....S. Jackson.....Choice Selection.................. 8:00 P.M.
MOVIE OPERATORS' CLUB......S. Jackson...Learn to operate a 16mm project. 8:00 P.M.

WEDNESDAY, DEC. 9...ENLISTED MENS' WIVES......N. Jackson......luncheon. 12:00 Noon
FAMILY RELATIONS DISCUSSION GROUP....N. Jackson.....Ladies only........ 1:00 P.M.
CAMERA CLUB........W. Grundy... 7:30 P.M.
TALK......"Reading Can Be Fun"...Cpl. Art. Bronstein.....W. Grundy..... 7:30 P.M.
CONTRACT BRIDGE.............W. Grundy................................... 7:30 P.M.
SWING SESSION...........................W. Grundy........................ 8:00 P.M.
PARTY NIGHT.......S. Jackson............Games, contests, movie.......... 8:00 P.M.

THURSDAY, DEC. 10...ENLISTED MENS' WIVES.....N. Jackson.....HIKE....... 9:30 A.M.
EIGTH GRADERS......N. Jackson... 3:30 P.M.
PROFESSOR QUIZ........W. Grundy... 7:15 P.M.
SEWING STRIPES FOR SOLDIERS..........N. Jackson.....Hostesses on duty... 7:30 P.M.
MOVIE...........W. Grundy... 7:45 P.M.
ADVANCED SHORTHAND CLASS...........W. Grundy............................ 7:45 P.M.
REGIMENTAL DANCE.........S. Jackson........208th F. A. .... 8:00 P.M.

FRIDAY, DEC. 11 ...ENLISTED MENS' WIVES.....N. Jackson.................. 10:30 A.M.
CANTEEN BOYS & GIRLS....N. & S. Jackson....Games, Dancing at Sports A.. 1:30 P.M.
PHOTOGRAPHY & CAMERA GUILD.......S. Jackson............................ 8:00 P.M.
MUSIC APPRECIATION...............S. Jackson...........Choice.......... 8:00 P.M.
HOUSE PARTY.......W. Grundy.....Bingo, games, refreshments............. 8:00 P.M.
DON'T WRITE........S. Jackson.......Talk A Letter Home.......... 9:00 to 10:00 P.M.

SATURDAY, DEC. 12 ...OPEN HOUSE.....N. Jackson.....Soldiers & friends.. 7:00 P.M.
MOVIE.......................W. Grundy.................................... 7:30 P.M.
DISCUSSION GROUP........W. Grundy........."The Unconquered People"...... 7:30 P.M.

As Camp Forrest and William Northern Army Airfield swelled to over 30,000 soldiers, the National United Service Organizations (USO) announced that the federal government would build four recreation clubs in Tullahoma. National Catholic Community Service, the Salvation Army, the Jewish Welfare Board, and the YMCA each operated a club, and the federal government purchased a local judge's former residence to serve as these organizations' administrative offices. The new facilities were inviting spaces, featuring large lounges with fireplaces, refreshment stands, parlors, social halls, meeting rooms, and screened porches. Dedication ceremonies held on January 25, 1942, included addresses by both civilian and military leaders. The clubs proved popular immediately with military personnel and civilians. During their first year of operation, more than two million groups and individuals visited. In the image shown, a USO handbill advertises the wide variety of activities available at the Tullahoma centers. (Courtesy of Bill Brown.)

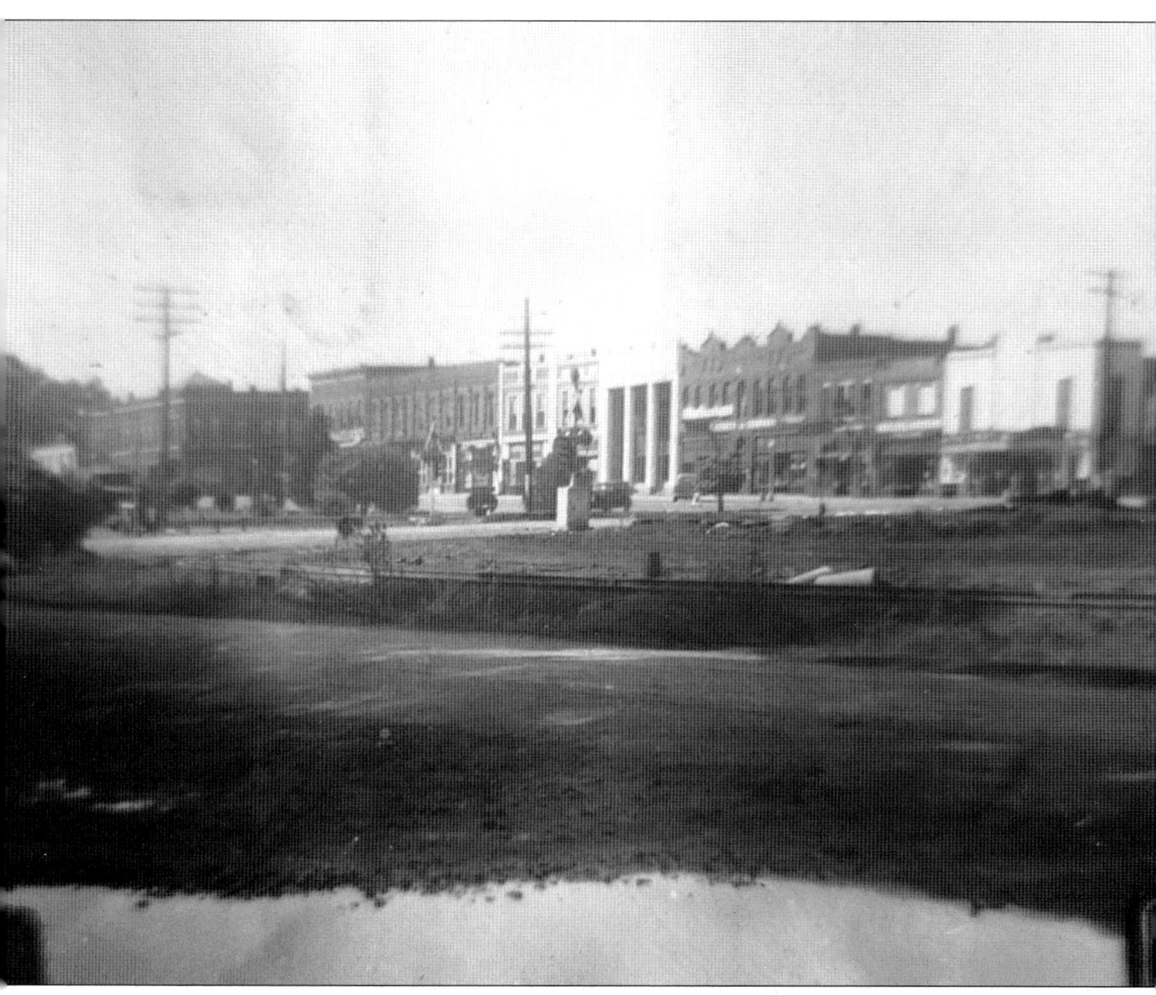

The arrival of Camp Forrest transformed Tullahoma overnight. Before the war, the town's population was just 4,500, but it swelled to an average of 75,000 as soldiers, civilian workers, and their families flooded the area. Despite the dramatic influx, personnel director Whitelaw R. Leath of the Hardaway-Creighton Company and Mayor Don Campbell noted that the city remained orderly, with few drinking or gambling problems. Pictured here is Atlantic Street, celebrated as the widest street in the world, stretching 330 feet across and one and a half miles long. In the spring of 1940, Mayor Campbell boasted to reporters about the city's industries: sporting goods manufacturers, a shoe industry, a renowned bedspread company, and 19 other local businesses, including Lannom Manufacturing (sporting equipment), M.R. Campbell and Company (baseball bats and golf shafts), Campbell and Dann Company (hardwood flooring), and the Tennessee Overall Company (clothing). (Courtesy of Dr. Paul Wylie family.)

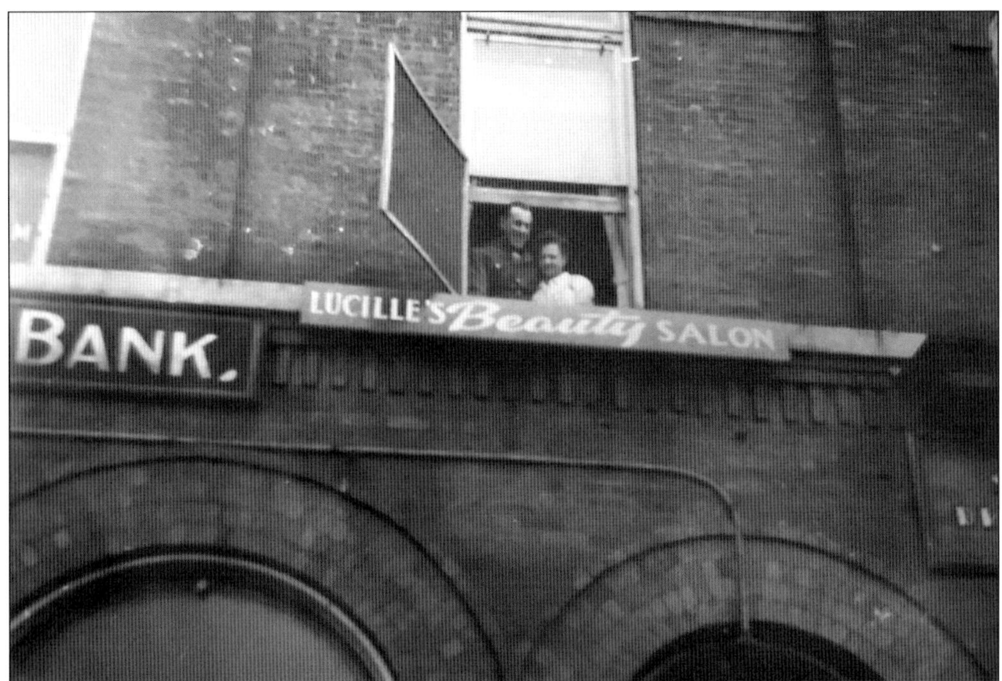

The wartime boom at Camp Forrest triggered explosive growth in Tullahoma. As thousands of soldiers and workers arrived, businesses sprang up overnight. City officials reported that more than 32 new businesses opened, along with the construction of 32 new homes and two apartment buildings with federal grant assistance. Shops of every kind filled the town, from restaurants to beauty parlors like Lucille's. But the sudden influx of people also overwhelmed Tullahoma's infrastructure, leading to sanitation problems and strained city services. To address these challenges, the federal government invested approximately $2 million in improvements, expanding utilities and modernizing facilities to support the unprecedented population surge. The result was a transformed town that reflected both the opportunities and the pressures of hosting one of the Army's largest training centers. (Courtesy of CFF.)

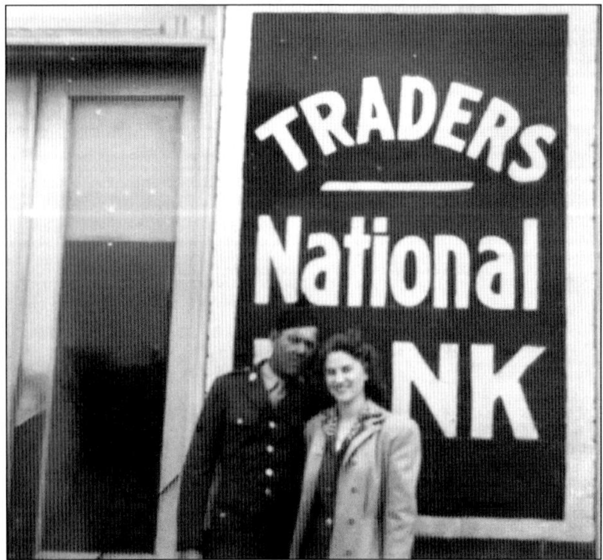

Financial institutions in Tullahoma reflected the town's growth well before the Army arrived. Traders National Bank opened its doors on May 1, 1889, on West Lincoln Street, and served as one of the community's early financial anchors. By World War II, there were two other banks in town: the First National Bank and the Farmers and Merchants Bank. These institutions supported local businesses, industries, and families during the population boom of the Camp Forrest years, when thousands of newcomers transformed the small town into a bustling wartime hub. (Courtesy of CFF.)

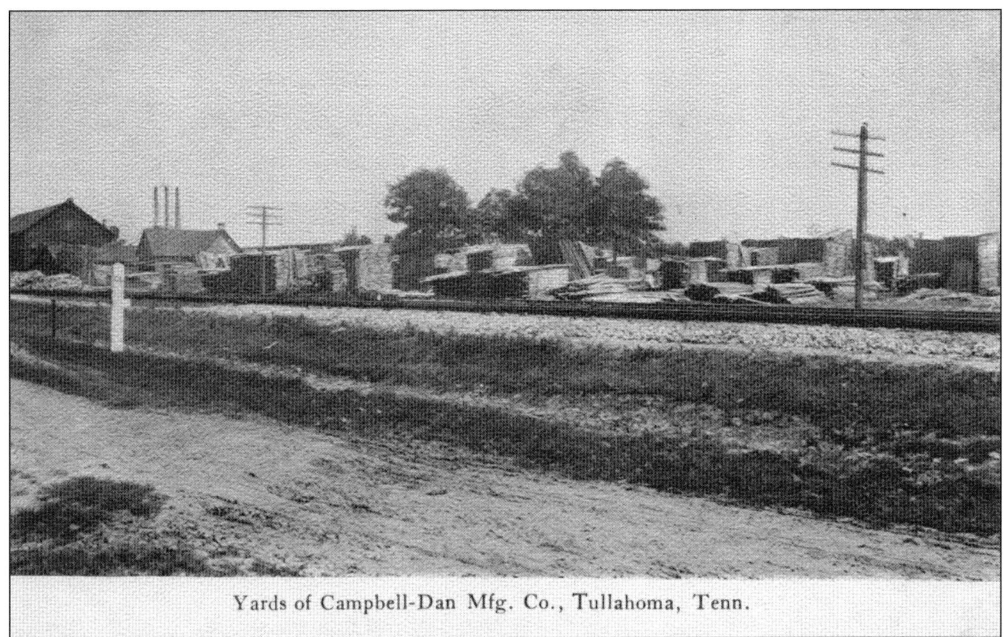

Industry and civic leadership were closely linked in Tullahoma during the wartime years. Campbell-Dann Manufacturing Company, a major producer of hardwood flooring, was among the town's largest employers. One of its owners, Donald B. Campbell, played a leading role in both business and civic life from the 1930s through the late 1960s. He served as president of M.R. Campbell Company, Inc., managed Campbell and Dann Company, Inc., and held office as mayor of Tullahoma from August 1938 to August 1946. During his tenure, the city experienced unprecedented growth with the arrival of Camp Forrest. Sen. Tom Stewart even sent Campbell a telegram announcing federal approval to expand Camp Peay into a permanent US Army post. (Courtesy of CFF.)

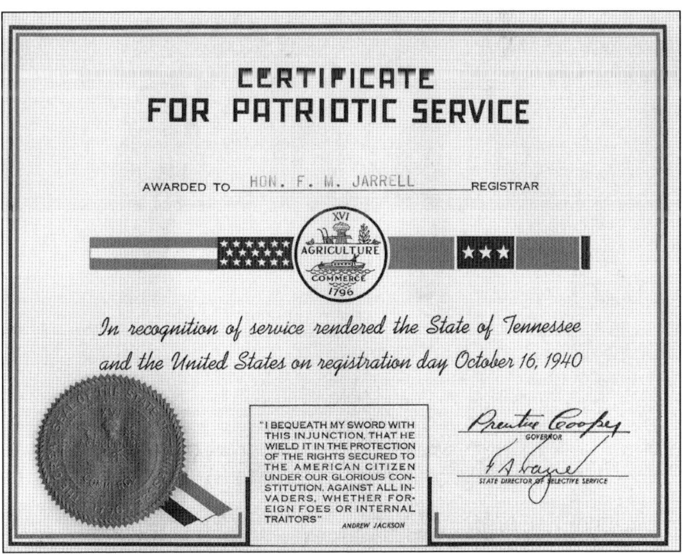

CERTIFICATE
FOR PATRIOTIC SERVICE

AWARDED TO HON. F. M. JARRELL REGISTRAR

XVI
AGRICULTURE
COMMERCE
1796

In recognition of service rendered the State of Tennessee and the United States on registration day October 16, 1940

"I BEQUEATH MY SWORD WITH THIS INJUNCTION, THAT HE WIELD IT IN THE PROTECTION OF THE RIGHTS SECURED TO THE AMERICAN CITIZEN UNDER OUR GLORIOUS CONSTITUTION, AGAINST ALL INVADERS, WHETHER FOREIGN FOES OR INTERNAL TRAITORS" ANDREW JACKSON

GOVERNOR

STATE DIRECTOR OF SELECTIVE SERVICE

Patriotism in Middle Tennessee remained strong throughout World War II. Citizens adjusted to wartime restrictions, coped with the disruptions caused by large-scale military maneuvers, and adapted to the influx of soldiers and war workers. More than 300,000 men and women from Tennessee served in uniform in World War II, while countless others contributed through industry, agriculture, volunteerism, and home-front sacrifices. (Courtesy of CFF.)

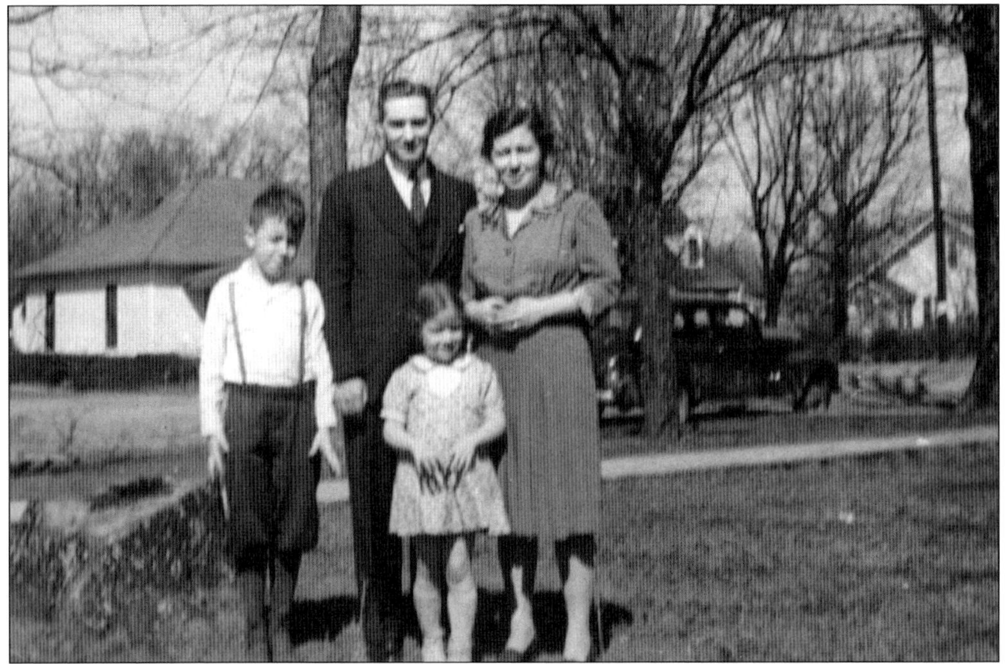

Pastor Roscoe S. Thompson of the First Christian Church in Tullahoma was both a spiritual leader and a dedicated civic figure during the war years. Known for counseling and befriending soldiers stationed at Camp Forrest, he offered support and guidance to those far from home. Beyond his ministry, Thompson chaired the Defense Recreation Committee, served as president of the Tullahoma Rotary Club, and presided over numerous dedication ceremonies and community receptions across the region. His leadership exemplified the close ties between the local community and the military. Shown here with his wife Rebecca, daughter Sarah, and son James, Pastor Thompson's influence extended from his congregation to the thousands of soldiers training nearby. Below is a church bulletin from a Christmas 1942 service held in a Camp Forrest chapel, reflecting the strong role of faith in sustaining morale during wartime. (Above, courtesy of Sarah Johnson; below, courtesy of CFF.)

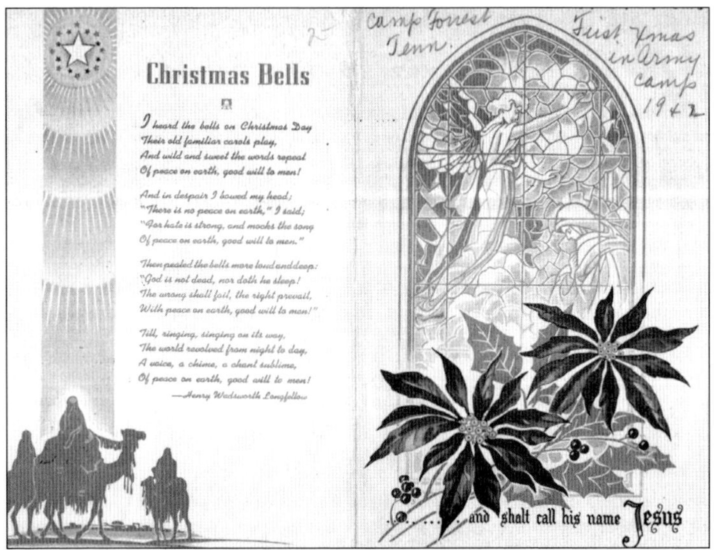

Christmas Bells

I heard the bells on Christmas Day
Their old familiar carols play,
And wild and sweet the words repeat
Of peace on earth, good will to men!

And in despair I bowed my head;
"There is no peace on earth," I said;
"For hate is strong, and mocks the song
Of peace on earth, good will to men."

Then pealed the bells more loud and deep:
"God is not dead, nor doth he sleep!
The wrong shall fail, the right prevail,
With peace on earth, good will to men!"

Till, ringing, singing on its way,
The world revolved from night to day,
A voice, a chime, a chant sublime,
Of peace on earth, good will to men!

—Henry Wadsworth Longfellow

Camp Forest Tenn.

First Xmas in Army camp 1942

. . . . . and shalt call his name Jesus

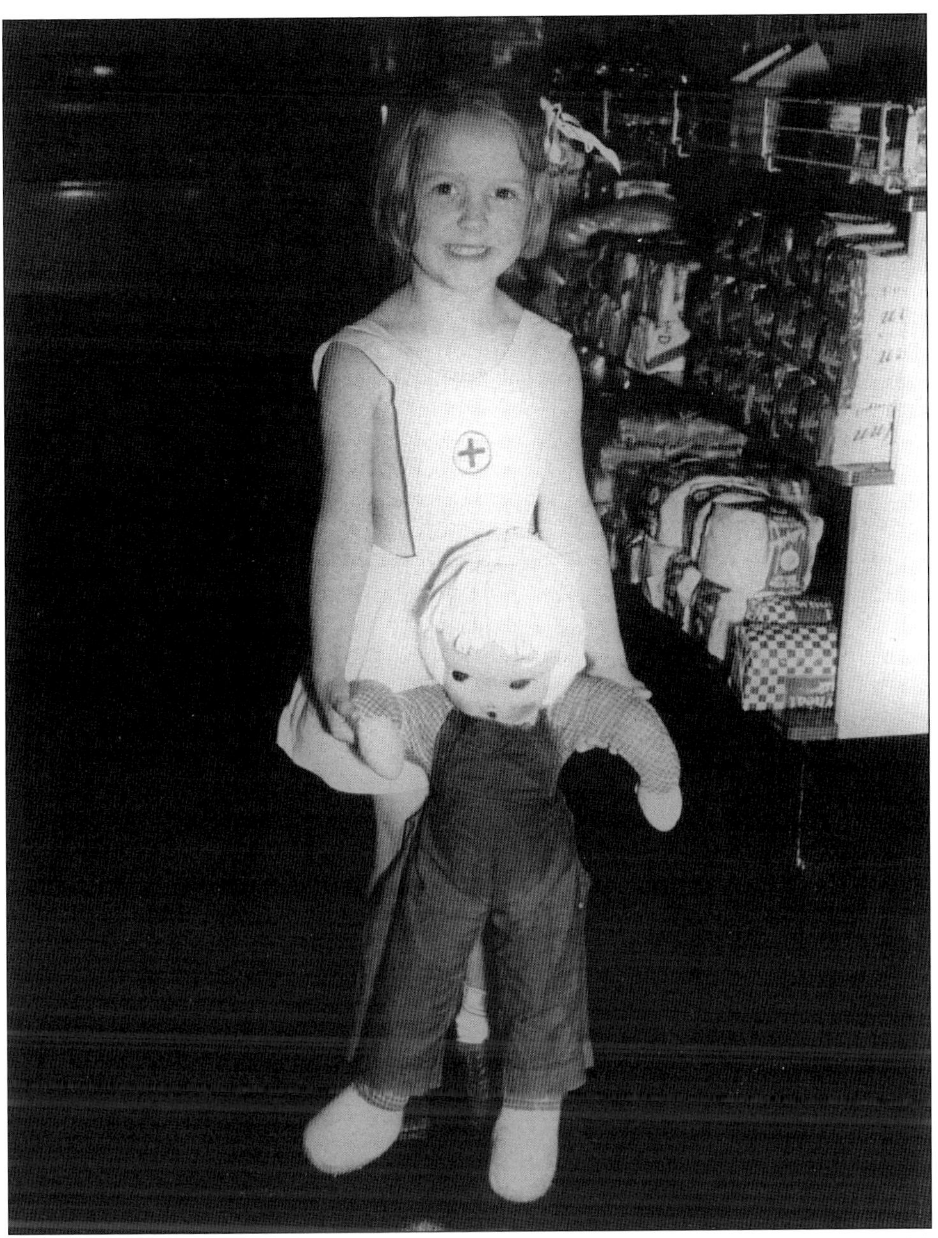

The war years touched even the youngest members of the Tullahoma community. Pictured here is four-year-old Dorothy (Dot) Couch (later Watson) with her favorite doll at her family's grocery store, Couch's. During the war, the Couch family opened their home to several women who worked at Camp Forrest, including a young nurse who left a lasting impression on Dot. Each day the two would play together, tending to the "broken bones" of Dot's dolls. The nurse even made her a white pinafore dress and cap with a hand-embroidered red cross, which Dot proudly wears in this photograph. Though the nurse eventually returned home, she never knew she had planted the seed of a vocation. The kindness and compassion she showed inspired Dot's lifelong path of service as a teacher, a nurse, and a volunteer. Reflecting on her childhood, Dot later wrote: "We never know what seeds we are planting and what they might sprout and grow into!" (Courtesy of Dorothy Couch Watson.)

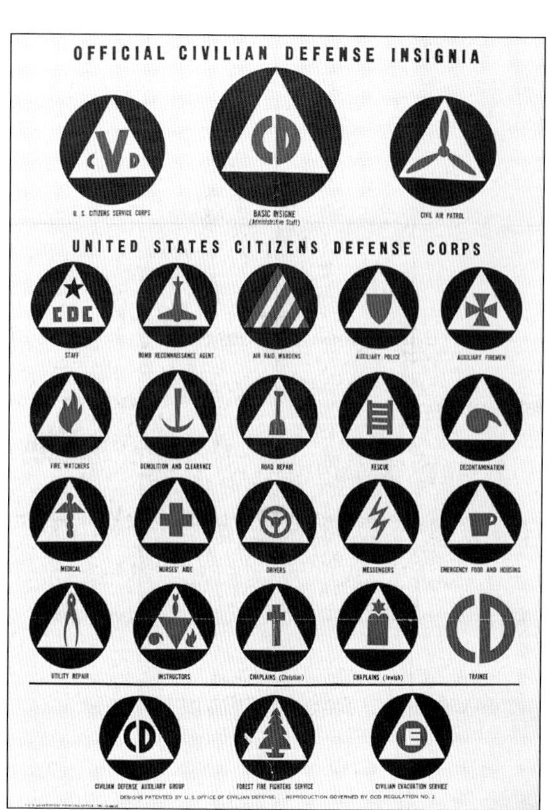

This poster, created in 1942 by the US Office of Civilian Defense, explained the official insignia used to identify members of the United States Defense Corps. The federal government, in cooperation with state and local authorities, organized a broad system of volunteer positions to support essential war-related tasks on the home front. Civilian defense workers performed duties ranging from air raid wardens and fire watchers to medical support and communications. Clear identification through standardized insignia ensured both recognition and authority, helping coordinate the massive volunteer effort that kept American communities prepared and resilient during wartime. (Courtesy of Northwestern University Library.)

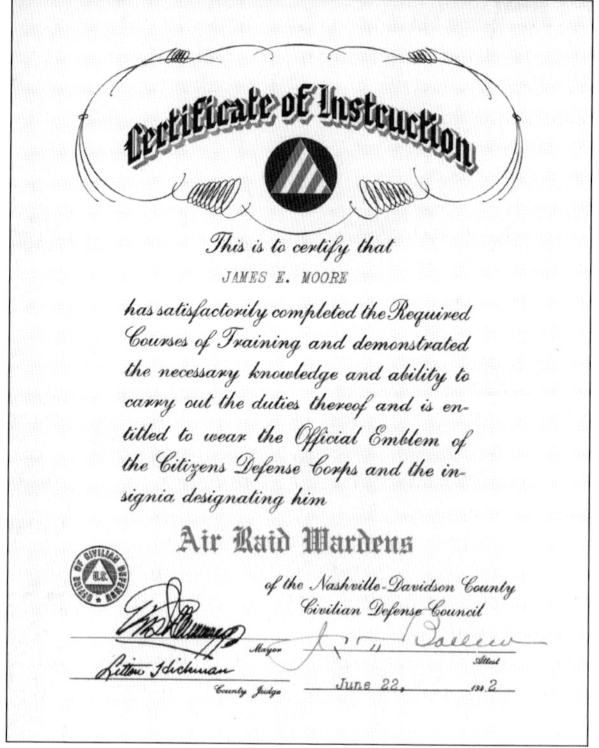

Certificate of Instruction

This is to certify that

JAMES E. MOORE

has satisfactorily completed the Required Courses of Training and demonstrated the necessary knowledge and ability to carry out the duties thereof and is entitled to wear the Official Emblem of the Citizens Defense Corps and the insignia designating him

Air Raid Wardens

of the Nashville-Davidson County Civilian Defense Council

Mayor — *Attest*

County Judge — June 22, 1942

Civilian volunteers served as air-raid wardens throughout World War II, playing a critical role in home-front defense. Their duties included educating communities about blackout procedures and the steps to take in the event of an air raid. At night, wardens patrolled neighborhoods to ensure compliance with blackout regulations designed to make towns less visible to potential enemy aircraft. Individuals who violated these rules risked fines issued by local Civil Defense Boards. Though enemy bombers never reached the Tullahoma skies, the presence of air-raid wardens reinforced vigilance, preparedness, and the sense that every citizen had a part to play in national defense. (Courtesy of North Carolina Digital Heritage Center.)

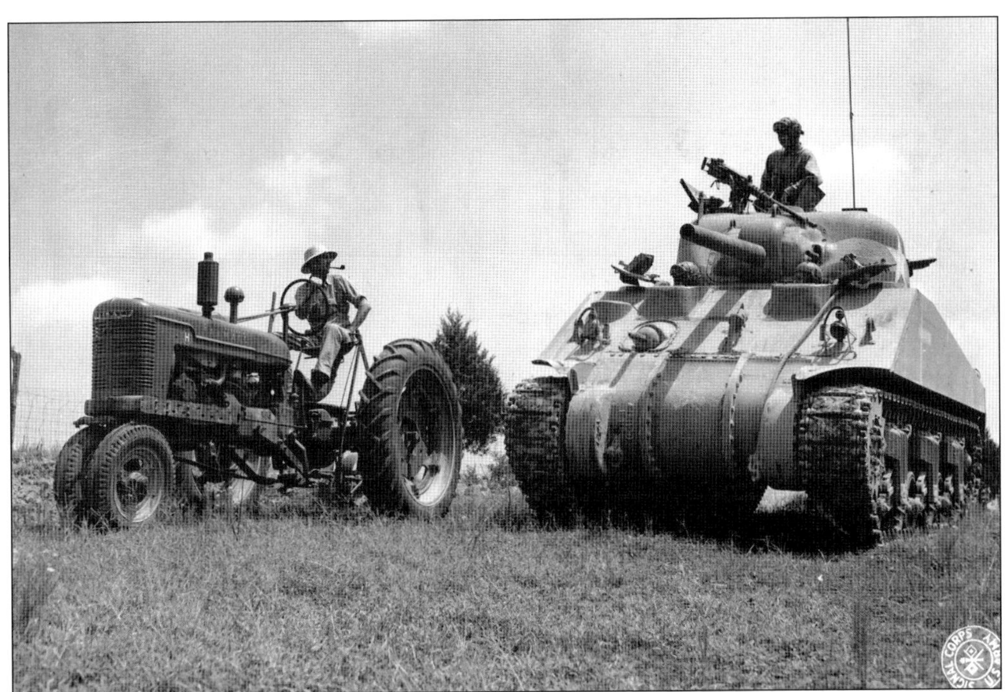

Wartime training in Middle Tennessee often brought soldiers and civilians face to face in unexpected ways. During large-scale maneuver exercises in the fall of 1943, it was not unusual for tank crews to ask locals for directions across the unfamiliar countryside. In one such moment, Allen Bass of Lebanon, Tennessee, was working on his tractor when a tank commanded by Sgt. Judd W. Wiley pulled alongside. Exchanges like this highlighted both the scale of the Tennessee Maneuvers and the good-natured interactions that often occurred between soldiers in training and the civilians whose farms, roads, and communities became part of America's preparation for war. (Courtesy of John Allan.)

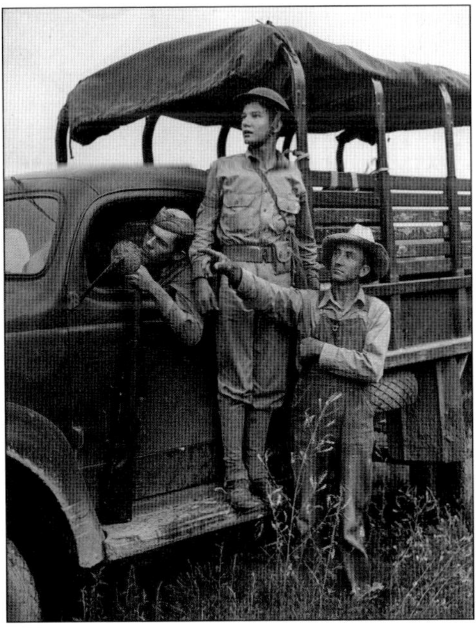

The Tennessee Maneuvers brought the realities of war to the farmlands and small towns of Middle Tennessee. In the 1941 exercises, some 77,000 soldiers engaged in simulated "combat" across a 600-square-mile area. The war games tested tactics, leadership, and coordination in a setting that blended military training with everyday civilian life. Here, a farmer provides two soldiers with directions during a lull in the maneuvers. These large-scale exercises served as a realistic prelude to the battles they would soon face overseas, sharpening their skills while underscoring the cooperation between soldiers in training and the local communities hosting the war games. (Courtesy of CFF.)

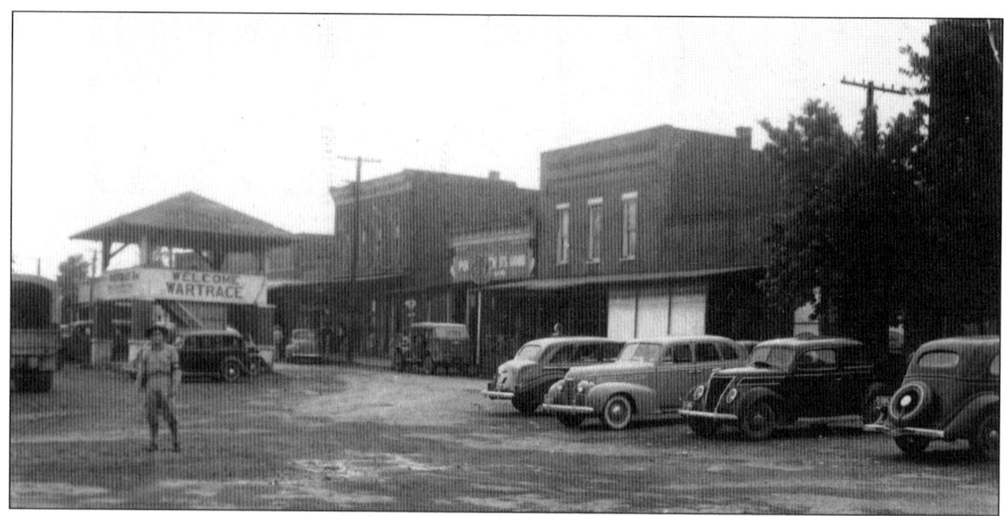

In May 1941, the quiet farming community of Wartrace, Tennessee, found itself hosting the second "Yankee invasion" of the South. Wartrace was 25 miles from Camp Forrest and home to just 550 residents. The 27th Infantry Division, numbering 21,000 men in 18 detachments, spread encampments from Wartrace to nearby Normandy. The division was preparing for large-scale maneuvers popularly called the "Battle of Tennessee." For the townspeople, the sudden influx of troops, who were primarily from northern states, transformed their daily routines and landscapes. For the soldiers, the rolling fields and rural roads of Middle Tennessee became proving grounds, offering realistic conditions for the massive training exercises that readied them for service overseas. (Courtesy of CFF.)

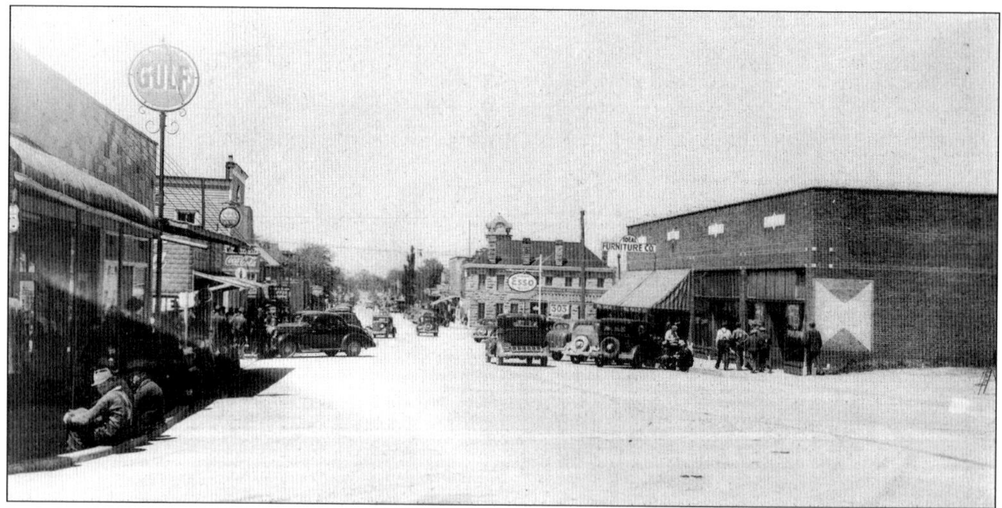

Ninety-three miles from Camp Forrest, the Civilian Conservation Corps (CCC) site at Crossville, Tennessee, was converted by the federal government into a prisoner of war camp during World War II. The Crossville facility opened in November 1942 and was unique as it was the only POW camp in the United States designated to hold German and Italian officers. The camp operated under strict rules of the Geneva Convention, providing housing, work details, and opportunities for cultural and educational activities. The Crossville POW camp remained in operation until December 1945, when the last prisoners were repatriated. Its legacy reflects both the scale of wartime internment in the United States and the complex human dimensions of global conflict brought to rural Tennessee. (Courtesy of CFF.)

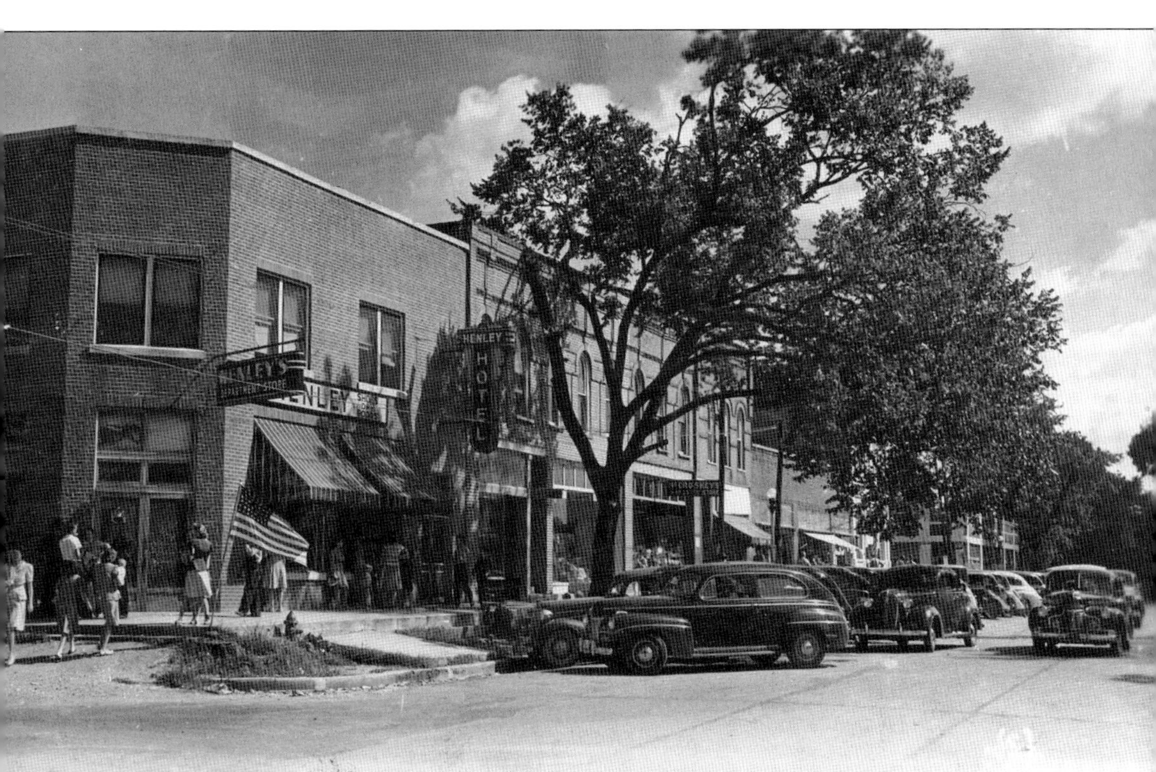

Manchester, the county seat of Coffee County, lies 19 miles from Camp Forrest. During the war years, the town saw a dramatic influx of military families and civilian workers seeking housing and employment. On weekends, the population swelled even further as soldiers arrived in search of entertainment. It was common for citizens to invite soldiers into their homes to visit and enjoy a home-cooked meal. For many soldiers, it was the first time they had encountered southern hospitality. The economic effects on the area were substantial: Coffee County Clerk J.F. Brantley noted that revenue rose during the war due to licenses issued for new businesses, many of them from out of state, catering to soldiers, their families, and base employees. However, when the War Department later eliminated training at Camp Forrest, he estimated that Coffee County lost 40 percent of its business, and the number of marriage licenses dropped sharply once the soldiers were gone. In 1941, Manchester also played a direct role in the Tennessee Maneuvers, when the Second Army Headquarters operated out of the high school gymnasium, serving as a hub for 50 newspaper reporters and photographers covering the war games. (Courtesy of John Allan.)

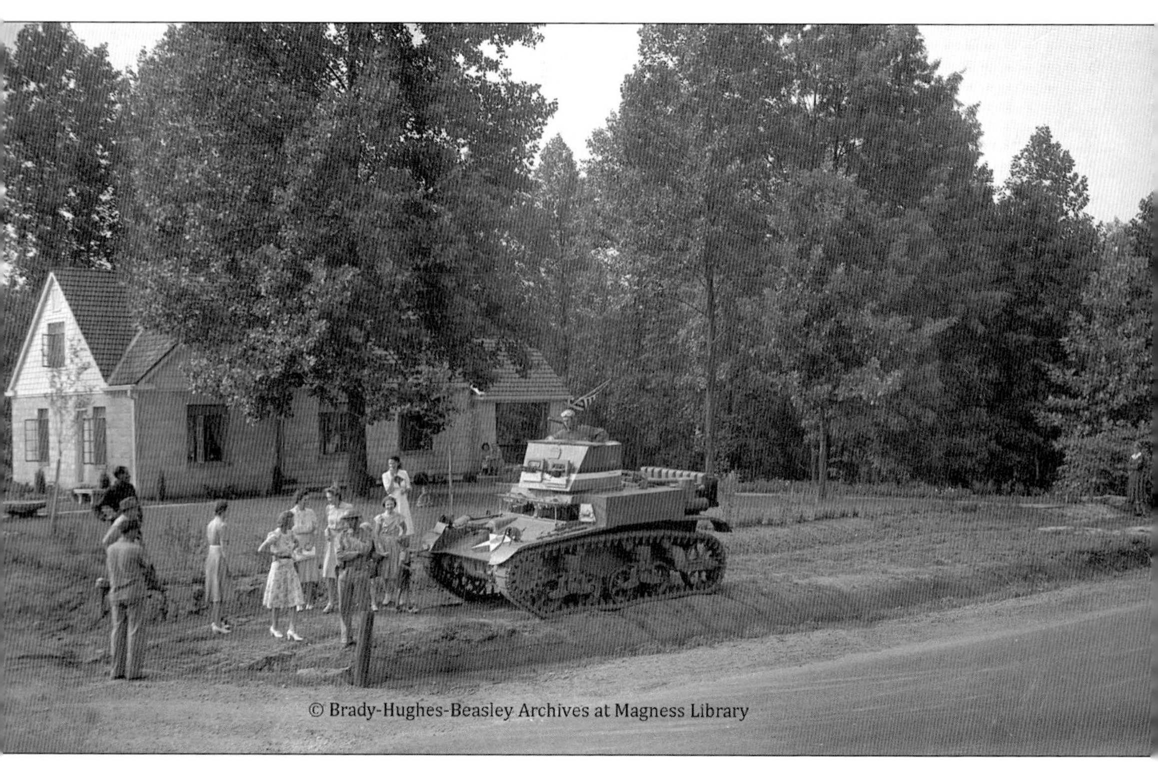

Military traffic reshaped daily life in Middle Tennessee during the war years. Convoys of Army vehicles traveling to and from Camp Forrest had priority on public roads, often halting civilian traffic for 30 minutes or more as long lines of trucks, jeeps, and tanks passed through towns. Pedestrians had to wait before crossing streets with passing convoys, since the heavy vehicles could not stop quickly or maneuver around obstacles. For residents, these delays became part of the wartime routine, a reminder of the scale of training and preparation taking place in their own communities. While sometimes inconvenient, the convoys symbolized the constant movement of men and materiel necessary to prepare an army for global war. (Courtesy of Brady-Hughes-Beasley Archives at Magness Library.)

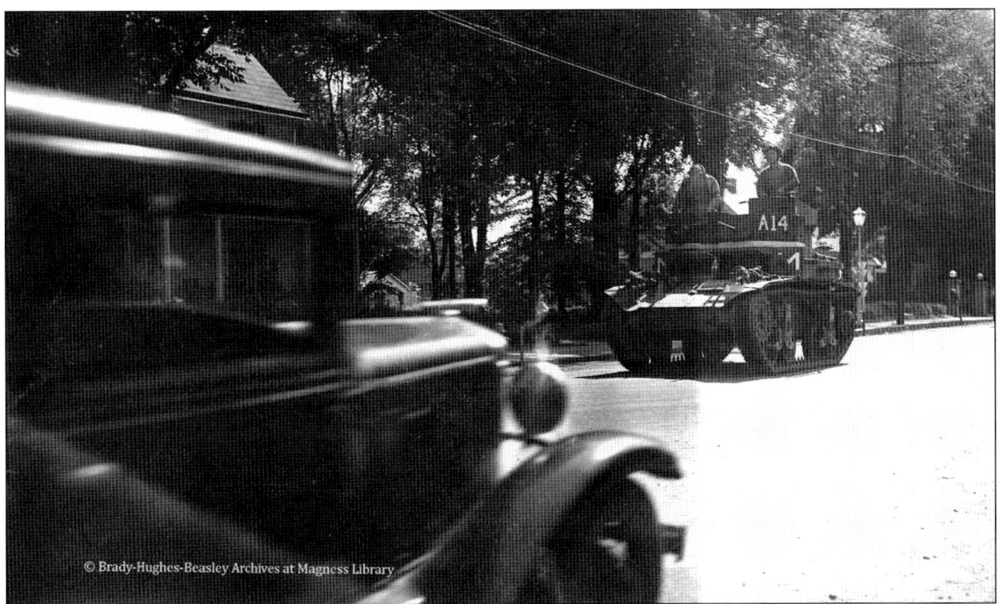

The rapid expansion of Camp Forrest placed enormous strain on the infrastructure of numerous area counties. By 1942, the federal government financed the construction of new roads throughout the surrounding counties to relieve congestion and reduce accidents caused by heavy military traffic. These new routes were restricted to military use only but were turned over to the state for civilian use after the war. Local and state leaders also proposed extending Camp Forrest Road three miles north of Manchester to further improve access. On January 29, 1942, the new concrete road officially opened, and its "first vehicle" was a plane that made an emergency landing. After the war ended, the federal government lifted restrictions, allowing civilians to use many of the roads originally built to serve the Army. (Courtesy of Brady-Hughes-Beasley Archives at Magness Library.)

Abbreviations

Title	Abbreviation
Brigadier General	Brig. Gen.
Captain	Capt.
Colonel	Col.
Corporal	Cpl.
First Lieutenant	1st Lt.
General	Gen.
Governor	Gov.
Lieutenant	Lt.
Lieutenant Colonel	Lt. Col.
Lieutenant General	Lt. Gen.
Major	Maj.
Major General	Maj. Gen.
President	Pres.
Private	Pvt.
Private, First Class	Pfc.
Representative	Rep.
Senator	Sen.
Sergeant	Sgt.
Staff Sergeant	S. Sgt.
Sergeant, First Class	Sfc.
Sergeant Major	Sgt. Maj.
Second Lieutenant	2nd Lt.
Tech Sergeant	T. Sgt.
Technician, First Grade	T1g.
Technician, Fourth Class	T/4
Technician, Fifth Class	T/5